**USA
TODAY**

LOGIC
SUPER CHALLENGE 2

Can't get enough of USA TODAY puzzles?

You can play:

- In the USA TODAY newspaper

- At puzzles.usatoday.com

- By downloading the FREE USA TODAY app (Get it on Google Play or iTunes)

- By downloading the FREE USA TODAY Crossword app (Get it on Google Play or iTunes)

USA TODAY

LOGIC
SUPER CHALLENGE 2
200 PUZZLES

Andrews McMeel
PUBLISHING®

Solving Tips

The next few pages have all the instructions you'll need to tackle all the puzzles in this book. They may look a little complicated but you'll soon get the hang of things.

Logic Problems

With each standard problem we provide a chart that takes into account every possibility to be considered in the solution. First, you carefully read the statement of the problem in the introduction, and then consider the clues. Next, you enter in the chart all the information immediately apparent from the clues, using an **X** to show a definite **no** and a ✓ to show a definite **yes**. You'll find that this narrows down the possibilities and might even reveal some new definite information. So now you re-read the clues with these new facts in mind to discover further positive/negative relationships. Be sure to enter information in all the relevant places in the chart, and to transfer newly discovered information from one part of the chart to all the other relevant parts. The smaller grid at the end of each problem is simply a quick-reference chart for all your findings.

Now try your hand at working through the example below—you'll soon get the hang of it.

EXAMPLE

Three children live on the same street. From the two clues given below, can you discover each child's full name and age?

Clues

1. Miss Brown is three years older than Mary.
2. The child whose surname is White is 9 years old.

Solution

Miss Brown (clue 1) cannot be Brian, so you can place an **X** in the Brian/Brown box. Clue 1 tells us that she is not Mary either, so you can put an **X** in the Mary/Brown box. Miss Brown is therefore Anne, the only possibility remaining. Now place a ✓ in that box in the chart, with corresponding **X**'s against the other possible surnames for Anne.

If Anne Brown is three years older than Mary (clue 1), she must be 10 and Mary, 7. So place ✓'s in the Anne/10, Brown/10 and Mary/7 boxes, and **X**'s in all the empty boxes in each row and column containing these ✓'s. The chart now reveals Brian's age as 9, so you can place a ✓ in the Brian/9 box. Clue 2 tells us that White is 9

years old too, so he must be Brian. Place a ✓ in the White/9 box and **X**'s in the remaining empty boxes in that row and column, then place a ✓ in the Brian/White box and **X**'s in all the remaining empty boxes in that row and column. You can see now that the remaining unfilled boxes in the chart must contain ✓'s, since their rows and columns contain only **X**'s, so they reveal Green as the surname of 7-year-old Mary.

Anne Brown, 10.
Brian White, 9.
Mary Green, 7.

The solving system for the puzzles that don't have grids is very similar. Read through the clues and insert any positive information onto the diagram. Then read through the clues again and use a process of elimination to start positioning the

	Brown	Green	White	7	9	10
Anne	✓	X	X	X	X	✓
Brian	X			X		X
Mary	X			✓	X	X
7	X					
9	X					
10	✓	X	X			

	Brown	Green	White	7	9	10
Anne	✓	X	X	X	X	✓
Brian	X	X	✓	X	✓	X
Mary	X		X	✓	X	X
7	X		X			
9	X	X	✓			
10	✓	X	X			

remaining elements of the puzzle. You may find it easier to make a few notes about which elements of the puzzle you know are linked but that cannot yet be entered on the diagram. These can be positioned once the other examples of those elements are positioned. If you find it difficult to know where to begin, use the starting tip printed upside down at the foot of the page.

Battleships

Before you look at the numbers around the grid, there are a number of squares you can fill in from the starter pieces given. If an end piece of a ship is given, then the square next to it, in the direction indicated by the end, must also be part of a ship. If a middle piece is given, then the pieces on either side must also be ship parts; in this instance, you need some more information before you can decide which way the ship runs. Also, any square that is adjacent to an end piece (apart from those squares in the direction of the rest of the ship), any square touching the corners of a middle piece, and all squares around destroyers (one-square ships) must be sea.

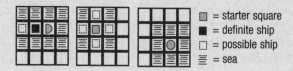

□ = starter square
■ = definite ship
◻ = possible ship
≡ = sea

Now, look at the numbers around the grid and eliminate rows and columns in which the large aircraft carrier might be. Either from this or by looking at the next consequences of the remaining possibilities, you should be able to position this ship. Now fill in the sea squares around the carrier and move on to the smaller ships.

Domino Search

Starting this puzzle is just a matter of finding one domino (number pair) that is unique in the grid. It is often easiest to look for the double numbers first (0 0; 6 6). When you have discovered one or more of these unique possibilities, you will find that their position in the grid forces you to place one or more dominoes in order to fill in the shape of the grid left. Cross off all these dominoes in the check-grid for future reference. Now, look at the dominoes you have managed to fill in and check around the grid, especially near the edge of the grid or next to dominoes already positioned, where the possibilities are reduced, to find other examples of those number pairs. Since you have already positioned that domino, you know that the second example you have found is not a pair and the domino must run in one of the other possible directions. Carry on in this vein, finding dominoes and then eliminating possibilities elsewhere in the grid until the puzzle is cracked.

Logi-5

Start by looking at the intersection of columns and rows that contain at least two starter letters, preferably more, and then use the "shapes" to further eliminate possible letters from that intersection square. You may well find that you can now position at least one letter exactly. There is one more "trick" to help: If, in your eliminating, you find two squares in a row or column, each of which must contain one of the same pair, then the other squares in the row or column cannot contain those letters and can be eliminated.

Sign In

When solving Sign In puzzles, the clues that aren't there are just as important as the ones that are. In the second row of our example puzzle, the 5 can only be positioned in column two, since placing it elsewhere in that row would mean that a 6 would have to be entered according to the signs. Following the 5, a 4 can now be written in below it. Now here's where the clues that aren't there come into play. If the 2 was placed in either of the shaded squares, either a 1 or 3 must be next to it. And there is no + or − sign linking these two squares. Therefore the 2 must be placed at the top.

Sudoku

The basic Sudoku puzzle is a 9 × 9 square grid, split into 9 square blocks, each containing 9 cells. Each puzzle starts off with roughly 20 to 35 of the cells filled in with any of the numbers 1 to 9. There is just one rule: The rest of the cells must be filled in with the missing numbers from 1 to 9 so that no number appears twice in any row, column, or 3 × 3 block. Use the numbers provided to eliminate places where the same number can't appear. For example, if there is already 1 in a cell, then 1 cannot appear again in that same row, column, or 3 × 3 block. By scanning all the cells that the various 1 values rule out, often you can find where the remaining 1s must go.

Killer Sudoku

This puzzle uses the solving skills of Sudoku, but in addition, the digits within each dotted-line shape imposed on top of the Sudoku grid must add up to the number in the top left corner of each shape. No digit may be repeated within a dotted-line shape. Look for the unique digit answers in the dotted-line shapes. For example, two squares totaling 17 must contain a 9 and an 8. Two squares totaling 4 must contain a 1 and a 3, as two 2s would not be allowed. Don't get so involved in the totals that you forget to use normal Sudoku solving methods as well.

Battleships

Do you remember the old game of battleships? These puzzles are based on that idea. Your task is to find the vessels in the diagram. Some parts of boats or sea squares have already been filled in, and a number next to a row or column refers to the number of occupied squares in that row or column. The boats may be positioned horizontally or vertically, but no two boats or parts of boats are in adjacent squares— horizontally, vertically, or diagonally.

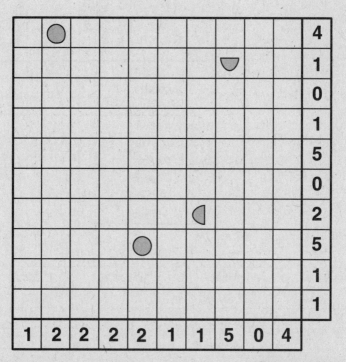

Acceptance . . .

The annual Netherlipp Movie Awards are coming to the end; the awards for best performances, best product placement, and best hairdo have been handed out, and we are left with only three to go. From the clues, can you work out who won each of the final three awards for what scene in which movie?

Clues

1. The dog-training movie *Hound of Music* was given the award for best extra, but it wasn't given to Jenny Jenman.

2. The park scene in the cut-rate monster movie *Lizard of Oz* received an award; the award for best cut-out (that's a scene which ended upon the cutting room floor) was given to a scene on a street.

3. Barry Barman won his award for his part in the wet weather exploitation movie *Sinnin' in the Rain*.

	Barry Barman	Jenny Jenman	Rick Rickman	Park	Stadium	Street	Hound of Music	Lizard of Oz	Sinnin' in the Rain
Best cut-out									
Best extra									
Best outtake									
Hound of Music									
Lizard of Oz									
Sinnin' in the Rain									
Park									
Stadium									
Street									

Award	Winner	Scene	Movie

USA TODAY

. . . Speeches

As with all awards ceremonies, the recipients of the prizes like to stand at the presentation lectern and, through tears of joy, thank all and sundry for the help and support they have offered. From the clues, can you work out which three disparate people each award winner thanked?

Clues

1. "This is such a surprise," sobbed Rick Rickman, "I should first of all like to thank my agent, newsagent that is . . ."

2. One person thanked their neighbor and their dad, and one thanked their hairdresser and their grandma but no one thanked both their grocery boy and their teacher—that would be silly.

3. "I need to say a big thank you to Ernie, my plumber," said Jenny Jenman through a flood of tears; she didn't thank her mom, but only because she was dragged off the stage before she got around to it.

	Grocery boy	Newsagent	Neighbor	Hair dresser	Plumber	Teacher	Dad	Grandma	Mom
Barry Barman									
Jenny Jenman									
Rick Rickman									
Dad									
Grandma									
Mom									
Hair dresser									
Plumber									
Teacher									

Winner	First	Second	Third

Drive and Deliver

Keighshire Carriers is a delivery company that can move everything from a small package to the contents of a six bedroomed house. Today, five of their small-truck drivers are on the roads of Keighshire making deliveries to various places. From the clues, can you discover who is driving which make of truck, his load, and his eventual destination?

Clues

1. The Ford, which is a lovely shade of "titanium," is en route to Crispin Parva, but neither it nor the Leyland, which is painted in a delicate shade of "snow," are carrying boxes of shoes.

2. Neither Nigel's truck nor Terry's is the one carrying autoparts, and none of these three vans is going to Upper Crispin, nor is Terry driving a Leyland truck.

3. Colin is delivering electrical domestic appliances but is not at the wheel of a Leyland.

4. The TVs are destined for a small shop in Churchminster, while the talc-colored Mercedes is full of washing-machines.

5. Sam and his marble-colored Fiat are not on their way to Brandywell.

6. Dean is delivering food.

Driver	Make of truck

	Fiat	Ford	Leyland	Mercedes	Renault	Auto parts	Food	Shoes	TVs	Washing-machines	Brandywell	Churchminster	Crispin Parva	Upper Crispin	Wallingfen
Colin															
Dean															
Nigel															
Sam															
Terry															
Brandywell															
Churchminster															
Crispin Parva															
Upper Crispin															
Wallingfen															
Auto parts															
Food															
Shoes															
TVs															
Washing-machines															

Load	Destination

Leading Ladies

After a series of tough auditions, five amateur actresses have been cast to star in the latest production by their local amateur dramatic societies. From the clues given, can you work out each one's full name, where the society to which she belongs is based, and what play she is going to star in.

Clues

1. Ms. Vickers, who has been given the part of the heroine in *Wait Until Dark*, isn't appearing in the production in Storbury.

2. Selma isn't Miss Oliphant, who does not belong to the Netherlipp Amateur Dramatic Society.

3. Maureen is playing Sheila Birling in *An Inspector Calls* but not in Colnecaster.

4. The girl who has been cast as Joan of Arc in *The Lark* in Churchminster isn't Veronica.

5. Davina's surname is Young; Gloria, who lives in Storbury and has been a member of the Amateur Dramatic Society since she was twelve, has a surname one letter longer than that of the actress who's playing Eliza Doolittle in *Pygmalion*, which isn't being staged in Netherlipp.

First name	Surname

	Ervine	Keen	Oliphant	Vickers	Young	Churchminster	Colnecaster	Netherlipp	Stonekeigh	Storbury	An Inspector Calls	Pygmalion	Romeo and Juliet	The Lark	Wait Until Dark
Davina															
Gloria															
Maureen															
Selma															
Veronica															
An Inspector Calls															
Pygmalion															
Romeo and Juliet															
The Lark															
Wait Until Dark															
Churchminster															
Colnecaster															
Netherlipp															
Stonekeigh															
Storbury															

Society	Play

Give Up the Ghost

Borbridge Rectory is famous as one of the most haunted houses in Britain, which is the most haunted country in the world. Last month's visit to the rectory by five amateur ghost hunters did nothing to damage that reputation. From the clues below, can you work out where each of the ghost hunters encountered a Borbridge Phantom, how they described it, and what particularly gruesome detail of its appearance stuck in their minds?

Clues

1. Eric Stone met a ghostly Butler while one of the female ghost hunters encountered the transparent figure of an old woman dressed in mid-Victorian style clothing.

2. It was not the apparition of a young country girl which was covered in blood.

3. It was a man who saw a ghost in the rectory's shadowy and ominous looking entrance hall and it was the headless phantom which manifested itself in the drawing room.

4. Annie Nash didn't have her grisly confrontation in the library.

5. Neither the he ghost which Bruce Oaks saw in the rectory kitchen nor the phantom Nun which appeared in the conservatory, dodging between the potted palms and the orange trees, was the figure whose throat had been cut from ear to ear (or, perhaps, there to there).

6. The apparition which terrified David Ross had a fleshless grinning Skull instead of a face.

Hunter	Room

	Conservatory	Drawing room	Entrance Hall	Kitchen	Library	Butler	Nun	Old woman	Soldier	Young girl	Covered in blood	Headless	Skull faced	Throat cut	Transparent
Annie Nash															
Bruce Oaks															
Cindy Price															
David Ross															
Eric Stone															
Covered in blood															
Headless															
Skull faced															
Throat cut															
Transparent															
Butler															
Nun															
Old woman															
Soldier															
Young girl															

Ghost	Feature

An Actor's Life

This is the heart-warming story of five girls from Northchester who, having been glued to Saturday evening TV for most of their lives, desperately wanted to be in showbusiness. When they grew up all fulfilled their ambitions—sort of—by getting a job at the city's famous Variety Theater. From the clues, can you work out each young lady's full name, what she originally wanted to be, and her job at the Variety?

Clues

1. Judy, who as a youngster wanted to be a pop singer (and performs regularly with her guitar and hat in Northchester High Street), doesn't have an on-stage job at the Variety.

2. Ms. Hayes' original ambition was to be a concert pianist, and she can often be heard playing the upright during sing-alongs at the Dog and Duck in Station Road.

3. The would-be actress who currently works as an usherette at the Variety has a surname beginning with a consonant.

4. The girl who has grown up to become producer of the new show at the Variety has an odd number of letters in her first name and an even number of letters in her surname, which is the same as that of the theater's owner.

5. Paula Edison never had any ambition to be a ballerina.

6. Ms. Miller is a dancer in the chorus of the Variety's latest show; her first name appears in the alphabetical list before Miss Smith's but after that of the girl who's employed as the comedian's stooge in the show, losing her skirt, and getting a custard pie in the face six evenings a week plus a matinee on Saturday.

First name	Surname

	Edison	Hayes	Miller	Oates	Smith	Actress	Ballerina	Comedian	Pianist	Pop singer	Barmaid	Chorus dancer	Producer	Stooge	Usherette
Anita															
Denise															
Gillian															
Judy															
Paula															
Barmaid															
Chorus dancer															
Producer															
Stooge															
Usherette															
Actress															
Ballerina															
Comedian															
Pianist															
Pop singer															

Ambition	Job

Sign In

Each row and column is to contain the digits 1-6. The given signs tell you if a digit in a cell is plus 1 (+) or minus 1 (-) the digit next to it. Signs between consecutive digits always work from left to right or top to bottom. Examples: 3 + 4 or 2 ALL occurrences of consecutive digits have been marked by a sign.

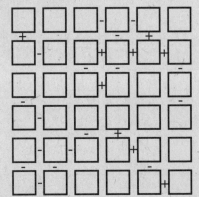

Sudoku

Complete this grid so that each column, each row, and each marked 3 X 3 square contains each of the numbers 1 to 9.

				9	3	2		
		7						3
	8						9	6
				5			6	9
5			1		6	7		
3				8		4		
4				6	1			8
		5	2					
	1	2	4			9		

Uke Can Do

The four ukuleles shown here hanging on the wall of the Music Makers instrument shop in Netherlipp Mall are no longer there, as each has been bought by a customer this morning. From the clues, can you work out who bought which ukulele, for what price, and for what reason?

Clues

1. Doris has bought the ukulele for herself, to learn how to play.

2. The $45 ukulele has been bought by a man who has a collection of musical instruments that has just got one larger; the concert-sized instrument was bought by a woman.

3. The tenor ukulele cost $5 more than the one bought by Alec but $5 less than the one bought by the experienced player to play in a band.

4. The instrument bought as a present was on the wall immediately to the left of the cheapest instrument.

Buyers: Alec; Briony; Colin; Doris
Reasons: collection; learn to play; play in band; present
Prices: $35; $40; $45; $50

Baritone

Tenor

Concert

Soprano

Starting tip: Work out who bought the ukulele for their collection.

Withdrawal Symptoms

Along the High Street this evening five bank customers are inserting their cards into ATM's to get some cash for the night's entertainment. From the clues, can you work out which bank each is using, their individual PIN numbers, and the amount of cash each is withdrawing?

Clues

1. Mr. Mclean has tapped in 4630 (his last two house numbers) to withdraw half the amount being taken from the Westshire Bank ATM by a customer whose number is not 4061 (the last four digits of their telephone number).

2. Miss Hanson is withdrawing more than the customer whose number is 3989 (their birthday, 3rd of September 1989).

3. Mr. Doyle is not the Lancashire Bank customer with the number 3162 (their age when the card was first used and then doubled).

4. Mrs. Bradley is a customer of the Bank of East Anglia.

5. The largest amount is being withdrawn from the Mercia Bank machine, but the smallest amount is not being withdrawn from the Midminster.

6. One customer has keyed in 6757 (their mother's birthday) to take out $20.

Bank	Customer

	Mrs. Bradley	Mr. Doyle	Miss Hanson	Mrs. Kerr	Mr. Mclean	3162	3989	4061	4630	6757	$10	$20	$40	$80	$160
East Anglia															
Lancashire															
Mercia															
Midminster															
Westshire															
$10															
$20															
$40															
$80															
$160															
3162															
3989															
4061															
4630															
6757															

CASINO BANKING

TAKE CASH

DOUBLE OR QUITS

PIN	Amount withdrawn

Gun Running

In the first quarter of the twentieth century the man known as Henri Dumas, although no one is sure if that was his real name, was the most notorious gun runner, controlling the illegal sale of weapons in much of the world. His history is little known and no one can be absolutely sure how and where he spent his time. However, some recent research has provided a little information. From the clues, can you work out the name and occupation he used to cover his identity in each of the listed years and where he was based at that time?

Clues

1. Henri wasn't in Montevideo in 1905 nor was that the year in which he posed as Diego Palotra from Mexico City, which wasn't the identity he used when passing himself off as a journalist.

2. In 1909 Henri was based in a European capital living under the name Vasco Carmona.

3. It was in 1913 that he posed as an industrial chemist to a certain laboratory whose experimental compounds could be adapted for military use.

4. In New York Henri passed himself off as an engineer working on a design for a floating bridge; in Brussels he was known as Axel Carlsen.

5. It wasn't in Oslo, where Henri was based in 1917, that he assumed the identity of Roman Catholic priest Father Sean Daley.

Date	Name

	Axel Carlsen	Diego Palotra	Erich Korner	Sean Daley	Vasco Carmona	Chemist	Engineer	Journalist	Priest	Rifle maker	Brussels	Montevideo	New York	Oslo	Paris
1905															
1909															
1913															
1917															
1921															
Brussels															
Montevideo															
New York															
Oslo															
Paris															
Chemist															
Engineer															
Journalist															
Priest															
Rifle maker															

Occupations	City

Great Sheikhs

It has been quite some years since we paid a visit to the oil-rich sheikhdom of Bonanzah. Over the last five years the ruling sheikh has paid out gratuities to five junior sheikhs who have each impressed him in some way. (The local Bonanzahan currency, the gusha, is made up of one hundred driblets, but no one deals in driblets any more.) From the clues, can you name the sheikh honored in each year, work out the amount of the award he was granted, and say for what achievement he was given it?

Clues

1. Sheikh Hays-el-rod, who used his water-divining talent to find waterholes in the arid Bonanzah desert, was rewarded with a grant of 2,500 gushas more than the most recent recipient of the sheikh's bounty.

2. The largest gratuity was paid out to the sheikh who bravely defended a desert oasis against a band of marauding nomads.

3. The 12,500 gushas reward was paid to Sheikh Ratl-en-rol, who was not the trainer of the Sheikh of Bonanzah's successful string of race horses.

4. The reward paid out in 2011 was exactly 10,000 gushas.

5. The sheikh who won the prestigious Bonanzah camel derby in the year 2013, who was not Sheikh Yahand, was rewarded by a gratuity consisting of an exact number of thousands of gushas.

6. Sheikh Adu-bel-sichs gained the Sheikh of Bonanzah's favor in 2014.

Year	Sheikh

	Sheikh Adu-bel-sichs	Sheikh Hays-el-rod	Sheikh Mahfist	Sheikh Ratl-en-rol	Sheikh Yahand	5,000 gushas	7,500 gushas	10,000 gushas	12,500 gushas	15,000 gushas	Defending oasis	Finding water	Sinking oil well	Training horses	Winning camel
2011															
2012															
2013															
2014															
2015															
Defending oasis															
Finding water															
Sinking oil well															
Training horses															
Winning camel															
5,000 gushas															
7,500 gushas															
10,000 gushas															
12,500 gushas															
15,000 gushas															

We've struck liquid gold! It's printer ink

Prize money	Achievement

Stonekeigh Spa

A new health club and spa facility has opened in a refurbished country hotel just outside Stonekeigh aimed at those wealthy Keighshire residents who find normal spa treatments and exercise sessions a little unpleasant or too much hassle to endure. The advertising flyer below has been mailed to homes in the more affluent areas describing the treatments available. From the clues, can you fill into each space the treatment it describes and the name of the spa employee who runs it?

Clues

1. The downhill exercise bike sessions (uphills are so tedious, don't you think?) are advertised in the right-hand column of the leaflet.

2. The clean mud wrap treatment, for those who don't like to get that icky dirt all over them, is numbered one higher than the session that will be provided by Douglas; Hector's session isn't advertised in position 2.

3. The virtual jogging (well, what's modern technology for if you can't send it for a run for you?) is shown immediately below Eleanor's session and immediately above the one offered by Archie.

4. The drypool swimming (for those who are a little nervous in the water) is shown in position 6; the session in position 5 will be run by Isobel; Claire isn't the staff member who will run the session in position 9.

5. Fiona will run the finger yoga classes for those who aren't yet ready for the full body thing; her sessions are advertised in one of the corner positions and immediately next to the cold steam room sessions (those hot affairs tend to make one a little warm, wouldn't you agree?), which isn't the subject of panel 9 on the flyer.

6. Stand-in aerobics (which isn't a spelling mistake for "standing," it's an aerobics session where customers can nominate a stand-in to do all that jumping and running on the spot for them) will be run by a man and is shown immediately above the session to be run by Jeffrey, which has an even number, unlike the weights watching session (also not a typing mistake but a session in which customers can watch other people lift weights), which will be run by a woman.

7. The ad for the calorie-free lunches prepared by the club's top chef (all the calories are free, no extra charge is made) is numbered three lower than the sessions organized by Bridget and is on the same horizontal row as the mental sauna (just sit there and think "hot").

Treatments: calorie-free lunches; clean mud wrap; cold steam room; downhill exercise bike; drypool swimming; finger yoga; mental sauna; stand-in aerobics; virtual jogging; weights watching

Staff members: Archie; Bridget; Claire; Douglas; Eleanor; Fiona; Gillian; Hector; Isobel; Jeffrey

1	2	3
4	**Stonekeigh Spa**	5
6		7
8	9	10

Starting tip: Begin by working out what is advertised in panel 8.

USA TODAY   21

An American Cousin

Miss Raffles, the sister of the more famous cracksman who appears regularly in these pages, had an American cousin, Annabelle Jemima Raffles, born in New Orleans, whose specialty was conning wealthy Western ranchers into entrusting her with their cash, and then vanishing into the sunset. In 1895, she conned five of them and got away with almost $1,000,000 in total. From the clues, can you work out which town she visited in each of the listed months, what she pretended to be, and the name of the local rancher she robbed?

Clues

1. Annabelle wasn't posing as a touring showbusiness performer when she robbed Rusty Cooper, whose ranch was just outside a community with a two-word name, in an even-numbered month of the year.

2. Annabelle pretended to be singer Lucille Lamour for the crime she undertook immediately before robbing Buck Wayne in Santa Fe, New Mexico.

3. Annabelle posed as actress Rachelle Raunche in Cheyenne, Wyoming, which she visited neither in June nor in the month in which she robbed "cattle king" Mason Hart.

4. Annabelle's theft of more than $300,000 from Gus Stewart took place the month after the crime in which she posed as private detective Drusilla Darling from the Pinkerton Agency.

5. Annabelle's robbery of Sam Autry while pretending to be army officer's widow Susannah Spicey didn't take place in March or during her stay in Tombstone, Arizona.

6. It wasn't in the month of August that Annabelle committed a crime in Dodge City, Kansas.

Month	Town

	Cheyenne	Dodge City	El Paso	Santa Fe	Tombstone	Actress	Detective	Heiress	Singer	Widow	Buck Wayne	Gus Stewart	Mason Hart	Rusty Cooper	Sam Autry
March															
May															
June															
August															
September															
Buck Wayne															
Gus Stewart															
Mason Hart															
Rusty Cooper															
Sam Autry															
Actress															
Detective															
Heiress															
Singer															
Widow															

Role	Victim

Housey-Housey

Mr. and Mrs. Johnson and their two growing kids have grown out of their town house in Colnecaster and need a new one. There are four adjacent houses for sale on the northern side of Storbury's Woodside Road in walking distance from the high school. From the clues, can you fill in the name of each house, the name of the family who is selling it, the name of the estate agents handling the sale, and work out which one the Johnsons have decided to buy?

Clues

1. Greengates, which is being sold through Norman's Estate Agents, is numbered two higher than the house the Johnsons finally decided to buy.

2. The house which Acme Estate Agents are selling for the Howard family isn't number 4 Woodside Road, which is known as Oakland.

3. The Johnsons' new home won't be next door to Rosebank.

4. The Miller family is selling Larksnest, but not through J and P Estate Agents.

5. The Coleman family's house, number 6, wasn't quite what the Johnsons were looking for.

House names: Greengates; Larksnest; Oakland; Rosebank
House vendors: Colemans; Howards; Millers; Stones
Estate agents: Acme; Gilmore's; J and P; Norman's

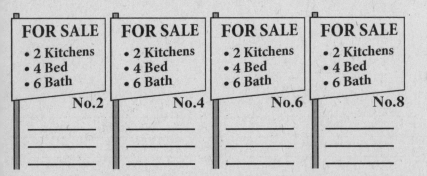

Starting tip: Decide which company is selling the Millers' house.

Domino Search

A standard set of dominoes has been laid out, using numbers instead of dots for clarity. Using a sharp pencil and a keen brain, can you draw in the lines to show where each domino has been placed? You may find the check grid useful—crossing off each domino as you find it.

4	5	4	1	2	1	5	2
3	0	6	1	3	4	3	0
2	5	4	4	1	4	5	5
6	6	0	6	0	0	1	2
3	3	4	1	5	3	6	2
6	2	1	3	5	2	0	4
3	5	6	6	0	2	0	1

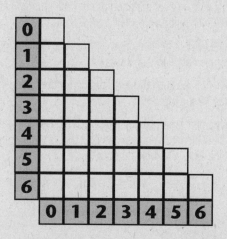

The Front Line

The South American republics of San Guinari and Banana Ria are at war again (or possibly still—the situation is not clear) and while the main fighting is along the river Orimoco, smaller forces are engaged at the Santa Maria border crossing in the far west. From the clues, can you fill in the names of the three men fighting on each side (I said the forces were small), each man's rank, and who, apart from his government (since you cannot live on army pay, even if you receive it), is employing them?

Clues

1. Juan Hernandez is in a foxhole next south in the Banana Rian line to the position occupied by the infantry sergeant; the man who supplements his income by smuggling arms for the terrorist group Red Dawn is serving in the San Guinarian force but isn't in the foxhole directly across no-man's land from the infantry sergeant.

2. The man who is providing information to the World Cable News Network (WCNN) occupies a position numbered one higher than that being used by the man who acts as a recruiter for mercenary leader Ivan Kozenko.

3. The paratrooper who has never actually jumped from a plane is fighting for San Guinari.

4. Francisco Lorca serves in San Guinari's marine corps, even though the country is land locked; his position is marked with an even number.

5. Matteo Costa, who receives from the CIA ten times the amount that the army pays him, is not the artillery gunner, who has a two pounder weapon but no ammunition; his position bears a higher number than that of Fidel Perez, who is not the local correspondent for the *New York Gazette.*

6. The rifleman, a member of his country's only Special Forces Unit, has a position between those of his two fellow countrymen.

7. Miguel Gomez is not in position 5; he is fighting for the force which is opposed to the one supported by the gunner.

8. The man employed part time by Luigi Carcano, who is a private in the infantry, is under cover at a position (not number 3) which has a higher number than Antonio Rojas, who isn't in foxhole number 1.

Names: Antonio Rojas; Fidel Perez; Francisco Lorca; Juan Hernandez; Matteo Costa; Miguel Gomez
Ranks: gunner; marine; paratrooper; private (infantry); rifleman; sergeant (infantry)
Other employers: CIA; Ivan Kozenko; Luigi Carcano; New York Gazette; Red Dawn; WCNN

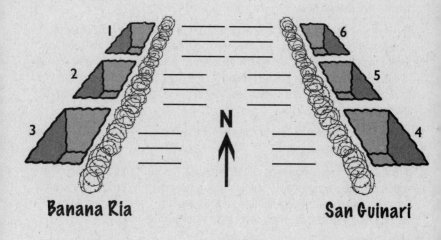

Banana Ria   San Guinari

Starting tip: Work out the rank of the man in position 3.

Holding On

Anna's afternoon off from work was not as relaxing as she'd hoped, as she needed to catch up on a few "life administration" phone calls. Each call involved negotiating a number of menus and then listening to a song on a loop interrupted with a friendly voice telling her how important she is. From the clues, can you work out to how many menus Anna had to respond to when calling each business, the song she was played over and over again, and the number of minutes it took for a human being to answer the phone?

Clues

1. The call to Keighshire Cover, her automobile insurance company, required driving through five menus; the call with the four-menu beginning didn't have the twenty-two-minute hold.

2. The wait on hold at the bank was accompanied by multiple playings of Gene Pitney's *24 Hours from Tulsa* (you'll probably get there faster that me!) and took longer than the call that involved the fewest menus but was shorter than the call in which Louis Armstrong sang *We Have All the Time in the World* (speak for yourself!); Louis Armstrong's voice wasn't part of the call answering system at the energy company.

3. The call with the most menus to negotiate resulted in the longest wait to get through to a human being.

4. It took Crispin Travel—who she called to discuss her vacation plans to anywhere without a phone connection—twenty minutes to answer the phone; this wasn't the call in which she negotiated three menus and then listened a few times to Bananarama's *Robert De Niro's Waiting* (he's not the only one!).

5. On the call that took eighteen minutes to answer, Anna gave up complaining and simply joined in with Diana Ross's *I'm Still Waiting.*

Business	Menus

	2 menus	3 menus	4 menus	5 menus	6 menus	Hanging on the . . .	I'm Still . . .	Robert De Niro's . . .	24 Hours from . . .	We Have All . . .	18 minutes	20 minutes	22 minutes	24 minutes	26 minutes
Bank															
Auto insurance															
Energy company															
Phone company															
Travel agent															
18 minutes															
20 minutes															
22 minutes															
24 minutes															
26 minutes															
Hanging on the . . .															
I'm Still . . .															
Robert De Niro's . . .															
24 Hours from . . .															
We Have All . . .															

Song	Minutes

Back Home

The five children of Liam and Kathleen Casey from Ballydrum in rural Ireland have all ventured overseas to seek their fortunes, but they've kept in touch, and this St. Patrick's Day they'll all be at home with their parents, who are celebrating their Ruby Wedding the same week. From the clues, can you work out what job each of the young Caseys does, where they live, and what present they've brought for their parents' anniversary?

Clues

1. It isn't the young Casey who lives and works in Britain who has bought Liam and Kathleen a new tea set for their anniversary.

2. The painting of a sailing ship in an Atlantic storm is a gift to the older Caseys from their son who now lives in the United States.

3. Neither the young Casey who has his own building business in Brazil nor Niall is giving his parents an anniversary gift of wine.

4. Sheilah Brady, nee Casey, now lives in Australia, in an even more rural spot.

5. The Caseys' oldest son, who's a soldier, isn't giving them the painting.

6. Father Declan Casey, a parish priest in his adopted home town, isn't giving his parents wine.

7. The police officer who's giving an anniversary gift of jewelry—cuff links for Liam and a bracelet for Kathleen—isn't Bridget Casey, who doesn't live in Britain.

First name	Occupation

	Builder	Folk-singer	Police officer	Priest	Soldier	Australia	Brazil	Britain	Spain	USA	Candlesticks	Jewelry	Painting	Tea set	Wine
Bridget															
Declan															
Kevin															
Niall															
Sheilah															
Candlesticks															
Jewelry															
Painting															
Tea set															
Wine															
Australia															
Brazil															
Britain															
Spain															
USA															

Country	Gift

Money for Old . . .

Ann Teak, proprietor of The Jumble Sale, a small shop of curiosities in the village of Longmell Ford in Suffolk, had a good week last week. As well as a number of high-priced individual sales, she managed five "double dealings" where a married couple purchased two slightly overpriced items, one chosen by the husband and one by the wife. From the clues, can you work out which two items she sold on each of the listed days, and the name of the couples, all of whom were visiting tourists, who bought them?

Clues

1. The Georgian carriage lamp was chosen by the woman who came in on Monday, who wasn't Mrs. Yurkowitz from Philadelphia; on Tuesday, the customers were the Fujitas from Tokyo in Japan.

2. The 18th-century French mirror was sold two days before the Bergs from Oslo, Norway, made their purchases; the German music box was purchased the day after the loving cup.

3. Mr. McAndrew, the gentleman from Auckland, New Zealand, chose an 18th-century Brown Bess musket.

4. The husband of the Thursday couple bought himself an old naval telescope that might, Ann wasn't sure, have been used by one of the officers of HMS *Victory* at the battle of Trafalgar.

5. Mrs. Hofmann from Essen bought herself a tallboy after the style of Sheraton (probably a long way after).

6. One gentleman bought a Stringer and Woodward walnut case grandmother clock for himself and a marble bust of Lord Nelson (probably) for his wife.

Day	Husband's purchase

	Clock	Loving cup	Musket	Tantalus	Telescope	Bust	Lamp	Mirror	Music box	Tallboy	Berg	Fujita	Hofmann	McAndrew	Yurkowitz
Monday															
Tuesday															
Thursday															
Friday															
Saturday															
Berg															
Fujita															
Hofmann															
McAndrew															
Yurkowitz															
Bust															
Lamp															
Mirror															
Music box															
Tallboy															

Mum, Grandma's just been on Antiques Roadshow

Really? What did she take?

Grandad

Wife's purchase	Surname

Great Expectations

One particular week each of our old friends from the Drones Club was dragged off to an event which was not his particular cup of tea in order to accompany an elderly aunt. Far from complaining, out loud at least, our five heroes made a great show of interest, as each had great expectations of a large legacy at some point in the future and had no intention of rocking that boat. From the clues, can you work out on which day which Drone escorted which Aunt to what event?

Clues

1. The flower show took place later in the week than the event to which Gerald Huntington escorted his Aunt Euphemia.

2. Aunt Victoria went out the day after the unwilling escort was Rupert de Grey.

3. Edward Tanqueray attended the art exhibition with his elderly relative.

4. Aunt Millicent's escort was not Archie Fotheringhay, who did not carry out his family obligation on Monday.

5. It was Aunt Priscilla who insisted on being escorted round the tapestry exhibition; this was not on Friday.

6. Montague Ffolliott performed his spell of duty on Thursday.

7. The opera was attended on Wednesday evening.

8. Aunt Constance had her nephew dancing attendance on Tuesday.

Day	Drone

	Archie Fotheringhay	Edward Tanqueray	Gerald Huntington	Montague Ffolliott	Rupert de Grey	Aunt Constance	Aunt Euphemia	Aunt Millicent	Aunt Priscilla	Aunt Victoria	Art exhibition	Ballet	Flower show	Opera	Tapestry exhibition
Monday															
Tuesday															
Wednesday															
Thursday															
Friday															
Art exhibition															
Ballet															
Flower show															
Opera															
Tapestry exhibition															
Aunt Constance															
Aunt Euphemia															
Aunt Millicent															
Aunt Priscilla															
Aunt Victoria															

Aunt	Outing

Logi-5

Each line, across and down, is to have each of the letters A, B, C, D, and E, appearing once. Also, every shape—shown by the thick lines—must also have each of the letters in it. Can you fill in the grid?

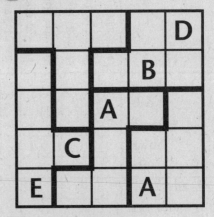

Killer Sudoku

The normal rules of Sudoku apply. In addition, the digits in each inner shape (marked by dots) must add up to the number in the top corner of that box.

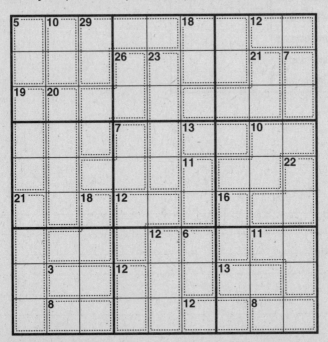

Battleships

Do you remember the old game of battleships? These puzzles are based on that idea. Your task is to find the vessels in the diagram. Some parts of boats or sea squares have already been filled in, and a number next to a row or column refers to the number of occupied squares in that row or column. The boats may be positioned horizontally or vertically, but no two boats or parts of boats are in adjacent squares—horizontally, vertically, or diagonally.

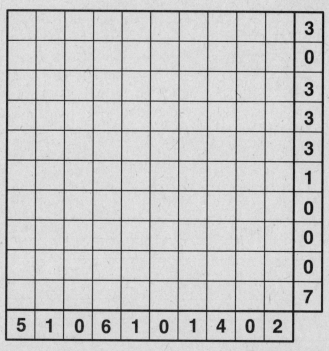

Aircraft carrier:

Battleship:

Cruiser:

Destroyer:

										3
										0
										3
										3
										3
										1
										0
										0
										0
										7
5	1	0	6	1	0	1	4	0	2	

Marriage Knot

Last Saturday, newspapers across the country reported a very unusual wedding at the Church of St. Thomas Didymus in Churchminster, when five men who each have a twin sister each married the twin sister of one of the other men, but without any of the men's sisters marrying the brother of the woman her brother had married. (Have you got all that clear? Good—I'm glad somebody has.) From the clues, can you work out the full name of each groom and the forename and maiden surname of his bride?

Clues

1. David's new wife, whose name isn't Julie, was formerly Miss McAlpine; her brother was married to Sarah on Saturday.

2. Nigel married Carol.

3. The former Tessa Haines didn't marry Peter Cammack.

4. Keith's new wife's maiden surname is the same as Karen's married surname.

5. The Mr. Purchan who married the former Miss Cammack isn't Simon.

Groom	Surname

	Surname										Maiden name				
	Cammack	Haines	McAlpine	Purchan	Tweedale	Carol	Julie	Karen	Sarah	Tessa	Cammack	Haines	McAlpine	Purchan	Tweedale
David															
Keith															
Nigel															
Peter															
Simon															
Maiden name Cammack															
Haines															
McAlpine															
Purchan															
Tweedale															
Carol															
Julie															
Karen															
Sarah															
Tessa															

Bride	Maiden name

An Expert Writes

When age catches up with those who have been blessed with athletic ability, one of the avenues open to them to earn a living is to write about the sport they've recently left. Five such sportsmen are featured here. From the clues, can you work out what type of sportsman each new journalist was, the name of the paper for which he now writes, and the city in which it is published?

Clues

1. Eddie Gordon was a reasonable marathon runner, winning both the Vancouver and Cape Town Marathons in his day; he isn't the former sportsman who now writes words of wisdom for the *Miami Record*.

2. Tom Zalewski from Toronto, who works for a paper in his home city, isn't the former boxing champion who now writes about his sport in the *Sun Times*.

3. Nick Pauly, who works for the weekly magazine *World of Sports*, didn't use a stick or a club in his sport.

4. The retired sportsman who competed in the decathlon in two Olympic Games in the 1990s but didn't win a medal now lives in London and writes for a publication published in that city.

5. The former ice hockey star doesn't work for one of two publications published in a city in the USA.

6. Randy Spring could never get the hang of golf as an amateur, let alone as a professional; he doesn't write for the publication based in San Diego in the USA, which isn't the *Journal*.

Sportman	Sport

	Boxing	Decathlon	Golf	Ice hockey	Marathon	Adelaide	London	Miami	San Diego	Toronto	Journal	Record	Sports News	Sun Times	World of Sports
Bernard Corrio															
Eddie Gordon															
Nick Pauly															
Randy Spring															
Tom Zalewski															
Journal															
Record															
Sports News															
Sun Times															
World of Sports															
Adelaide															
London															
Miami															
San Diego															
Toronto															

City	Paper

Is It Art?

Art dealer Walt Tizzett specializes in modern art, the sort that leaves many people puzzled, and has recently managed to persuade Marston Bagshot, the retired city bigwig who lives at Crispin Manor, to part with some of his wealth. Below are details of five recent acquisitions. Can you work out for which trendy gallery Tizzett was acting when he sold each piece, the name of the artist, what the work of art consists of, and how much Marston paid for each?

Clues

1. The Ivan Rippov piece, a stainless steel pyramid, was not from the Huddwinker Gallery but cost twice as much as the piece Walt Tizzett persuaded Marston Bagshot to buy from the Schamm Gallery.

2. The work by Monty Banks from the Foni Gallery cost $5,000 less than the piece from the Schamm.

3. The waste basket full of cans (carefully filled, not just thrown in) cost Marston more than the broken glass in a frame.

4. The pile of old automobile tires was priced at $10,000; it was not the work of Artie Fishall, who was also not responsible for the waste basket of cans.

5. The broken glass in the frame was on display at Fake Modern until Tizzett sold it to Bagshot.

6. Marston had to pay more for the Con Swindell work than for that by Esau Hoakes.

Gallery	Artist

	Artie Fishal	Con Swindell	Esau Hoakes	Ivan Rippov	Monty Banks	Broken glass	Waste basket	Pile of tires	Steel pyramid	Yellow kettle	$5,000	$10,000	$15,000	$20,000	$25,000
Fake Modern															
Foni															
Huddwinker															
Pinchbeck															
Schamm															
$5,000															
$10,000															
$15,000															
$20,000															
$25,000															
Broken glass															
Waste basket															
Pile of tires															
Steel pyramid															
Yellow kettle															

Good job we didn't finish unpacking it

TURNER PRIZE

1ST

Work	Price

Spelling Schools

The popularity of a certain well-known junior wizard over the past decade or so has led many people to believe that the schools mentioned in those stories are the only ones in the country. That's far from the truth, as there are many academies offering magical courses to would-be sorcerers and spell-casters. Below are details of five lucky candidates who have won places at these institutions. Can you work out at which establishment each is a pupil, their main areas of study, and the professor looking after each?

Clues

1. Larry Lester is at Porkwens Academy, but not to study invisibility (he couldn't see any point in that); Prof. Deerkey instructs in wandwork, but not at Porkwens or Hamboils.

2. Lottie Baxter is not at Boarpocks and isn't being taught by Prof. McTavish, who is not a specialist in flying.

3. Barry Carter is a pupil of Prof. Tumbledown.

4. Carrie Foster is studying potions and has had to promise not to practice on her little brother.

5. One of the five is attending Sowrash Academy to study fortune-telling—no one saw that coming.

6. Prof. Squirrel is a fellow of Gruntpimples Academy.

Pupil	Academy

	Boarpocks	Gruntpimples	Hamboils	Porkwens	Sowrash	Flying	Fortune-telling	Invisibility	Potions	Wandwork	Deerkey	McTavish	Snoop	Squirrel	Tumbledown
Barry Carter															
Carrie Foster															
Gary Dexter															
Larry Lester															
Lottie Baxter															
Deerkey															
McTavish															
Snoop															
Squirrel															
Tumbledown															
Flying															
Fortune-telling															
Invisibility															
Potions															
Wandwork															

Area	Professor

Hounds and Homes

The families living at numbers 2 to 8 Newfoundland Terrace in Netherlipp each have a pet dog. From the clues given below, can you name the family at each house and their dog, and identify the latter's breed?

Clues

1. The Kennell family lives at the house immediately to the right of the one which is home to Ricky, the Dalmatian.

2. The Barkers' house has a lower number than the one where the bulldog lives.

3. Butch lives at number 4.

4. The family at number 6 owns the Labrador.

5. The spaniel, who is not called Simba, belongs to the Doggetts.

Families: Barker; Doggett; Kennell; Yapp
Dogs: Butch; Jack; Ricky; Simba
Breeds: bulldog; Dalmatian; Labrador; spaniel

Starting tip: Start by working out where Ricky lives.

Domino Search

A standard set of dominoes has been laid out, using numbers instead of dots for clarity. Using a sharp pencil and a keen brain, can you draw in the lines to show where each domino has been placed? You may find the check grid useful—crossing off each domino as you find it.

0	0	3	1	2	3	0	6
2	0	5	2	4	4	0	2
6	1	5	3	1	3	5	4
5	2	2	6	2	2	6	1
6	6	4	3	5	0	4	4
0	1	4	6	1	6	3	1
0	1	3	5	4	5	3	5

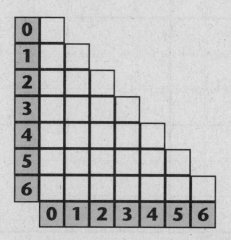

Logi-5

Each line, across and down, is to have each of the letters A, B, C, D, and E, appearing once. Also, every shape—shown by the thick lines—must also have each of the letters in it. Can you fill in the grid?

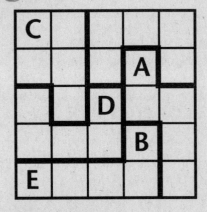

Killer Sudoku

The normal rules of Sudoku apply. In addition, the digits in each inner shape (marked by dots) must add up to the number in the top corner of that box.

11		14	16	17	8		14	
21						22		
	8	13	5	21				7
					12		12	
12					4			12
8		13		21		17		
3	14					10		22
	21	12	8					
			14		3		10	

World View

The small shop World of Globes in Stonekeigh Mall (or it could be Globe of Worlds) has five globes in its small window display. Each globe is a different diameter and has used a different color to depict the areas of seas and oceans. From the clues, can you work out the size and sea color for each?

Clues

1. The 9-inch globe uses the traditional blue for the watery bits.

2. The stainless steel globe has a silver sea; it is immediately to the left of the globe that uses a creamy white for the oceans and immediately right of the globe with the 7-inch diameter, which isn't globe 2.

3. Globe 1 is larger than the one with the yellow sea (and not just for the Yellow Sea) but is smaller than its immediate neighbor.

4. The largest globe, which doesn't feature a red sea (not even for the Red Sea) is globe 4; the smallest globe isn't globe 3.

Diameters: 6 inches; 7 inches; 8 inches; 9 inches; 10 inches
Sea colors: blue; red; silver; white; yellow

Starting tip: Begin by positioning the smallest globe.

Student Quarters

Number 8 Park Road in Goatsferry is a large house divided into five student accommodation modules all occupied by female students. By and large, the modules are identical, with the same furniture, the same books, and so on—but each of the girls has a pet gerbil and some items pertaining to her slightly unusual hobby. From the clues, can you work out which student lives in each module, the name of her animal companion, and the nature of her hobby?

Clues

1. The student in number 5 has a hobby (or peculiarity) of constantly seeking new flavors of fruit tea, which is the only thing she ever drinks (so long as you don't count pina colada, that is); Princess' owner is a keen woodworker and spends her spare time making things for her module and her friends.

2. Iona Hertford is the proud owner of Poppy, who is not red but a sort of sandy color, as all the gerbils are; Nora Merton rests her mind from the study of Law by reading westerns, especially those of Louis L'Amour.

3. Regina is the resident gerbil in module 3; Spot—named because he or she (no one has bothered to check) doesn't have any—and his or her owner occupy a higher numbered module than Lynne Keble but a lower numbered one than the student who investigates UFO sightings and contacts and is sure that most of her roommates are aliens of some sort.

4. Cassie Balliol is neither the Jane Austen–loving owner of Darcy nor the collector of cacti, who has a lower number than the one where Darcy lives, but not module 2; Yvonne Wadham is not in module 4.

Module	Student

	Cassie Balliol	Iona Hertford	Lynne Keble	Nora Merton	Yvonne Wadham	Darcy	Poppy	Princess	Regina	Spot	Collects cacti	Fruit teas	Reads westerns	UFO watcher	Wood worker
1															
2															
3															
4															
5															
Collects cacti															
Fruit teas															
Reads westerns															
UFO watcher															
Wood worker															
Darcy															
Poppy															
Princess															
Regina															
Spot															

Gerbil	Hobby

The Klashers

The latest arrivals on children's television are the Klashers, five cuddly creatures living on a faraway moon and communicating with each other using a kazoo-type sound. From the clues, can you discover their names, their individual colors, the distinctive item of clothing each wears, and the job each performs around the house?

Clues

1. Luni is yellow, but Dipi is neither pink nor green.

2. The green Klasher neither wears an apron, which is the cook's accessory, nor is responsible for the gardening.

3. The Klasher who wears the top hat is not pink; he, she, or it doesn't drive the others around and doesn't do the laundry.

4. It's the purple Klasher who does the laundry but doesn't wear wellies while doing it.

5. Dafi cleans the house but doesn't sport the top hat.

6. Bati always wears the sou'wester, while the red Klasher wears the waistcoat.

Name	Color

	Green	Pink	Purple	Red	Yellow	Apron	Sou'wester	Top hat	Waistcoat	Wellies	Cleaning	Cooking	Driving	Gardening	Laundry
Bati															
Dafi															
Dipi															
Gaga															
Luni															
Cleaning															
Cooking															
Driving															
Gardening															
Laundry															
Apron															
Sou'wester															
Top hat															
Waistcoat															
Wellies															

Clothing	Job

USA TODAY 53

Great Eastshire Menu

Somebody at Albion TV has come up with a brilliant idea for yet another cookery program, and five chefs, all equally qualified, are competing to become the presenter. (Actually, the producer's already decided to give the job to his girlfriend, but they don't know yet.) From the clues, can you work out the particularly distinctive aspect of each chef's appearance, the style of cookery in which he specializes, and in what part of Eastshire he runs a small but incredibly popular restaurant?

Clues

1. The man with the goatee beard cooks nouvelle cuisine; neither Tim Sweet-Bredd nor the fish specialist whose restaurant is called Heart and Sole insists on dressing in green.

2. The man with the shaven head has a restaurant in Storbury; he has no hyphen in his surname and is neither Dirk D'Essert nor the specialist in British traditional fare.

3. Angus Bannock is an expert in Oriental cookery; Perry Rasher is recognized by his unusual facial hair.

4. The man whose restaurant is in Brightbourne cooks only vegetarian food.

5. Jay Hammond-Eggz, who wears his hair in a tightly-braided pigtail, does not have a restaurant in Meadowland.

6. Perry Rasher, who runs Chez Longue in Colnecaster, is not an expert in fish cookery.

7. Tim Sweet-Bredd does not cook traditional British food.

Name	Appearance

	Walrus mustache	Dresses in green	Goatee beard	Pigtail	Shaven head	British traditional	Fish	Nouvelle cuisine	Oriental	Vegetarian	Brightbourne	Colnecaster	Meadowland	Middlehampton	Storbury
Angus Bannock															
Dirk D'Essert															
Jay Hammond-Eggz															
Perry Rasher															
Tim Sweet-Bredd															
Brightbourne															
Colnecaster															
Meadowland															
Middlehampton															
Storbury															
British traditional															
Fish															
Nouvelle cuisine															
Oriental															
Vegetarian															

NOUVELLE CUISINE
Chip Shop

Tiddler & Chip.........£25
Mushy Pea..............£15
Mini Pizza (serves 12)....£20

Specialty	Location

yAbe

The reverse of eBay, which is of course yAbe, is not a list of items people are prepared to pay you to take away (wouldn't that be good?) but is a place where people hunting specific items can advertise their desires. The five people listed here are avid collectors of very specific items. From the clues, can you work out the home of each collector and what items made by whom they collect?

Clues

1. The avid collector Oscar Oared lives in Dover.

2. Sophia Storem, who has a small but very select collection of paperweights (particularly unsightly and not very weighty) and is advertising for more, is not the collector from Penzance who collects things by Katherine Trimble Latimer, but only because she's their married daughter; Mrs. Latimer doesn't make guitars, not even bad ones.

3. Stanley Stox's collection is not comprised of anything to read or with which to write.

4. The first edition novels by the little-known and little-revered author Amelia Jansen Barclay (to be honest, first editions are all there ever are, as the initial print runs are never repeated) are not collected by Kate Kerlecht.

5. Penny Pylup, who has never lived in Carlisle, collects items crafted (if that's the word) by Olivia Sanders Tasker, which not even Ms. Tasker does, knowing junk when she sees it.

6. Penny Pylup isn't the resident of Lincoln who is advertising for artisan-made fountain pens, which release ink in a veritable fountain should you be unwise enough to add any; the fountain pen maker isn't Jeremiah Pendleton Wilmott.

Collector	Home

	Carlisle	Dover	Leicester	Lincoln	Penzance	Copper pots	First editions	Fountain pens	Guitars	Paperweights	AJ Barclay	JP Wilmott	KT Latimer	OS Tasker	PB Watchman
Kate Kerlecht															
Oscar Oared															
Penny Pylup															
Sophia Storem															
Stanley Stox															
AJ Barclay															
JP Wilmott															
KT Latimer															
OS Tasker															
PB Watchman															
Copper pots															
First editions															
Fountain pens															
Guitars															
Paperweights															

Item	Maker

Detectives Storey

Sam Storey is a literary agent in the city of New York and has recently acquired five new clients, each one a real-life detective of some sort who's working on a book about a fictional detective . . . of some sort. From the clues, can you work out the name and employer of each of the real-life detectives, and the name and occupation of the fictional investigator he or she has created?

Clues

1. The detective whose book features Sergeant Lucy Regan of the Internal Affairs Division (IAD) of an unnamed metropolitan police department, whose job is investigating fellow cops, isn't employed by a police department.

2. Dave Carey's book, which isn't about Patsy-Ann Bowen, features a federal agent belonging to a special task force working against organized crime.

3. Wendy Vance is the creator of Maisie Hovik.

4. John Kengo is a senior investigator for the Stern Detective Agency; it isn't the Vice Squad detective from the Miami Police who has created a private eye character.

5. The New York police officer, whose fictional investigator is not called Andy Gomez, and the detective who is writing a book about a small-town police chief are both male.

6. The investigator for Diamond Insurance, whose book is about a Military Police detective, isn't Moira Penn, whose fictional creation is female.

Real	Employer

	Boston police	Diamond Insurance	Miami police	New York police	Stern Agency	Andy Gomez	Carl Van Damm	Lucy Regan	Maisie Hovik	Patsy-Ann Bowen	Federal agent	IAD officer	Military Police officer	Police chief	Private eye
Dave Carey															
John Kengo															
Moira Penn															
Saul Rossi															
Wendy Vance															
Federal agent															
IAD officer															
Military Police officer															
Police chief															
Private eye															
Andy Gomez															
Carl Van Damm															
Lucy Regan															
Maisie Hovik															
Patsy-Ann Bowen															

Fictional	Occupation

Sign In

Each row and column is to contain the digits 1-6. The given signs tell you if a digit in a cell is plus 1 (+) or minus 1 (-) the digit next to it. Signs between consecutive digits always work from left to right or top to bottom.
Examples: 3 + 4 or 2
ALL occurrences of consecutive digits have been marked by a sign.

Sudoku

Complete this grid so that each column, each row, and each marked 3 X 3 square contains each of the numbers 1 to 9.

6				2				9
8				1				
	5	2	9					
5		1			2			
4		8	7				5	6
			9		8			
	2			5	7	3		
		5			7			
			8	4		9	5	

Daily Exercise

Back in the early 1960s four mob bosses from different cities were arrested by the FBI, and as a reward for giving information about the activities of the others, each was sentenced to 99 years. The picture below shows the four at their daily exercise in the smallest of America's federal prisons at Smalltown, Arizona. From the clues, can you fill in each prisoner's name, mob nickname, and the town he used to run?

Clues

1. Prisoner 2 is not the man called Don Bedelio, who was formerly the mob boss of Providence, Rhode Island.

2. The St. Louis gang leader was nicknamed Muscles, because he knew where to hire some.

3. The man who used to run the underworld in Tulsa, Oklahoma, is prisoner 4, who is not Frankie "the Spider" Fabiani.

4. Prisoner 1 is Tony Sambani; Pistols is not the nickname of prisoner 3.

Mob bosses: Don Bedelio; Frankie Fabiani; Joey Miliano; Tony Sambani
Nicknames: Crazy man; Muscles; Pistols; Spider
Cities: Detroit; Providence; St. Louis; Tulsa

Starting tip: Begin by placing Don Bedelio in the line-up.

Roman Vacation

Five recently retired couples are enjoying a long Mediterranean cruise, and the ship has steamed into the port of Civitavecchia for a day's visit to the ancient city of Rome. From the clues, can you work out where each couple went and what item the male half lost during the excursion and where?

Clues

1. Mr. Thomas embarrassed his wife at the Trevi Fountain by singing about three coins, tossing in three euros, and then trying to fish them out again; he didn't leave his item on a seat.

2. "You left your phrase-book in the taxi," said one man's wife. "You put it down after trying to translate, 'How much? We wanted to ride in the car, not buy it!' and forgot to pick it up again."

3. One man returned from the Pantheon without his prized, bright orange, floppy hat, much to his wife's delight—she had been looking for somewhere to lose the thing for days.

4. "Pass the sunblock," said Mr. Simkin to his wife. "You've got it," she replied. "You had it in your hand." "We'll have to buy some more," he said. "That stuff was no good anyway."

5. Mr. Grey rushed out of a diner quickly before anyone noticed the tiny tip he'd left but left something more valuable behind in the process.

6. It wasn't Mr. and Mrs. Lewes who alighted from the bus at the Forum and watched it pull away with something they owned still on board; Mr. Shepherd didn't lose anything in a means of transport and still has all his sunglasses.

7. The item left at the Spanish Steps wasn't made of paper; the postcards weren't left behind at the Colosseum.

Couple	Destination

	Colosseum	Forum	Pantheon	Spanish Steps	Trevi Fountain	Hat	Phrase book	Postcards	Sunblock	Sunglasses	Bus	Diner	Ice-cream stall	Seat	Taxi
Grey															
Lewes															
Shepherd															
Simkin															
Thomas															
Bus															
Diner															
Ice-cream stall															
Seat															
Taxi															
Hat															
Phrase book															
Postcards															
Sunblock															
Sunglasses															

Lost	Location

A Book by Its Cover

Five celebrity autobiographies are currently on sale in Foylstones book shop in Netherlipp Mall, and each has a title chosen to catch the eye and massage the writer's ego. From the clues, can you discover the egotistical title of each book, the name of the author, his or her profession, and the cover price of each volume?

Clues

1. Guy Fuller's autobiography is entitled, apparently without any compunction, *The Fuller Story*; Caleb Ritty is a soccer player for Netherlipp United, whose regular bans for violent conduct have left him with plenty of time to write.

2. *Speaking Personally* is on sale at $16.99, but its author is not the 18-year-old pop singer whose autobiography (which mainly covers the "nursery years") is priced lower than *Quite a Life*.

3. The radio presenter's book, *Talking of Me*, has a lower cover price than Hugh Jeago's.

4. The former senator's autobiography is only $15.99 (which is an interesting use of the word "only"), but its author is not Ed Biggar.

5. *I Say!* isn't the $17.99 volume.

6. Emma Starr's autobiography is for sale at $18.99.

Title	Author

	Ed Biggar	Guy Fuller	Hugh Jeago	Caleb Ritty	Emma Starr	$15.99	$16.99	$17.99	$18.99	$19.99	Footballer	MP	Opera singer	Pop singer	Radio presenter
I Say!															
Quite a Life															
Speaking Personally															
Talking of Me															
The Fuller Story															
Soccer player															
Senator															
Opera singer															
Pop singer															
Radio presenter															
$15.99															
$16.99															
$17.99															
$18.99															
$19.99															

This is Ian Mytee with his new book "Me, Me, Me, Me, Me!" What's it about, Ian?

Price	Profession

Beaux on Board

An acquaintance of our five old friends the Regency Beaux was a dandy with a maritime bent, named Beau Spritt. When the Napoleonic Wars were safely concluded, the latter enjoyed summer cruises on his yacht, during which one of our Beaux was invited along with a young lady whose acquaintance he was eager to pursue. From the clues, can you say which Beau was invited aboard in each year, and name the girl he was interested in and her father's rank or occupation?

Clues

1. Matilda, whose father was an ambassador at the court of St. James, was a guest on a cruise in a later year than the one on which Beau Nydel was invited.

2. Beau Legges and the admiral's daughter, who was not Augusta, were both Beau Spritt's guests in the year before Caroline went cruising.

3. Beau Belles was an earlier guest of Beau Spritt's than Beau Tighe.

4. Charlotte, whose father was not the rich merchant, was the young lady who appealed to Beau Streate; their cruise was not the first or last of the five.

5. 1817 was the year in which Sophia was invited to travel on Beau Spritt's yacht.

6. The earl's daughter was the prize catch aboard Beau Spritt's yacht in 1818; she was not being pursued by Beau Belles.

Year	Beau

	Beau Belles	Beau Legges	Beau Nydel	Beau Streate	Beau Tighe	Augusta	Caroline	Charlotte	Matilda	Sophia	Admiral	Ambassador	Baronet	Earl	Rich merchant
1816															
1817															
1818															
1819															
1820															
Admiral															
Ambassador															
Baronet															
Earl															
Rich merchant															
Augusta															
Caroline															
Charlotte															
Matilda															
Sophia															

Lady	Father

On Report

Sophie is a pupil at Stonekeigh High School and was a little wary when she took her report card home at the end of the term. To her surprise, her parents were, on the whole, quite pleased with it, though the grades she received varied between A and C+. From the clues, can you work out which grade she was given by which teacher in each of the five listed subjects, and say which summarizing comment each teacher appended?

Clues

1. The A grade was naturally the one matched by the comment "excellent," while the A- was not accompanied by the comment "works hard."

2. The grade given by Mr. Dingle was not as good as the science grade but higher than the one which drew the comment "intelligent."

3. "A steady worker" was Mrs. Carter's assessment of Sophie.

4. Sophie received a B+ from her French teacher.

5. In history, Sophie was given a grade immediately higher than the one she received for math, which she is not taught by Miss Roberts.

6. The B grade was awarded by Mrs. Jefferson.

7. The English teacher, Mr. Fletcher, awarded Sophie the grade immediately higher than the one which preceded the comment "solid progress."

Subject	Grade

	A	A-	B+	B	C+	Mrs. Carter	Mr. Dingle	Mr. Fletcher	Mrs. Jefferson	Miss Roberts	A steady worker	Excellent	Intelligent	Solid progress	Works hard
English															
French															
History															
Math															
Science															
A steady worker															
Excellent															
Intelligent															
Solid progress															
Works hard															
Mrs. Carter															
Mr. Dingle															
Mr. Fletcher															
Mrs. Jefferson															
Miss Roberts															

REPORT

It's been redacted for security reasons

Teacher	Comment

Poster Boys

Wanted posters for notorious outlaws have gone up in five Wild West towns. From the clues, can you discover where each poster has been nailed up, the crime for which each outlaw is wanted, and the reward being offered?

Clues

1. Scotty McRae is wanted in Harris Falls, and the reward being offered is $300 more than that for the cattle rustler.

2. The $400 reward is being offered in Little Pine, but not for the capture of Hank Gilmore.

3. The reward being offered for the murderer is $100 more than the sum on the posters in White River, where an even number of hundreds of dollars is being offered.

4. Zack Monroe is a train robber.

5. The reward for Link O'Reilly is $600.

6. The bank robber is wanted in Gibbsville, but $500 is not the sum to be paid.

Town	Outlaw

	Hank Gilmore	Baxter Gould	Scotty McRae	Zack Monroe	Link O'Reilly	Bank robbery	Cattle rustling	Horse stealing	Murder	Train robbery	$400	$500	$600	$700	$1,000
Gibbsville															
Harris Falls															
Little Pine															
White River															
Yellow Creek															
$400															
$500															
$600															
$700															
$1,000															
Bank robbery															
Cattle rustling															
Horse stealing															
Murder															
Train robbery															

Crime	Reward

Piece of Cake

Alice Flower runs a small bakery in the Farnwyde industrial estate just outside Stonekeigh. She has a couple of employees hard at work baking but, currently, has to make the deliveries herself. Today she had five orders to deliver but found herself delayed on the narrow and winding roads of Keighshire by a slow moving vehicle of some sort. From the clues, can you say to which customer each order was being delivered, which vehicle delayed Alice's small truck, and for how many minutes she was delayed?

Clues

1. Mr. Simnel of Lower Crispin had ordered a large wedding cake for his daughter's nuptials; Alice wasn't held up on the way to deliver this by the backhoe moving from one building site to another but was held up for five minutes longer than when she was on her way to Mrs. Dundee in Wallingfen and five minutes shorter than when making the delivery of four dozen cup cakes for a party.

2. The route to Mrs. Angel's house in Great Crispin was blocked for a short time while an tractor-trailer performed a 378-point turn in the road.

3. The delivery of the birthday cake ordered by a man for his wife's fiftieth birthday was delayed for ten minutes but wasn't the one held up by the truck making it's deliveries along a narrow lane.

4. The tenth birthday cake arrived a little later than Alice had planned after she had sat irritably drumming on her steering wheel while a tractor made its serene way along a country road between two fields.

5. The horse trailer, apparently empty but still tootling along at a slow pace, held up Alice for a quarter of an hour.

6. The route to Mr. Eccles in Crispin Parva wasn't the one that involved the shortest delay.

Customer	Cake

	Anniversary cake	Birthday cake 10th	Birthday cake 50th	Cup cakes	Wedding cake	Tractor-trailer	Horse trailer	Backhoe	Truck	Tractor	5 minutes	10 minutes	15 minutes	20 minutes	25 minutes
Mrs. Angel															
Mr. Battenburg															
Mrs. Dundee															
Mr. Eccles															
Mr. Simnel															
5 minutes															
10 minutes															
15 minutes															
20 minutes															
25 minutes															
Tractor-trailer															
Horse trailer															
Backhoe															
Truck															
Tractor															

Vehicle	Minutes

Out of the Game

Albion TV is making a new series about sportsmen or women who have gone from fame and fortune to obscurity because of some unfortunate incident. From the clues, can you work out the name of each subject chosen so far, his or her former sport, what happened, and what he or she does now?

Clues

1. Diane Frost owns the Green Lion pub in Storbury; none of Diane, the former BMX rider, or the sports star who is now employed by a charity was involved in a divorce scandal.

2. The squash player's prospects were ruined when it came out they had taken a bribe to lose a match; the person who now breeds dogs was banned for life for drugging an opponent to ensure a place in the final of the All Eastshire Cup.

3. Neither Penny Robins, who has never played football nor the sports star who has been blacklisted after libeling their manager is either the BMX rider or the former star who is now employed as a sports teacher.

4. Both Brian Cooper, who was once a top javelin thrower, and Tommy Warton are self-employed, running their own businesses because no one else will give them a job.

5. Jane Martin, who received a twenty-year ban for punching the umpire, wasn't a professional football player.

Sports star	Sport

	BMX cycling	Football	Javelin	Squash	Tennis	Bribery scandal	Divorce scandal	Drugged opponent	Libeled manager	Punched umpire	Charity worker	Dog breeder	Freelance journalist	Pub owner	Sports teacher
Brian Cooper															
Diane Frost															
Jane Martin															
Penny Robins															
Tommy Warton															
Charity worker															
Dog breeder															
Freelance journalist															
Pub owner															
Sports teacher															
Bribery scandal															
Divorce scandal															
Drugged opponent															
Libeled manager															
Punched umpire															

That's excellent! Next week we'll do "letting go."

Reason	Present job

Collection Day

The residents of Benefice Avenue in Netherlipp have answered the request to donate nearly new clothing and other items to a charitable group and have placed them outside their houses for collection. From the clues, can you name the family at each number, the main items of clothing in the sacks, and the other items in the boxes?

Clues

1. The box outside 9 Benefice Avenue contains toys.

2. The Grays live next door to the family who has donated a few pairs of rarely worn shoes, who don't live at number 7.

3. The Greenes live between the family who has donated a box of books and the family who has filled their bag with nearly new woollen sweaters; the family that is giving the books is not the same one that has filled the bag with T-shirts.

4. The Brauns live at a lower number than the family who has found a number of sweatshirts to donate; the Whytes have filled their bag with pants which are now too big for them after a spate of family dieting.

Surnames: Braun; Gray; Greene; Whyte
In the bags: sweaters; sweatshirts; pants; T-shirts
In the boxes: books; DVDs; shoes; toys

Starting tip: Work out who lives at 11 Benefice Avenue.

Battleships

Do you remember the old game of battleships? These puzzles are based on that idea. Your task is to find the vessels in the diagram. Some parts of boats or sea squares have already been filled in, and a number next to a row or column refers to the number of occupied squares in that row or column. The boats may be positioned horizontally or vertically, but no two boats or parts of boats are in adjacent squares—horizontally, vertically, or diagonally.

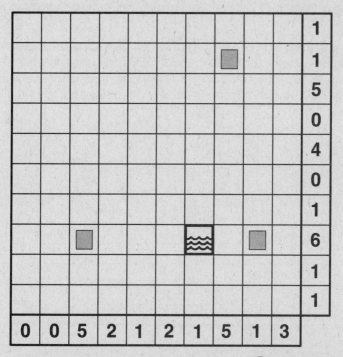

Aircraft carrier:

Battleship:

Cruiser:

Destroyer:

Plane Investigations

Shingle Bay is an area of southwest Ireland. Five aircraft of different nationalities crashed off its coast between 1941 and 1945, all on some form of military flight, and these planes are now being investigated by teams of historians and divers for an Albion TV documentary series. From the clues, can you work out where each plane crashed, its type, when it crashed, and the name of the man in charge of the investigation?

Clues

1. The Douglas C47—the American-built transport known as the Dakota—which crashed owing to pilot error in March, 1945, is not being investigated by Charlie Beaufort's team.

2. The Junkers JU52/3M, a big, three-engined, German transport plane, is being dealt with by Ulrich Tasman, whose grandfather flew one just like it; Owen North's team is not working on the plane that went down in the shallows known as Seal Bay.

3. It was in 1944 that one aircraft hit the water in the shadow of Rocky Point while trying to make an emergency landing, almost exactly one year after the crash being investigated by Don Coral and his team; the German Messerschmitt Bf110 fighter didn't crash in 1942.

4. The Westland Lysander—a communications aircraft much used for special secret operations—crashed near Mariners Haven after running out of fuel, but not in 1943; Tom Solomon's men are diving close to Viking Head, but not on the wreck of either the Douglas C47 or the British Short Stirling four-engined bomber.

Location	Plane

	Douglas	Junkers	Messerschmitt	Short Stirling	Westland	1941	1942	1943	1944	1945	Charlie Beaufort	Don Coral	Owen North	Tom Solomon	Ulrich Tasman
Devil's Rock															
Mariners Haven															
Rocky Point															
Seal Bay															
Viking Head															
Charlie Beaufort															
Don Coral															
Owen North															
Tom Solomon															
Ulrich Tasman															
1941															
1942															
1943															
1944															
1945															

Year	Archaeologist

That's the Ticket

Sylvester Stubbs collects tickets or parts of tickets that he has used himself and displays many of them in frames on the walls of his home. From the clues, can you work out the details of the tickets in the frame below: the month in which it was issued and the location, service, or performance to which it allowed him access? (For clarity, tickets 3, 4, and 5 are the three square ones.)

Clues

1. The ticket from Sylvester's visit to the Netherlipp Opera House, which wasn't in April, to see the Keighshire Body Builders' Amateur Operatic Society's performance of the *Barbell of Seville* is shown immediately below the ticket dated June and immediately to the right of the one allowing access to the theme park Walton Towers, based on a long-running imported TV series; the June ticket and the Walton Towers ticket are different shapes.

2. The ticket to the local derby football game between Netherlipp United and Stonekeigh Rovers (and to the pitch invasion that would inevitably happen halfway through the second half) is numbered twice that of the ticket issued to Sylvester in November.

3. The ticket to the Mega Multiscreen Maxidrome Movieplex movie house to see the blockbuster *Admission Impossible,* in which our hero spends two hours looking for a way in, was issued the month after ticket number 3 and the month before the ticket to the Netherlipp Grand Theater to see the Bard's little-performed sequel *A Nightmare in Fall.*

4. Ticket number 1 was issued one month after ticket number 9, which wasn't for the train journey between Netherlipp and Upper Crispin, which isn't on the top row of tickets; ticket number 6, which wasn't issued in October, wasn't issued the month before the visit to the Netherlipp State Museum.

5. Ticket 2 allowed Sylvester in to the big top to see the trapeze flyers and high wire walkers of the circus; ticket 4 is dated September 21.

6. The ticket dated in August, which isn't one of the three square tickets and isn't immediately below the museum ticket, is a memento of Sylvester's trip to see the Turnoff Prize entrants at Netherlipp's Modern Art Gallery.

Tickets: art gallery; movie house; circus; football game; museum; opera house; theater; theme park; train journey

Months: March; April; May; June; July; August; September; October; November

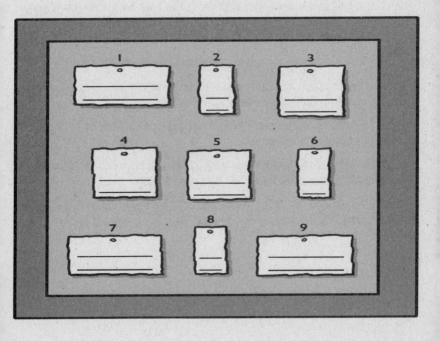

Starting tip: Begin by deciding which numbered ticked is dated November.

Very Special Days

Kay Terring is Northchester's leading organizer of wedding receptions, and this month has been booked to run the wedding celebrations for five rather out-of-the-ordinary marriages. From the clues, can you work out the name of the bride and groom concerned in each of them, where the actual ceremony will take place, and what Kay is charging for doing the reception?

Clues

1. Kay's bill for the reception at the Netherlipp United football stadium after Jon Ireton and his bride, both dressed in United colors, have been united (as it were) in matrimony on the center spot of the pitch will be lower than the one for the former Liz Monk's do.

2. Rachel Shaw's reception is going to cost her parents exactly $6,000.

3. Mark Lewis' reception is going to cost $7,200; he isn't the gentleman who will be getting married in the basket of a hot-air balloon.

4. Clare Dane and her husband-to-be have arranged for their wedding to be on the shore of a beautiful woodland lake.

5. Kay's bill for the small, families-only reception after the wedding at the stately home called Northchester Towers will be a mere $4,800.

6. The cost of the reception after the marriage of Alison Bell to Simon Ryder will be $1,200 more than what Kay is charging Nick Murphy's in-laws-to-be.

Bride	Groom

	Daniel Clark	Jon Ireton	Mark Lewis	Nick Murphy	Simon Ryder	Football ground	Hot-air balloon	Lake shore	Stately home	Tudor chapel	$4,200	$4,800	$5,400	$6,000	$7,200
Alison Bell															
Clare Dane															
Emma Finch															
Liz Monk															
Rachel Shaw															
$4,200															
$4,800															
$5,400															
$6,000															
$7,200															
Football stadium															
Hot-air balloon															
Lake shore															
Stately home															
Tudor chapel															

I think the word you're looking for is "Just."

MERELY MARRIED

Location	Cost

Sunday Celebs

The *Sunday Clarion*, Netherlipp's Sunday newspaper covering the Keighshire area, contains a color magazine called *Keigh Facts* with interesting information and photos of local celebrities. Ed Snooper is the editor of *Keigh Facts* and has five teams of reporters and photographers who gather the information. From the clues, can you name the leader of each team, the type of celebrities they are focusing on this week, and the deadline that Ed Snooper has given them for the delivery of their article?

Clues

1. Horace Hack, who leads the Nightclub Sweep team lying in wait outside nightclubs for celebrities who look the worse for wear, has a later deadline for his article than the team targeting TV stars this week and an earlier one than Sally Scoop and her team need to meet.

2. The Home Stalking team, nestling in bushes outside celebrity homes hoping to catch them off guard, which is led by a woman and is focusing on movie stars this week, doesn't have the Thursday afternoon deadline.

3. The article about the politicians is due the day after the Office Stalkers are due to deliver their piece after milling about outside various workplaces but the day before Stan Scribe and his team are due to place their article on Ed Snooper's desk.

4. The Diner Crew, who hang around outside posh restaurants and fashionable coffee shops, need to deliver their article on Thursday; the Dumpster Divers, who don plastic gloves to delve through the contents of celebrities' garbage cans, are not the team hoping to expose an athlete or two; the piece about the athletes is not due on Thursday morning.

5. Stella Stringer has an afternoon deadline.

Team	Leader

	Horace Hack	Sally Scoop	Stan Scribe	Stella Stringer	Will Wright	Athletes	Movie stars	Politicians	Pop stars	TV stars	Wednesday a.m.	Wednesday p.m.	Thursday a.m.	Thursday p.m.	Friday a.m.
Dumpster Divers															
Diner Crew															
Home Stalkers															
Nightclub Sweep															
Office Stalkers															
Wednesday a.m.															
Wednesday p.m.															
Thursday a.m.															
Thursday p.m.															
Friday a.m.															
Athletes															
Movie stars															
Politicians															
Pop stars															
TV stars															

Celeb type	Deadline

Van Guard

The Storbury Mobile Homes Center is a major trailer dealer and on the forecourt of their headquarters (a small hut on the road to Northchester) four trailers are displayed—all clamped and anchored into position, in case anybody tries to move them—they lost one that way last summer! From the clues, can you fill in on the diagram the make and model of each trailer, and say how many berths it has?

Clues

1. The Explorer, which is the 6-berth model, is immediately right of the mobile home made by Lynewood.

2. The Colorado has more berths than the Olympus.

3. Trailer A is the Northwest, which is not a 4-berth.

4. The Arundel trailer is immediately left of the 2-berth trailer.

5. The Meteor is a product of Eldorado Trailers Ltd.

Manufacturers: Arundel; Eldorado; Lynewood; Northwest
Models: Colorado; Explorer; Meteor; Olympus
Berths: 2; 4; 5; 6

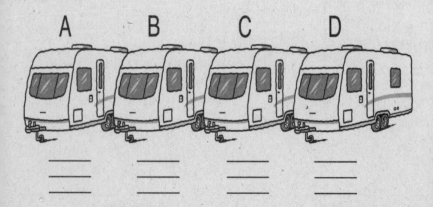

Logi-5

Each line, across and down, is to have each of the letters A, B, C, D, and E, appearing once. Also, every shape—shown by the thick lines—must also have each of the letters in it. Can you fill in the grid?

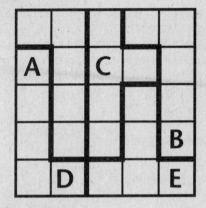

Sudoku

Complete this grid so that each column, each row, and each marked 3 X 3 square contains each of the numbers 1 to 9.

			3					
		9					6	5
	8		7			4	3	
2		4	9	1		5		7
			2			1	9	
								2
		6	8	4				
	3	1		7				4
	4		1		2		5	8

Battleships

Do you remember the old game of battleships? These puzzles are based on that idea. Your task is to find the vessels in the diagram. Some parts of boats or sea squares have already been filled in, and a number next to a row or column refers to the number of occupied squares in that row or column. The boats may be positioned horizontally or vertically, but no two boats or parts of boats are in adjacent squares—horizontally, vertically, or diagonally.

Aircraft carrier:

Battleship:

Cruiser:

Destroyer:

										1
			≈							**4**
										1
										4
										3
										0
										1
										1
										0
	≈									**5**
3	**1**	**3**	**2**	**0**	**0**	**0**	**2**	**2**	**7**	

Mixed Drinks

Tom Collins is the owner of Combinations, a cocktail bar in Stonekeigh Town Square that is famous for its new creations. Tom has just made six of these dubious concoctions for a group of over-intrepid customers. From the clues, can you work out the spirit and unusual mixer in each glass on the tray? (For clarity, glass 4 is directly in front of 1, 5 is in front of 2 and 6 is in front of 3.)

Clues

1. The rum is in the glass immediately behind the one containing vinegar; the tequila is in the glass directly in front of the one with the dash of ketchup.

2. The brandy and custard concoction is in the glass numbered twice that of the one with the vodka.

3. Glass 5 contains a good slosh of chicken stock but no whisky, which isn't the spirit in the glass directly in front of the one with the liberal squirt of Worcestershire sauce.

4. The gin is in one of the glasses on the back row of the tray; glass 3 has no mustard.

Spirits: brandy; gin; rum; tequila; vodka; whisky
Mixers: chicken stock; custard; ketchup; mustard; vinegar; Worcestershire sauce

Starting tip: Work out what spirit accompanies the chicken stock.

Read the Signs

The *Netherlipp Clarion* runs an astrology column by the famous star sign interpreter Horace Cope which is read by many, including the five members of the Overseas Underdevelopment Department at GloboCorp. Horace's foretellings always follow the same pattern. He has some good news for each sign and some bad news, about which he is oddly specific. From the clues, can you say which GloboCorp worker's birthday falls within which star sign (given in order through the calendar year) and the two parts of their forecast?

Clues

1. Cora's birthday is on July 31, which makes her a Leo.

2. Anne, whose birthday is later in the year than her colleague whose horoscope includes the worrying news that their pet will have some health problems connected to the left front paw (not least because they don't have a pet), is being told she will meet an old friend.

3. Eric has been warned to expect an unexpected expense for an item made of PVC or possibly wrought iron; Bill isn't the worker whose horoscope drew some suspicious glances by foretelling a career advancement.

4. One person was told to expect some news from overseas and warned that they will lose something small and silvery on a form of public transport.

5. The staff member who looked glum when told of a sudden increase in workload when all their colleagues decide to take a vacation together isn't covered by the star sign next after that of the person who, apparently, is heading for a hot romance.

6. The Pisces staff member will miss an important appointment with a person from Guatemala or, possibly, Stonekeigh; the good news for the Scorpio, which was about a sudden windfall, was tempered by calls from the rest of the office: "The next round's on you!!"

Staff member	Sign

	Pisces	Aries	Gemini	Leo	Scorpio	Career advance	Meet old friend	Overseas news	Romance	Windfall	Increased workload	Lose item	Miss appointment	Pet's health	Unexpected expense
Anne															
Bill															
Cora															
Dawn															
Eric															
Increased workload															
Lose item															
Miss appointment															
Pet's health															
Unexpected expense															
Career advance															
Meet old friend															
Overseas news															
Romance															
Windfall															

Positive	Negative

Serve You Right

In the dining room at the Stonekeigh Academy, five lunch ladies, wearing football padding and helmets, are lined up nervously waiting to serve lunches to the angry rabble impatiently milling beyond the locked door. Details of the first five children to pass along the serving counter are given below. Can you discover the name and year of each and work out which lunch lady is serving which item?

Clues

1. Annie is serving the beans from behind a visor (a bean in the eye is no fun at all), but Kay is on neither the potatoes nor the pies.

2. Neither Shelley, who is in 8th grade, nor the child in 9th grade is having potatoes but only because they won't fit on the already overflowing plate.

3. Nicky is not in 10th grade or 11th grade and isn't being served pies; he is also not the 7th grade pupil being served at arm's length by Mavis.

4. The 10th grade child, who is not Rosie, is having a large helping of peas—not to eat of course; a pea is the ideal fork-launched missile.

5. Lee is having fish sticks for lunch.

6. Wendy is serving Matthew.

Lunch lady	Food

	Beans	Fish sticks	Peas	Pies	Potatoes	Lee	Matthew	Nicky	Rosie	Shelley	7th grade	8th grade	9th grade	10th grade	11th grade
Annie															
Hazel															
Kay															
Mavis															
Wendy															
7th grade															
8th grade															
9th grade															
10th grade															
11th grade															
Lee															
Matthew															
Nicky															
Rosie															
Shelley															

Seems to be going down well today

Pupil	Year

Fruitless Following

When a private detective is struggling for leads on a case, he has to take any opportunity that presents itself. This was the situation earlier this morning with each of the five private dicks in the Southern Californian town of San Angelo, into whose lives we often peer. While pondering their cases and going about their morning, each detective spotted a person whom they thought they recognized and set off to follow, each of them ending up in San Angelo's Central Park where, coincidentally, the five suspects all gathered at a picnic table where they laid out and ate lunch. From the clues, can you say who each detective followed, from where, and the case he is currently working on?

Clues

1. One of the detectives spotted a suspicious man with a dog, and, since his current dog-napping case had no leads (if you'll pardon me), he decided to follow him anyway; this detective is behind a tree on the same side of the central path as the detective whose corruption in local government case was in need of some greasing.

2. Mike Mallet spotted a likely suspect in the Kwikee Mart grocery store buying cold meats and bread and decided to follow.

3. Nicky Nail is currently poking his nose out from behind a tree on the right of the path (as we view the picture); Dick Drill, whose leads on his missing persons case have all disappeared, is directly across the central path from Ricky Wrench, who has followed a man to the park.

4. The detective secreted behind tree number 1, who hadn't followed the man with the basket (a picnic basket it turns out), is hoping to add some sparkle to his case concerning the theft of a collection of diamond jewelry; the detective behind tree 5 had followed his suspect ever since he spotted them at the bus station.

5. One detective had spotted a very suspicious character wearing a straw hat buying bottles of lemonade at O'Malley's bar and had decided to see where he went.

6. The man who had carefully tailed his quarry all the way from San Angelo railway station is further away from us as we look at the picture than the man who has followed the woman with the parasol.

7. The woman carrying the package, who isn't the suspect in the case of infidelity, is being followed by the detective behind the tree numbered one higher than the detective who spotted a potential lead alighting at the tram stop and has been on their tail ever since.

8. Tree 4 is hiding Spike Spanner from the view of the innocent picnickers.

USA TODAY

Detectives: Dick Drill; Mike Mallet; Nicky Nail; Ricky Wrench; Spike Spanner
Following: man in straw hat; man with basket; man with dog; woman with parasol; woman with package
From: bus station; Kwikee Mart; O'Malley's bar; railway station; tram stop
Cases: corruption; diamond theft; dog-napping; infidelity; missing person

Starting tip: Begin by name the man behind tree 3.

Court in the Act

After a session at the juvenile court last week, five of the offenders, having been found guilty, were assigned to the care of probation officers as part of their sentence. From the clues, can you say which offense each of the five, whose names have been changed to avoid the embarrassment of the families, committed and fully identify the probation officer to whom each was referred?

Clues

1. Jonathan was found guilty of taking a vehicle without the owner's consent and leaving it in a ditch, also without the owner's consent.

2. Probation Officer Rachel Atkins did not follow up the disorderly conduct offense.

3. Marlon was not the shoplifter who "forgot" to pay for his bag of pick'n'mix; the shoplifter's probation officer was Martin, who is not Nathan.

4. The man into whose charge Christian was assigned and the man looking after the youth found guilty of vandalism of an unresponsive vending machine have first names of equal length.

5. The drunk in public offense was the crime of which the client of James, who is not Holloway, was convicted—he was celebrating after being found not-guilty of a similar offense the week before.

6. Farouk's probation officer was Lowther; the former had not been charged with a disorderly conduct offense.

Client	Offense

	Drunk in public	Disorderly conduct	Shoplifting	Taking without . . .	Vandalism	Barry	James	Nathan	Pamela	Rachel	Atkins	Berryman	Holloway	Lowther	Martin
Christian															
Craig															
Farouk															
Jonathan															
Marlon															
Atkins															
Berryman															
Holloway															
Lowther															
Martin															
Barry															
James															
Nathan															
Pamela															
Rachel															

First name	Surname

Lippie Service

We are lucky to be able to reveal advance information about some of the nominees for this year's Netherlipp Film Festival Awards, the Lippies 2019. From the clues, can you discover for which award each person has been nominated, the title of the film concerned, and the month it was released during the year?

Clues

1. Rachel Morris has been nominated for an award for the November film, which has a two-word title, while Miranda Kemp is up for the Best Actress Lippie.

2. A woman has been nominated for the Best Director award for her film *The Marked Man*.

3. Hugh Talbot has not been nominated for work in special effects; the film being rewarded for its effects, released in May 2019, is not *One Rainy Day*.

4. The nominated costume designer worked on a film released four months after the one for which Imogen Penn has been nominated.

5. *Desert Ice* is not one of the films up for the Lippie for Best Score.

6. *Queen of Manhattan* was released last July.

Month	Film

	Desert Ice	Funny Business	One Rainy Day	Queen of Manhattan	The Marked Man	Costume design	Director	Leading actress	Score	Special effects	Miranda Kemp	Duncan McKee	Rachel Morris	Imogen Penn	Hugh Talbot
May															
July															
September															
November															
January															
Miranda Kemp															
Duncan McKee															
Rachel Morris															
Imogen Penn															
Hugh Talbot															
Costume design															
Director															
Leading actress															
Score															
Special effects															

Award	Nominee

Domino Search

A standard set of dominoes has been laid out, using numbers instead of dots for clarity. Using a sharp pencil and a keen brain, can you draw in the lines to show where each domino has been placed? You may find the check grid useful—crossing off each domino as you find it.

1	6	6	1	4	5	5	4
2	0	4	3	1	1	6	2
3	3	3	5	0	3	2	0
6	2	5	2	6	0	6	6
3	4	5	0	0	1	4	3
0	4	1	3	5	2	2	4
2	0	5	5	1	6	1	4

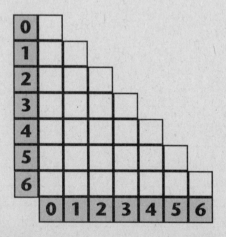

Art Dekko

Mike Angel runs the "Isms" evening art class at Stonekeigh College for new artists trying to come to grips with styles of painting. He currently has five students who are daubing away trying to fit into a genre. From the clues, can you name the would-be artist behind each canvas and say in what "ism" he or she is painting?

Clues

1. Bonny Kneah is daubing away immediately between the artist striving for impressionism and Matt Ease.

2. Dave Inchy is hoping to express some expressionism; artist 4 isn't the would-be pointillist.

3. Della Kwah is painting the canvas numbered twice that of the artist hoping to join the Dadaist movement.

4. The artist in the middle of the line is painting in what they hope is the cubist style; Donna Tellow is not the artist behind canvas number 5.

Artists: Bonny Kneah; Dave Inchy; Della Kwah; Donna Tellow; Matt Ease
Isms: cubism; Dadaism; expressionism; impressionism; pointillism

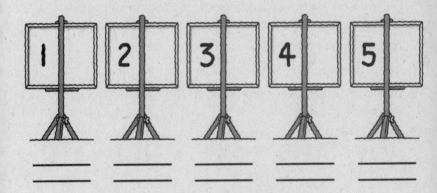

Starting tip: Begin by naming artist 5.

Odometer

The four cars lined up outside Honest Harry's second-hand automobile dealership on the main road just outside Wallingfen each had different "guaranteed mileages" on the odometer. Harry guarantees they've all done these numbers of miles . . . at least. From the clues, can you work out the exact mileage shown on each car's odometer and identify its make and color?

Clues

1. Each of the digits 0 to 9 appears twice in all, while no car's mileage contains a repeated digit, and no two digits appear in the same position on two different odometers.

2. Auto 2 has done less than 30,000 miles according to its odometer, while none of the four cars has yet reached a total of 50,000.

3. The first number on the odometer of automobile 3 is two lower than the one in the same position on automobile 1, whose odometer also displays an 8.

4. The blue car, which is next to the Fiat in the line, has the largest total on its odometer, while the red car's second digit on the odometer is a 9.

5. The third digit displayed on automobile 2 is the same as the last digit on automobile 4.

6. One zero is the third figure on one odometer, and the other is in the last position, but not on an adjacent vehicle.

7. The fourth number on the display of automobile number 1 is a 4.

8. The last three figures on the odometer of the black Volvo are 735.

9. There is no 7 showing on the odometer of the Audi, whose last digit on the odometer is a 1.

10. The digits 65 occupy those consecutive positions on the display of one car, while another's corresponding digits are 98.

Colors: black; blue; green; red
Cars: Audi; Fiat; Ford; Volvo
Digits: 0; 0; 1; 1; 2; 2; 3; 3; 4; 4; 5; 5; 6; 6; 7; 7; 8; 8; 9; 9

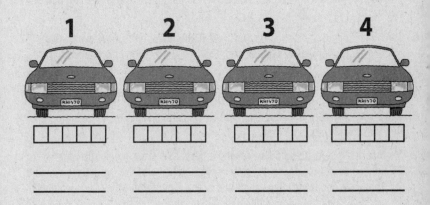

Starting tip: First work out the first digit on each car's odometer display.

Hot Wheels

Newtwick is an area of Northchester which has become notorious for a number of automobile thefts. Yesterday five vehicles were reported stolen, although all were recovered—or, at least, found—by the end of the day. From the clues, can you work out where each theft took place, what automobile was stolen, whose it was, and its condition on recovery?

Clues

1. The Ford, stolen from Spice Street, didn't belong to Mr. Mason.

2. Mr. Kennedy's Toyota was taken from outside his home, where he'd unwisely left it running.

3. The automobile taken from Herring Street was found late in the evening, burned out.

4. The automobile that crashed on the Great South Road in the early evening was neither the property of Mrs. Robins nor the Renault, which wasn't stolen from Myrtle Street.

5. Mr. Green's car, taken from Barracks Street, wasn't the one which was crashed.

6. The BMW was recovered, but only after it had been dismantled for spare parts and was about to be exported.

7. Mr. Mason's car, found by police raiding a garage used by a well-known local villain, had been repainted from gray to red; the name of the street from which it was stolen is one letter longer than that of the street from which the automobile found abandoned but undamaged was taken.

Street	Car

	BMW	Ford	Renault	Toyota	Volvo	Mr. Green	Mr. Kennedy	Mr. Mason	Mrs. Robins	Ms. Wells	Abandoned	Burned out	Crashed	Dismantled	Repainted
Barracks Street															
Herring Street															
Myrtle Street															
Spice Street															
York Street															
Abandoned															
Burned out															
Crashed															
Dismantled															
Repainted															
Mr. Green															
Mr. Kennedy															
Mr. Mason															
Mrs. Robins															
Ms. Wells															

I stole a smart car— It texted the police and picked me out in a line up

Owner	Recovered

Celebrity Sprouts

If you have found yourself left with a fridge-load of cooked or raw sprouts (after everyone politely declined the offer of second helping, or even first), you could, perhaps, do worse than try out these recipes dreamt up by some of the country's best-loved celebrity chefs. Aiming to "re-invent" the humble vegetable, they have picked a garnish and beverage to complement their delicious sprout-based treat. From the clues, can you connect each popular foodie with their new creation and all its trimmings?

Clues

1. "Sprout Ice Cream" will be the new must-taste flavor this summer—at least according to its developer, Ollie James; fortunately this is not the recipe that calls for a garnish of snails for its finishing touch and a pint of lager to help wash the slimy creatures down.

2. One chef garnishes his "Pulled Sprouts" dish—take a few cooked sprouts, rip apart, and arrange on the plate—with a side order of sliced turkey; its male inventor, apparently oblivious to his recipe's resemblance to the festive meal just past, is not French superchef Anton Petitchou.

3. Blokey New Zealander Don Corrode bizarrely recommends taking a glassful of sprout smoothie to wash down the rest of the sprouts in his recipe.

4. The drink matched with "Sprout Kiev" is vodka & tonic, appropriately enough—mostly because anyone who has spent the prescribed two hours stuffing a bucketful of sprouts with garlic butter is going to need a strong drink to recover.

5. The side dish called "Textures of Sprout" does not go with Celia Jones' new offering, which is not the gooey "Sprout Brownie"; both the brownie and Celia's dish are unsullied by snails.

6. Experimental food-artist Fleet Rosendal garnishes his dish with a sprinkling of freeze-dried sprout powder but doesn't recommend cranberry juice.

Recipe	Chef

	Don Corrode	Ollie James	Celia Jones	Anton Petitchou	Fleet Rosendal	Snails	Sprout foam	Sprout powder	Textures of sprout	Turkey slices	Cranberry juice	Green tea	Pint of lager	Sprout smoothie	Vodka & tonic
Pulled Sprouts															
Sprout Brownie															
Sprout Ice Cream															
Sprout Kiev															
Sprout Porridge															
Cranberry juice															
Green tea															
Pint of lager															
Sprout smoothie															
Vodka & tonic															
Snails															
Sprout foam															
Sprout powder															
Textures of sprout															
Turkey slices															

Garnish	Beverage

The Balloon Goes Up

Recently five people were treated to trips in hot-air balloons to mark different milestones in their lives. Although all had expressed a wish to make such a trip, their reactions to it varied greatly. Toward the end of each trip, adverse weather conditions blew up and, although they all landed safely, they did so in some unorthodox places. From the clues, can you work out all the details?

Clues

1. One of the male passengers felt airsick—unpleasant for both him and those on the ground; his ordeal ended in a field in a herd of cows.

2. The balloonist who ended in someone's back garden, who was not the flier who had just retired, was the same sex as the one who remained calm and serene.

3. David was terrified all the time he was aloft and for about a week and a half afterwards.

4. John's trip was not to mark his retirement, while Mary's adventure was paid for by her parents for passing her exams.

5. Ronald's flight, during which he did not express overexcitable enjoyment, ended when his balloon came down in the middle of a busy road.

6. The person who couldn't bear to look down was celebrating a big job promotion.

7. The birthday tripper, who was not Pauline, got wet when the balloon came down in a pond.

Name	Reason

	Birthday	Job promotion	Passing exams	Retirement	Ruby wedding	Airsick	Calm and serene	Couldn't look down	Enjoyed overexcitedly	Terrified	Beach	Garden	Herd of cows	Pond	Road
David															
John															
Mary															
Pauline															
Ronald															
Beach															
Garden															
Herd of cows															
Pond															
Road															
Airsick															
Calm and serene															
Couldn't look down															
Enjoyed overexcitedly															
Terrified															

Reaction	Landed

Cruise Missing

The five couples who are enjoying a long cruise and whom we have been following for a couple of issues are spending a few days on board between destinations. After a rough night at sea only one of each couple emerged the next day, their spouses suffering from a spot of seasickness and preferring to stay in bed, and are sharing a table to tuck into a light lunch before going to an afternoon's activity. From their conversation, can you work out what each is eating, what activity they will be doing, and a quote from their words?

Clues

1. When Mr. Grey sensitively noted, "This is delicious; my wife would have loved this, if she wasn't feeling ill," he wasn't talking about the asparagus; Mr. Grey wasn't spending the afternoon in the pottery class.

2. The woman who was crunching her way through a green salad and who would be spending the afternoon in the art class with the very attractive Bohemian teacher wasn't the cruiser who said of their spouse, "Oh, they'll be OK. I'll pop back later this afternoon, probably."

3. Mrs. Thomas, who planned to catch up on a few hours of sleep, wasn't the woman who looked down at the avocado she was enjoying and said, "You know, this is the precise color my husband turned last night."

4. "So what are you making in your cooking class?" asked one cruiser of another. "Cakes, I hope," came the reply. "This healthy lunch is getting me down a bit."

5. Mr. Simkin had chosen pea soup for lunch; it wasn't Mrs. Shepherd who asked as the plates were being taken away, "So . . . what time is tea served?"

Cruiser	Lunch

	Asparagus	Avocado	Green salad	Pea soup	Prawns	Art class	Cooking class	Pottery class	Quoits	Sleeping	Cakes, I hope	Color of husband	I'll pop back ...	What time is tea?	Wife would love ...
Mr. Grey															
Mrs. Lewes															
Mrs. Shepherd															
Mr. Simkin															
Mrs. Thomas															
Cakes, I hope															
Color of husband															
I'll pop back ...															
What time is tea?															
Wife would love ...															
Art class															
Cooking class															
Pottery class															
Quoits															
Sleeping															

Activity	Quote

A Charmed Life

A Charmed Life is the name of a stall in Northchester's Kirkdale Market which sells charms, fetishes and jujus from around the world. I am an avid customer and my collection of amulets has made me what I am today. Below is a picture of four of my talismans on a shelf in one of my many luxury residences (to prevent casual onlookers from stealing their powers, I keep them in boxes). From the clues, can you discover the color and composition of each mojo and the attribute it conveys?

Clues

1. The shell-encrusted power juju is immediately right of the feathered mojo.

2. The green talisman engenders wealth; it is somewhere right of the cloth amulet.

3. There is more than one place between the blue beady fetish and the love charm, which is not purple.

Colors: blue; green; red; purple
Materials: beads; cloth; feathers; shells
Qualities: fame; love; power; wealth

Starting tip: Decide the composition of the green charm.

Battleships

Do you remember the old game of battleships? These puzzles are based on that idea. Your task is to find the vessels in the diagram. Some parts of boats or sea squares have already been filled in, and a number next to a row or column refers to the number of occupied squares in that row or column. The boats may be positioned horizontally or vertically, but no two boats or parts of boats are in adjacent squares—horizontally, vertically, or diagonally.

Aircraft carrier:

Battleship:

Cruiser:

Destroyer:

										0
								◖		4
										1
			●						≈	4
										3
										3
										2
							▣			3
										0
										0
0	**3**	**0**	**3**	**1**	**4**	**1**	**3**	**2**	**3**	

Top Deck

The top deck of the bus from Upper Crispin to Stonekeigh is silent as its nine passengers are each deep in concentration, engrossed in whatever is on the screen of their mobile device. From the clues, can you work out the name of each passenger and the nature of the screen-based entertainment that is keeping them amused on the short journey?

Clues

1. Naomi is sitting immediately behind the person updating their personal profile on Mugbook.

2. Pamela, who isn't in position 8, is sharing a seat with the person browsing the SportsWatch sports website to see how Netherlipp Rovers got on last night; the person in seat 5, who isn't Ian, is reading the review of the offerings at the Mega Multiscreen Maxidrome Movieplex movie house on a movie website.

3. Martin is looking up something on the on-line reference Wigglypedia, which is like a more well-known site but a bit more rambling; Martin is not in a seat numbered one higher than the person posting Chirps on the social network site Chirrup, who is immediately behind the person playing Yourscraft.

4. Laura is sitting on the same side of the aisle as Kevin.

5. The person playing Scribble (an on-line combination of Scrabble and Pictionary) is not sitting on the front row of seats but is on the same row of seats as their neighbor Helen, who is not sharing a seat with Oliver.

6. The person playing the new on-line game sensation World of Peace, who has a seat numbered higher than Janice's, is on a seat next to the aisle, unlike the person perusing the music website, who is sitting on the row in front of the one where Janice is sitting.

Names: Helen; Ian; Janice; Kevin; Laura; Martin; Naomi; Oliver; Pamela

Entertainments: Chirrup messaging; movie website; Mugbook social media; music website; Scribble; sports website; Wigglypedia; World of Peace; Yourscraft

Starting tip: Begin by working out the names of the two women sharing the front-row seat.

Hospital Exit

St Sebastian's, Albion TV's hospital-based soap opera, has been assigned a new producer, and to make her mark on the show she has ordered scriptwriters to write out five characters—but without killing any of them off. They've done their best but . . . from the clues given, can you work who plays which character, and why and how they're being got rid of? (All actors play roles of their own gender.)

Clues

1. The character who vanishes (along with an aircraft full of other people) in the notorious Bermuda Triangle isn't cardiologist Dr. Ginger McKay.

2. The best the writers could think of to dispose of physician Dr. Patrick Mulligan was to have him decide to retire from medicine to take up a career as a psychic medium.

3. The character played by the actor who's been fired after being convicted of theft after being caught shoplifting will be abducted by aliens; he or she is not Dr. Scotty Gordon, the role played for five years by Peter Redman.

4. Dr. Jean Doumis is being given the heave-ho, because the actor's partying lifestyle had made them increasingly unreliable.

5. Bonnie Corder's character, who isn't Dr. CJ Forrest, is getting the boot after viewers' complaints about her immorality, dishonesty, and general obnoxiousness (the character's, that is, not Bonnie's—although . . .).

6. Dougie Eliot's character is emigrating to Australia to become a flying doctor; Larry Munro is not the actor who has angered the *St. Sebastian's* production team by demanding a pay raise.

Actor	Character

	CJ Forrest	Ginger McKay	Jean Doumis	Patrick Mulligan	Scotty Gordon	Demanding rise	Retired	Theft conviction	Unreliable	Viewers' complaints	Abducted by aliens	Became a psychic	Bermuda Triangle	Defected to Korea	Emigrated
Bonnie Corder															
Dougie Eliot															
Helen Gauss															
Larry Munro															
Peter Redman															
Abducted by aliens															
Became a psychic															
Bermuda Triangle															
Defected to Korea															
Emigrated															
Demanding rise															
Retired															
Theft conviction															
Unreliable															
Viewers' complaints															

Reason	Method

Lunch in the Park

It's lunchtime on a sunny day in Storbury and six young ladies employed in various departments of an IT company are enjoying their breaks in Oldfield Park, opposite the company HQ. From the clues can you fill in each one's name and say what she's doing and how long she's got before she should be back at her desk?

Clues

1. Diane Eliot is the next figure east of the young lady who still has thirty minutes left and the next one west from her workmate who's dozing.

2. Molly Lane has five fewer minutes of lunch break remaining than the woman who's eating an ice cream, but has more time in the sun left than figure B.

3. Carol Bell is the next figure east of the receptionist, who is due to be back at work in ten minutes.

4. Sue Ross has five fewer minutes of break left than the company employee who's talking on her cell, who is more than one place east of Sue; Vicky Unwin has five minutes more break left than figure E.

5. The young lady with only five minutes of her lunch hour left, who dislikes and never eats bananas, is next west of the one with thirty minutes left; the most recent recruit to the company, who is reading a book, is further east than either of the first two women but somewhere west of the one with fifteen minutes of break left.

6. Figure D, who isn't the one with fifteen minutes left, has five minutes less of her break left than figure E but five minutes more than figure F.

Names: Carol Bell; Diane Eliot; Jill Irving; Molly Lane; Sue Ross; Vicky Unwin
Activities: dozing; eating banana; eating ice cream; listening to music; reading; talking on cell
Break times remaining: 5 mins.; 10 mins.; 15 mins.; 20 mins.; 25 mins.; 30 mins.

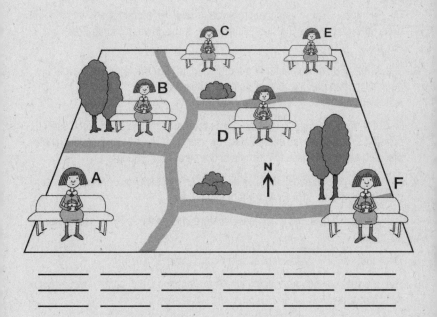

Starting tip: Work out how long woman D has left of her lunch break.

USA TODAY   119

Area 52

You've probably heard of Area 51, the secret base in the USA where the remains of crashed UFOs are said to be stored—but what about Area 52, the British equivalent, camouflaged as a small, remote railway station on the Keighshire Moors? From the clues, can you work out the details of the five wrecks stored there: when and where in the country it came down, what it (originally) looked like, and how it was brought down to Earth?

Clues

1. The cylindrical UFO—sometimes referred to as a flying drainpipe—was the first to be delivered to Area 52; the machine that came down at Taurus Green was the last.

2. One of the UFOs flew straight into the ground in 1967 while trying to avoid the attentions of an RAF interceptor fighter; neither this crash nor the one in 1981 took place on the slopes of Trantor Fell.

3. One UFO fell into British scientists' hands after being disabled by some sort of onboard explosion seven years before the classic flying saucer-type machine crashed; neither of these two events occurred at Pern Bridge.

4. It was the flying dumbbell that collided with an electricity pylon fourteen years after the triangular UFO (or flying fan) came down.

5. The UFO which flew into a hill near Marsford was neither a flying saucer nor a flying fan.

6. The spherical UFO, or flying pea, didn't come down in 1974.

7. The UFO that crashed after being struck by lightning didn't come down anywhere near Moonbury.

Date	Location

	Marsford	Moonbury	Pern Bridge	Taurus Green	Trantor Fell	Cylinder	Dumbbell	Flying saucer	Sphere	Triangle	Avoided fighter	Collided with pylon	Explosion	Flew into hill	Lightning
1960															
1967															
1974															
1981															
1988															
Avoided fighter															
Collided with pylon															
Explosion															
Flew into hill															
Lightning															
Cylinder															
Dumbbell															
Flying saucer															
Sphere															
Triangle															

Shapes	Downed by

Rs and Js

Iris Sadleigh-Penham is a writer of romantic fiction with a bardic bent—the hero and heroine are invariably star-crossed lovers whose disapproved-of romance always ends in tears. Nevertheless these are hugely popular, and Iris now does her writing on a plush veranda overlooking the Caribbean Sea. From the clues, can you work out the titles of I. Sadleigh-Penham's five most recent works and name the hero and heroine who make up the unhappy pair featured in each tale?

Clues

1. The heart-rending, some might say depressing, tale of Raymond and Jeanette was published the year after *Amour No More*.

2. Julia was the ill-fated heroine of the novel which immediately preceded *A Heavy Heart*.

3. *The Last Goodbye* was the title which first appeared in 2011 (and has singularly failed to say goodbye at all, having been in print ever since).

4. Roland was the tragic hero of the next novel after the one featuring the doomed Roger.

5. The book published in 2013 recounted Rupert's ruined romance, which was not with cursed Jayne.

6. *The Loneliest Nights* was the novel immediately preceding the one describing woeful Rory's unhappy affair.

7. The luckless Josephine was jilted at the altar in the most recent novel by I. Sadleigh-Penham.

Year	Novel

USA TODAY

	A Fond Farewell	A Heavy Heart	Amour No More	The Last Goodbye	The Loneliest Nights	Raymond	Roger	Roland	Rory	Rupert	Jacqueline	Jayne	Jeanette	Josephine	Julia
2011															
2012															
2013															
2014															
2015															
Jacqueline															
Jayne															
Jeanette															
Josephine															
Julia															
Raymond															
Roger															
Roland															
Rory															
Rupert															

Hero	Heroine

Take a Part

Minor movie actress Donna Prima has been offered starring roles in five films soon to go into production by Ivywood Productions in Netherlipp. All roles pay very well, but there are certain other pros and cons that she has to consider. From the clues, can you work out the title of each script Donna's been sent, what type of film it is, and what factors there are in favor and against her accepting the role?

Clues

1. *Deep Water*, which isn't a horror film, has a director who's really hot at the moment—his last four films have been nominated for Lippies—but doesn't include any of Donna's ex-boyfriends to complicate things.

2. The thriller is based on a blockbuster book that was top of the bestseller list for months; *Road Hog* isn't the film which offers Donna the chance to appear with a really hot co-star.

3. The movie that has an absolutely brilliant script with some really great lines for Donna but is a remake of a picture that did well in the '60s (and remakes of good movies are always a hostage to fortune) isn't the science-fiction movie *Blue Devil*.

4. The producer of the war movie, which is going to be shot entirely in the studio but doesn't have a great script, is unfortunately one of Donna's numerous ex-boyfriends.

5. *Night Watch* involves extensive nude scenes, and Donna really prefers to limit that sort of thing.

Working title	Type of movie

	Comedy	Horror	Science fiction	Thriller	War	Based on bestseller	Great locations	Great script	Hot co-star	Hot director	Ex-boyfriend directs	Ex-boyfriend producer	Low budget	Nude scenes	Remake
Blue Devil															
Deep Water															
Night Watch															
Road Hog															
Wild Wings															
Ex-boyfriend directs															
Ex-boyfriend producer															
Low budget															
Nude scenes															
Remake															
Based on bestseller															
Great locations															
Great script															
Hot co-star															
Hot director															

Pro	Con

Cruising Home

The last stop on the itinerary of the five cruise liner couples we've been following for a few months is the Moroccan port of Tangier. While the female halves of the couples are preparing things for the flight home, they have sent their husbands on a mission to the nearby bazaar to pick up one last present for a member of their family. From the clues, can you work out what each man was sent to buy, what he ended up buying, and what excuse he gave for failing to follow orders?

Clues

1. Mr. Simkin was sent to buy a djellaba and left singing the line "Striped djellabas we can wear at home" from *Marrakech Express*.

2. One man stood looking very sheepish as his wife tried to understand his actions. "I asked you to buy a tagine," she said as calmly as she could manage. "Yes, I know," he replied, "but what exactly is a tagine?"; this wasn't Mr. Thomas, who returned from his shopping trip, which wasn't to buy a small wooden jewelry box, with a brass lantern and a ready-prepared excuse for not buying what he'd been asked to.

3. The man who had been told to buy a small rug, who wasn't Mr. Shepherd, staggered back up the cruise-liner's gangplank carrying a large roll of carpet looking both proud of himself and a little nervous at the same time; this wasn't Mr. Lewes, who offered the well-tried excuse "I thought you said . . ." without any real hope of it working but wasn't the man who had bought a snake charmer's basket.

4. "You bought a large box of spices," said one woman looking at her husband with bemusement, "so why didn't you also buy what I asked for?" "Well," replied her husband, "after buying the spices I didn't have any money left."

5. It wasn't Mr. Grey who cowered before his wife's stern gaze and said, "But . . . but . . . the salesman really was very insistent."

Man	Sent to buy

	Djellaba	Jewelry box	Leather bag	Small rug	Tagine	Basket	Box of spices	Coasters	Lantern	Large carpet	Insistent salesman	No money left	Thought you said . . .	Was a bargain	What is a . . .?
Mr. Grey															
Mr. Lewes															
Mr. Shepherd															
Mr. Simkin															
Mr. Thomas															
Insistent salesman															
No money left															
Thought you said . . .															
Was a bargain															
What is a . . .?															
Basket															
Box of spices															
Coasters															
Lantern															
Large carpet															

Bought	Excuse

I'm All Right Jack

Last week's *Stonekeigh Advertiser*'s Classified Ads could have a section entitled *Jacks of All Trades*, as by strange coincidence, five of its ads promoting local businesses were by tradesmen named Jack. From the clues, can you discover which trade each Jack is in, the name of the current clients of each, and the address where each is working today?

Clues

1. Jack Naylor is neither a builder nor a decorator, while the builder is neither working for Mr. and Mrs. Plummer at their home on Brick Road nor working on Tyler Street.

2. The Joyners do not live on either Millers Way or Cobblers Drive and are not employing the decorator.

3. The carpet layer is working on Cobblers Drive today, but not for Mr. and Mrs. Butcher.

4. Jack Gardner is working on Locksmith Lane, but not for the Joyners.

5. The sweep is clearing the chimney for Mr. and Mrs. Baker.

6. Jack Glaser is an electrician, and Jack Painter is working for Mr. and Mrs. Piper.

Tradesman	Trade

	Builder	Carpet Layer	Decorator	Electrician	Chimney Sweep	Mr. and Mrs. Baker	Mr. and Mrs. Butcher	Mr. and Mrs. Joyner	Mr. and Mrs. Piper	Mr. and Mrs. Plummer	Brick Road	Cobblers Drive	Locksmith Lane	Millers Way	Tyler Street
Jack Carpenter															
Jack Gardner															
Jack Glaser															
Jack Naylor															
Jack Painter															
Brick Road															
Cobblers Drive															
Locksmith Lane															
Millers Way															
Tyler Street															
Mr. and Mrs. Baker															
Mr. and Mrs. Butcher															
Mr. and Mrs. Joyner															
Mr. and Mrs. Piper															
Mr. and Mrs. Plummer															

I couldn't find the problem so I've relabeled it instead

OFF
OFF

Customers	Address

Troubled Waters

Peter Payshant is the resident Director of the Calm Seas apartment block in Stonekeigh. A couple of his neighbors rarely cause him problems—mostly because they live away for most of the year—but five householders regularly make complaints about trivial matters. Can you assign each malcontent to their correct apartment and, in doing so, discover Peter's own apartment and those of the two absent residents, say what each grumbler's current complaint is about, and identify the automobile they drive which, when spotted sitting outside the main entrance, warns Peter to avoid going out just at that moment?

Clues

1. The first floor is the only level where both apartments have householders who cause Peter problems; three of the five complainants live on the same side of the block.

2. Wilf Wynger, who lives higher in the block on the opposite side to Peter, is complaining about a puddle on the roof, which appears mysteriously, generally after some heavy rain.

3. If Peter goes out when a red Audi is parked in the driveway, he is bound to receive an earful from its owner complaining about people who park in the driveway; there is a separate floor between Tony's apartment and that of the Audi's owner.

4. Both the driver of the gray Mazda and Nora Newsance live somewhere below Peter, but not on the same floor as each other; the person who persistently requests the installation of self-opening doors in the main entrance does not drive the Mazda and isn't Paul Petty, who drives a white Ford.

5. The resident who drives the black Volkswagen lives in apartment 6.

6. Davina Dotty, who isn't the resident demanding new planters outside the main entrance, lives on the opposite side of the block to the resident who drives the red Audi.

Residents: Davina Dotty; Nora Newsance; Paul Petty; Tony Trubble; Wilf Wynger
Cars: red Audi; white Ford; gray Mazda; blue Toyota; black Volkswagen
Complaints: lighting in garage area; parking in driveway; planters beside entrance; puddle on
roof; self-opening doors

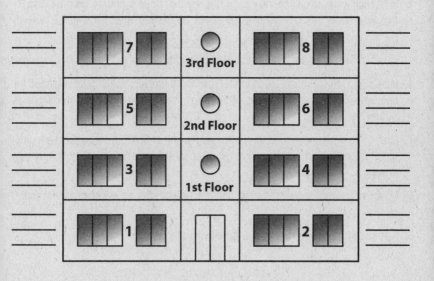

Starting tip: Work out which is Peter's own apartment.

After School

A number of after school activities are offered to the students at Stonekeigh Academy, and Sam decided he would like to attempt some. They are run by some of the dedicated teachers, whose interests extended beyond their normal subject. As a boy of only 12 years old, Sam was willing to try each of the activities for a few weeks, as thereafter he felt that life had to move on. From the clues, can you work out the number of weeks he attended each of the activities he chose, the teacher who ran it, and the subject that each teacher would normally teach?

Clues

1. Sam wasn't too struck by the dance classes and, since it quickly became clear that he'd never become the next Billy Elliot, he gave up after two weeks.

2. Mr. Abbot, who doesn't teach a language subject, offers after school guitar lessons; Sam attended the English teacher's after school activity for three weeks.

3. Mr. Gale isn't the French teacher who runs the judo club, which Sam attended for one week fewer than he did the activity organized by the history teacher Mrs. Barnes.

4. Miss Price, who doesn't teach science and is one of Sam's favorite teachers, had the pleasure of Sam's company in her after school sessions for an even number of weeks.

5. Miss Evans was delighted to have Sam attend her after school sessions for four weeks.

6. Sam didn't attend the chess club for exactly five weeks.

Activity	Weeks

	2 weeks	3 weeks	4 weeks	5 weeks	7 weeks	Mr. Abbot	Mrs. Barnes	Miss Evans	Mr. Gale	Miss Price	English	French	History	Math	Science
Chess															
Dance															
Drums															
Guitar															
Judo															
English															
French															
History															
Math															
Science															
Mr. Abbot															
Mrs. Barnes															
Miss Evans															
Mr. Gale															
Miss Price															

Teacher	Subject

Logi-5

Each line, across and down, is to have each of the letters A, B, C, D, and E, appearing once. Also, every shape—shown by the thick lines—must also have each of the letters in it. Can you fill in the grid?

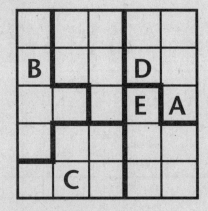

Killer Sudoku

The normal rules of Sudoku apply. In addition, the digits in each inner shape (marked by dots) must add up to the number in the top corner of that box.

14		11		23	11			
16						23		
7	20	13	9		11	30		
				13				20
9				20				
		15		15				10
22					4	5		
13			23			20	13	5
	10							

Apostrophe's

Know Your Onion's is a stall in Northchesters' Kirkdale Market which sells vegetable's at very reasonable price's but, in the tradition of greengrocer's, has no consideration for the niceties of punctuation. From the clue's, can you work out the position of each vegetable in the display and the price it fetches per pound (Know Your Onion's can't be doing with new-fangled kilogram's)?

Clues

1. The vegetable's that might be termed green's (cabbage's and lettuce's) are both on the left half of the stall.

2. The artichoke's cost as much as the cabbage's and lettuce's added together, the onion's and turnip's added together, and the carrot's and tomato's added together.

3. A dollar of each of the vegetable's in the bottom row would cost 50 cents more than the same quantity of those in the top row.

4. The pepper's are in position B.

5. The cabbage's are directly behind the artichoke's.

6. The tomato's cost 5 cents more than the turnip's, which are directly to their left and directly in front of the carrot's.

Vegetable's: artichoke's; cabbage's; carrot's; lettuce's; onion's; pepper's; tomato's; turnip's
Price's: 20 cents; 25 cents; 30 cents; 40 cents; 45 cents; 50 cents; 60 cents; 70 cents

Starting tip: Work out the price of the artichoke's.

Matter of Course

When our five old friends the Drones about town decided to play golf together one afternoon, each had his round interrupted at a different hole by an untoward occurrence, and each ended up with a rather large total of strokes taken at the end of the round, although that wasn't very unusual. From the clues, can you work out all the details?

Clues

1. It was at the unlucky thirteenth hole that one Drone spent some time digging his way out of a bunker; his final total was an odd number of strokes.

2. The monocle was mislaid as its owner searched for his ball further along the course than the incident involving Edward Tanqueray, who completed his round with a score of 108.

3. The score of 96 was achieved by the Drone who had to take a penalty when he lost his original ball in a hollow tree well off the fairway.

4. Archie Fotheringhay suffered the next mishap after his friend's ball had been taken by a squirrel.

5. The Drone whose score was 101 had problems at the eighth.

6. Montague Ffolliott tore a hole in the seat of his brand-new plus fours on some brambles as he searched for his ball; he took fewer strokes than Rupert de Grey.

7. Gerald Huntington got into difficulties on the tenth.

Drone	Mishap

	Bunker	Hollow tree	Lost monocle	Squirrel	Tore plus fours	Third	Eighth	Tenth	Thirteenth	Seventeenth	96	99	101	108	115
Archie Fotheringhay															
Edward Tanqueray															
Gerald Huntington															
Montague Ffolliott															
Rupert de Grey															
96															
99															
101															
108															
115															
Third															
Eighth															
Tenth															
Thirteenth															
Seventeenth															

Hole	Strokes taken

Subtitles

Albion TV has bought a job lot of cheap foreign films to show during their weeklong movie festival, but they've not received exactly what they were hoping for. The subtitles were supposed to be in English but are in the wrong language. Nevertheless, the movies have been paid for so will now be shown in the 1:00 a.m. slot over the coming week, in the hope that no one will notice. From the clues, can you work out each film's original language, its subtitle language, and when it will be shown?

Clues

1. *Paws*, a comedy set in a pet shop, will be announced as *Lappanna* in its Icelandic subtitles. It will be shown a day later in the week than *Fifty Grades of Shale*, a documentary on the geology of Netherlipp, but earlier than the Catalan film subtitled in Japanese.

2. Tuesday's film will be *Kitties Insane*, a romping adventure featuring a band of crazy cats. It is neither filmed in Afrikaans nor subtitled in Filipino.

3. Friday's offering is filmed in Bengali. It won't be *Six on the Settee*, about half a dozen couch potatoes in search of the TV remote, which will be screened the day after the movie with Hungarian subtitles.

4. *Slow and Serene*, a video diary of a boat trip down the Keighshire Canal, filmed in slow motion, which won't be the last show of the week, will be shown two days after the offering filmed in Dutch.

Day	Film

	Fifty Grades of Shale	Kitties Insane	Paws	Six on the Settee	Slow and Serene	Afrikaans	Bengali	Catalan	Dutch	Estonian	Filipino	Georgian	Hungarian	Icelandic	Japanese
Tuesday															
Wednesday															
Thursday															
Friday															
Saturday															
Filipino															
Georgian															
Hungarian															
Icelandic															
Japanese															
Afrikaans															
Bengali															
Catalan															
Dutch															
Estonian															

Have you picked a parrot?

No, I'll take some seed. I've decided to grow my own

PAW'S PETS

Language	Subtitles

Diving Expedition

Members of the Stonekeigh Scuba Diving Club made their own way to Brightbourne Cove last Sunday. They were particularly interested in this area of the southeast coast, as there were reports of a discovered wreck timelessly resting in the depths. After they arrived and after a briefing, the more inexperienced divers made their preparations for the dive, with the help of their more experienced dive buddies. From the clues, can you work out who the dive buddy was for each of the novice divers, what artifact or object of interest was discovered between each pair of divers, and the depth to which each pair dived?

Clues

1. Experienced diver Russ found a silver goblet, but not at 15m deep; Russ's novice wasn't Jon who, with the assistance of his dive buddy, who wasn't Kerry, bravely ventured to a depth of 32m.

2. Emily caught sight of the brooch that lay on top of a rusty piece of metal, which may have drifted away from the main wreck.

3. Marc and his novice dive, Gary, didn't dive to exactly 20 or 23 meters deep.

4. Ben didn't want to exceed 20m, as this was only his third dive outside of the swimming pool.

5. Pippa dived to a depth of 30m but wasn't Heather's dive buddy, who didn't find the old leather boot at 20m deep.

6. Tina didn't find the Roman coin.

Novice	Dive buddy

	Kerry	Marc	Pippa	Russ	Tina	Boot	Brooch	Coin	Goblet	Seal pups	15	20	23	30	32
Ben															
Emily															
Gary															
Heather															
Jon															
15															
20															
23															
30															
32															
Boot															
Brooch															
Coin															
Goblet															
Seal pups															

Object/subject	Depth (m)

Watch the Skies

Seamus Lesse is one of the keenest amateur astronomers in Keighshire, but occasionally he lets his enthusiasm run away with him. Taking advantage of a rare run of clear nights last week, he set up his telescope, hopeful as ever of making his name with the next great discovery; sadly he was to be disappointed. Can you work out on which night he observed each strange phenomenon, in which constellation it appeared—and what it actually turned out to have been after all?

Clues

1. It was on Wednesday that Seamus spotted something unusual in the constellation of Orion, but it wasn't quite as unusual as a UFO, the "sighting" of which occurred earlier than the night he got confused by a rogue firework.

2. On one night, Seamus thought he'd witnessed the birth of a supernova in the Square of Pegasus; this took place two days after his apparent discovery of a new moon of Jupiter—to be named after himself, naturally.

3. As an old hand, Seamus really should have thought of checking his telescope lens for wandering spiders before phoning Albion TV to warn of an imminent meteor strike on Stonekeigh college hall.

4. Not even Seamus could have mistaken the transit through Ursa Minor of British Airways flight 558 to Rome in the second half of the week for a passing comet, especially as he'd got embarrassingly overexcited about a possible comet on Monday night.

5. Seamus was fooled by the reflection of a motorcycle headlamp the night after his close encounter in the constellation Taurus, which itself occurred sometime after the misidentification of a weather balloon.

Night	Constellation

	Orion	Pegasus	Taurus	Ursa Major	Ursa Minor	Comet	Meteor	Moon of Jupiter	Supernova	UFO	Airplane	Firework	Motorbike lamp	Spider	Weather balloon
Monday															
Tuesday															
Wednesday															
Thursday															
Friday															
Airplane															
Firework															
Motorbike lamp															
Spider															
Weather balloon															
Comet															
Meteor															
Moon of Jupiter															
Supernova															
UFO															

Phenomenon	Explanation

Spinning Off

Albion TV's popular sitcom *Red Gables*, about five students at Goatsferry University who share a house on the outskirts of the town, has come to the end of its run, but the producers have decided to "spin off" each of the main characters into a series of his or her own. From the clues, can you work out the name of each character, what they've been studying at Goatsferry, the title of their spin-off series, and its basic premise?

Clues

1. In *City Lights*, one of the former students, having graduated, will move to London and have to find a home, a job and—ultimately—new friends.

2. Rather bizarrely, the new comedy series about the George Todd character will see him accidentally killed in the first episode and then follow his comic adventures as a new and naive ghost.

3. The male theology student will move on to a series in which he gets a job in the Religious Affairs Department of a major TV company and is shocked by the attitudes of his fellow workers; it will not be called *Number 7*.

4. The series given the title *Room 102* will feature the former Goatsferry School of Engineering student.

5. The spin-off series for the Brenda Owen character is to be called *Pinkies*.

6. In *Red Gables*, Kenny Young was studying archaeology.

7. The series in which one of the former students inherits a title—and a huge, semi-derelict estate—includes a number in its title.

8. The character from *Red Gables* who marries an ambitious politician isn't the ex-drama student, who isn't George Todd and won't be featured in *Number 7*.

Name	Subject

	Archaeology	Drama	Engineering	Medicine	Theology	City Lights	Hard Times	Number 7	Pinkies	Room 102	Becomes ghost	Gets job in TV	Inherits title	Marries politician	Moves to London
Brenda Owen															
Esther Reid															
George Todd															
Ian Vickers															
Kenny Young															
Becomes ghost															
Gets job in TV															
Inherits title															
Marries politician															
Moves to London															
City Lights															
Hard Times															
Number 7															
Pinkies															
Room 102															

Series title	Series idea

Curry Favor

Friday night is take-out night for the five students, and they like to try the different restaurants that Stonekeigh has to offer. They stumbled across a new one last week and each of the friends tried a different dish. As they looked at the menu, they noticed that each dish was represented by a different number of chilies, depicting the hotness and spiciness of the fare, with one chili being the mildest and five chilies being the hottest. From the clues, can you work out what each of the diners ordered, the number of chilies assigned to that particular dish, and the drink chosen to wash it all down?

Clues

1. Liam wasn't too sure if he would order his particular meal again, as it was rated an eye-watering five chilies and he spent a lot of the evening wiping his eyes; he didn't have the fruit juice, which also didn't wash down the four-chili rated dish.

2. The student who ordered the prawn meal, which wasn't the hottest dish, also asked for a large jug of water, most of which was drunk by the end of the meal; prawn meal wasn't Danny's order.

3. The fish dish was rated 3 chilies.

4. Alicia, who had the beer, ordered a dish that was represented by two chilies fewer than the number of chilies representing the vegetable dish.

5. Millie chose the bean meal; the eggplant meal wasn't the mildest dish.

6. The student who drank cola had a milder dish rating of only 2 chilies.

Name	Dish

	Eggplant	Bean	Fish	Mixed vegetable	Prawn	1	2	3	4	5	Beer	Cola	Fruit juice	Lager	Water
Alicia															
Danny															
Fran															
Liam															
Millie															
Beer															
Cola															
Fruit juice															
Lager															
Water															
1															
2															
3															
4															
5															

Chilies	Drink

Vacation Booking

Ivy Reeder loves historical novels, and when she went on vacation this year, she took her electronic device loaded with five, recommended by various friends and acquaintances. When she returned, she told me—in fairly blunt terms—that she hadn't thought much of any of them and the reasons why. From the clues, can you work out which book was recommended by each of Ivy's friends, the name of the author, and determine Ivy's considered opinion of it?

Clues

1. Ivy thought *Rupert's Woman* was "boring"; this isn't the Kate Lovel book recommended by Audrey.

2. Ivy considered the novel recommended by Patsy pornographic.

3. The recommender of *Empress* appears next in the alphabetical list after the friend who recommended the Lucy Mowiss novel; neither of these was the book Ivy said was infantile, which was the one recommended by a woman whose name is one letter shorter than that of the recommender of *Constantinople*.

4. Both *Passion Fruit* and the book that Jane urged Ivy to read were the work of writers with the same initial for first name and surname; the book recommended by Jane had, unlike the Greta Hallaby opus and the novel which Patsy recommended, more than one word in its title.

5. The woman who wrote *Lord of Eagles* has a shorter surname than the author of the book recommended by Zoe, which wasn't described by Ivy as mildly amusing.

6. Dawn didn't suggest the Coral Carey novel.

Friend	Title

	Constantinople	Empress	Lord of Eagles	Passion Fruit	Rupert's Woman	Coral Carey	Greta Hallaby	Kate Lovel	Lucy Mowiss	Saul Snape	Badly researched	Boring	Infantile	Mildly amusing	Pornographic
Audrey															
Dawn															
Jane															
Patsy															
Zoe															
Badly researched															
Boring															
Infantile															
Mildly amusing															
Pornographic															
Coral Carey															
Greta Hallaby															
Kate Lovel															
Lucy Mowiss															
Saul Snape															

e-library
Break Glass
in case of
power outage

Actual
Real
Book

Writer	Opinion

Battleships

Do you remember the old game of battleships? These puzzles are based on that idea. Your task is to find the vessels in the diagram. Some parts of boats or sea squares have already been filled in, and a number next to a row or column refers to the number of occupied squares in that row or column. The boats may be positioned horizontally or vertically, but no two boats or parts of boats are in adjacent squares— horizontally, vertically, or diagonally.

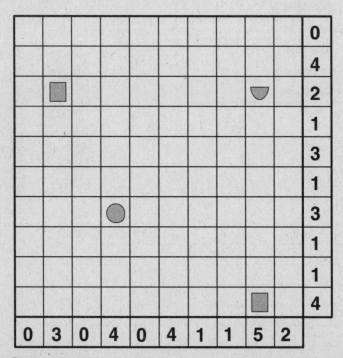

Sunny Specs

Sunny Specs is small kiosk on Brightbourne seafront selling trendy and, frankly, overpriced sunglasses. The part of the display we see here shows six different designs at six different prices. From the clues, can you work out the details?

Clues

1. The Shades model is priced $10 higher than the pair to the immediate right of them; the Poolwear design is immediately to the right of the Seafarer pair.

2. The Beachcool pair of sunglasses is on the same shelf as and is cheaper than the Glider pair; the EyeSpy pair is not the cheapest of these six.

3. The sum of the prices of the pairs on the top shelf is $25 higher than the sum of those on the bottom shelf; pair 3 is priced $5 lower than pair 5, and the $65 pair is immediately below the $70 pair.

Models: Beach cool; EyeSpy; Glider; Poolwear; Seafarer; Shades
Prices: $60; $65; $70; $75; $80; $85

Starting tip: Work out the prices of all the numbered pairs. Begin with pair 3.

Maiden Cruisers

These five young ladies have lived in different sea ports all their lives, watching cruise ships come and go and dreaming of sailing themselves. Their wishes have at last come true, as each is about to embark upon the luxury Sunflare liner *Moonshadow* on a 10-day cruise around the Mediterranean; it's not as fun as it sounds, though, as they are each due to join it as a member of the working crew. Still, you can't have everything. Can you match each lady with her home town and say which post she will be filling and at which sunny port along the way she will be embarking to take up her duties?

Clues

1. Pippa will be a chorus-line dancer in the cabaret; the cruise maiden who will join the ship at Naples is not going to be the IT Facilitator—responsible for explaining the ship's complex intranet system to baffled passengers.

2. Marie will start her new job when the *Moonshadow* calls at Barcelona.

3. The cruise maiden joining the ship at its last outward port in Santorini will be a cook in the galley; she is not Sandy, who does not come from Portsmouth or Southampton.

4. Jane was born and bred in Liverpool.

5. The cruise maiden from Harwich is joining the boat at Monte Carlo; her job will not involve one-to-one contact with the passengers.

6. Neither Jane nor Sandy is either the lady who is joining as a personal cabin steward dealing with passenger's daily needs or the one who will be joining the ship at Gibraltar; the new cabin steward is not from Southampton.

Maiden	Home town

	Felixstowe	Harwich	Liverpool	Portsmouth	Southampton	Cabin steward	Cook	Dancer	IT Facilitator	Receptionist	Barcelona	Gibraltar	Monte Carlo	Naples	Santorini
Jane															
Laura															
Marie															
Pippa															
Sandy															
Barcelona															
Gibraltar															
Monte Carlo															
Naples															
Santorini															
Cabin steward															
Cook															
Dancer															
IT Facilitator															
Receptionist															

Job	Joining port

Pool Party

In the mid-1960s Netherlipp's multinational GloboCorp Company employed a typing pool of nine women as shown in the diagram. From the clues, can you fully identify the woman in each position? (Lefts and rights in the clues are from our point of view as we look at the picture.)

Clues

1. As they sit at their desks, Alicia is immediately behind Ms. Myers and immediately right of Ms. Jordan.

2. Beverley works at the same table as Ines, who is not seated directly in front of or behind Eve; the two former are separated by Ms. Quigley.

3. Diane is in the row behind the woman named Ryan, but not immediately behind her.

4. Cassandra Orton, who is not in the back row, is directly in line to the left of Ms. Lawson.

5. The woman named Prentice uses the central typewriter in the middle row.

6. Ms. Kettley works in a higher-numbered position than Ms. Nolan.

7. Position 6 in the diagram is occupied by Harriet, whose surname contains an even number of letters.

8. Frances works diagonally behind and to the left of Gill.

First names: Alicia; Beverley; Cassandra; Diane; Eve; Frances; Gill; Harriet; Ines
Surnames: Jordan; Kettley; Lawson; Myers; Nolan; Orton; Prentice; Quigley; Ryan

Starting tip: Begin by placing Myers.

Steaks Are High

Anyone invited to dine "alfresco" on a summer's evening with experimental chef Steve Sizzell is likely to find himself offered rather more unusual barbecue fare than the normal run-of-the-mill lamb steaks and beef burgers: Steve delights in serving a varied selection of exotic meats sourced from his local artisan butcher's shop, all marinated to his own recipes—guaranteed to tempt the palate, or not as the case may be. Can you match tonight's guests with the steak and burger combination that Steve thought they would be sure to enjoy—and the more conventional drink they are drinking in an attempt to disguise the flavors?

Clues

1. One lucky diner was treated to the "perfect" combination of whale-burger and wombat steak.

2. Chester Chewett is attempting to conceal his half-eaten squirrel-burger among the branches of a nearby tree—back where it belongs.

3. The yak-burger was presented to the guest who had chosen cola to drink; the guinea pig on this occasion (now *there's* a thought) wasn't Charlie Chomp, who doesn't drink alcohol, although he might well start after tonight.

4. One of the guests is hoping that a few glasses of red wine will erase the taste—and the memory—of the alligator steak; fortunately Steve knows that alligator doesn't go well with wildebeest and never serves them together.

5. Gordon Guzzler can taste every parched desert mile in his tough old camel steak; he is avoiding orange juice, which Steve says doesn't suit its piquancy—nor that of any other hoofed animal, apparently.

6. Terry Trencher-Manne, who always drinks wine, especially at Steve's barbecues, has never eaten zebra and doesn't see any reason to start now; the person eating the emu steak isn't trying to drown it in white wine.

7. Nicky Nibble has stocked up with several bottles of soda water—it could be a long and uncomfortable night.

Guest	Steak

	Alligator	Camel	Emu	Wombat	Zebra	Bison	Squirrel	Whale	Wildebeest	Yak	Cola	Orange Juice	Red Wine	Soda Water	White Wine
Charlie Chomp															
Chester Chewett															
Gordon Guzzler															
Nicky Nibble															
Terry Trencher-Manne															
Cola															
Orange Juice															
Red Wine															
Soda Water															
White Wine															
Bison															
Squirrel															
Whale															
Wildebeest															
Yak															

Burger	Drink

Late Cut

The five chairs at the Clippity Doo Dah unisex hair salon in Netherlipp have all been booked this morning but all stand empty. Each of their intended occupants has called in to explain that they will be a few minutes late after encountering an unexpected delay. From the clues, can you work out the name of the customer who should be in each seat, the name of the stylist booked to deal with them, the delay each customer has encountered, and the number of minutes late they are when they walk through the door?

Clues

1. Barnaby, when he turns up, will be in the seat immediately to the right of that to be occupied by the customer who is stuck at home waiting for a delivery and immediately left of the chair where Justin's customers always sit; Justin's customer will be five minutes less late than Hannah's.

2. One customer has called in to say they will be five minutes late, as the bus they were on was running behind.

3. Annabel will be five minutes more late than the customer who has had an unexpected problem on the school run (a need to return home and collect homework) and five minutes less late than Kathryn's customer, who won't be in seat 4.

4. Eleanor will be having her locks preened in seat 3, eventually; the customer destined for seat 2 will settle themselves into it 10 minutes later than their allotted time.

5. Douglas, who will have a chair somewhere to the right of the one occupied by Imogen's customer, has called in to say that owing to circumstances beyond his control his arrival at the salon will be delayed by 20 minutes (Douglas travels a lot by rail and that sort of talk tends to wear off on you).

6. Gordon's customer has phoned in from their automobile saying that they are stuck in a traffic jam on the Netherlipp highway; they won't be the customer who will be delayed the most.

Customers: Annabel; Barnaby; Claudia; Douglas; Eleanor
Stylists: Gordon; Hannah; Imogen; Justin; Kathryn
Reasons: bus late; automobile won't start; delivery late; school run; traffic jam
Latenesses: 5 mins.; 10 mins.; 15 mins.; 20 mins.; 25 mins.

Traveling Player

Laurinda Locum is a skilled hand on the ivories and spends her days teaching little fingers to play scales. But in the evenings she is a performer playing organs in churches when the regular player is unavailable. Last week she was in demand and had five engagements in different churches around Netherlipp. From the clues can you say at what location she played on each day, the name of the organist she was standing in for, and the time at which she began her playing?

Clues

1. Laurinda's appointment at Christchurch was on an earlier day and at an earlier time than when she substituted for Christopher Peddle but on a later day and at a later time than when she played in place of Frank Flatts.

2. The 7 p.m. recital was later in the week than when Laurinda covered for Susan Pypes and earlier than the day she traveled to St. Jethro's Church.

3. The engagement at St. Mildred's Church, which wasn't the first of the week, began 15 minutes later in the evening than the one on the day that she replaced Charles Stopps, which was the day after she visited All Saints Church, which wasn't Wednesday, which wasn't the day with latest starting time.

4. On Monday Laurinda stood in for a man; on Tuesday she took the place of Joanne Keyes.

5. The recital at St. Seymour's did not kick off at 6:45 p.m.

Day	Church

	All Saints	Christchurch	St. Jethro's	St. Mildred's	St. Seymour's	Charles Stopps	Christopher Peddle	Frank Flatts	Joanne Keyes	Susan Pypes	6:30 p.m.	6:45 p.m.	7:00 p.m.	7:15 p.m.	7:30 p.m.
Monday															
Tuesday															
Wednesday															
Thursday															
Friday															
6:30 p.m.															
6:45 p.m.															
7:00 p.m.															
7:15 p.m.															
7:30 p.m.															
Charles Stopps															
Christopher Peddle															
Frank Flatts															
Joanne Keyes															
Susan Pypes															

Our organist is still on holiday, so we'll sing Hymn 569 — "Chopsticks"

Organist	Time

In the House

Netherlipp TV's Celebrity version of their reality TV series *In the House* has just reached its conclusion. Five celebrities with different claims to distinction were assembled together and then ejected one at a time, in what has become the traditional manner, following votes by the viewers. From the clues, can you fully identify and describe the five and work out in which order they were expelled from the household or, in one case, survived and won?

Clues

1. The TV personality was the next to be expelled from the household after Clyde Crowe.

2. The former politician, who is not Headstrong, was given a much larger majority in being voted off first than had ever been seen in the constituency at past elections.

3. The male radio presenter's surname is not Boast.

4. Pushey, who is not Linda, stayed longer in the household than the former international athlete but was not the eventual winner.

5. Loudleigh was still a member of the household after the departure of the gossip columnist from a tabloid newspaper, who was not voted off third.

6. Max was expelled at the end of the second session of voting.

7. Headstrong did not survive as long as Adrienne, who is not the gossip columnist.

First name	Surname

	Boast	Crowe	Headstrong	Loudleigh	Pushey	Former politician	Gossip columnist	Radio presenter	Retired athlete	TV personality	First	Second	Third	Fourth	Winner
Adrienne															
Clyde															
Linda															
Max															
Steve															
First															
Second															
Third															
Fourth															
Winner															
Former politician															
Gossip columnist															
Radio presenter															
Retired athlete															
TV personality															

Claim to fame	Order

Orbis in Urbis

Goatsferry University's Department of Parapsychology has sent a team of students out into the city center to investigate orbs, those mysterious blobs which occasionally appear in digital photographs and CCTV footage. From the clues, can you discover which landmark each student photographed, how many orbs they found, and what they surmised these phenomena to be?

Clues

1. Terry Pathic photographed 5 more orbs than were attributed to aliens but 5 fewer than were counted at the River Pits Institute, which investigates the configuration of stream beds and the like.

2. The display of 20 orbs was presumed to be the embodiment of the bright ideas floating above Goatsferry's great minds.

3. The student at the Radleian Museum deduced the orbs spotted there, of which there were fewer than one hundred, to be ghosts; this was not Claire Voyant, who spotted fewer orbs than Sy Kick (who did not spot the most), but more than the researcher who pointed their camera at the Bodmolean Camera which is sadly just a building and didn't point back.

4. Sue Pernatural photographed 10 fewer orbs than the student who attributed them to the presence of disembodied time travelers; neither the time travelers nor the aliens were discovered at the Ashcliffe Library.

5. One researcher was derided for blaming the orbs seen at Circus on the dust kicked up by the heavy traffic which gives Goatsferry its sobriquet of The City of Screaming Tires.

Student	Landmark

	Ashcliffe Library	Bodmolean Camera	Circus	Radleian Museum	River Pits Institute	5	10	15	20	113	Aliens	Dust	Ghosts	Ideas	Time travelers
Claire Voyant															
Misty Cal															
Sue Pernatural															
Sy Kick															
Terry Pathic															
Aliens															
Dust															
Ghosts															
Ideas															
Time travelers															
5															
10															
15															
20															
113															

Orbs	Explanation

In the Jug

On the table at a family barbecue are five jugs of mixed juices, each of which contains two flavors carefully blended together. From the clues, can you work out the two juices in each jug?

Clues

1. Each of the juices appears in two jugs and, perhaps obviously, all of the blends are different.

2. No two adjacent jugs contain the same flavor.

3. The sum of numbers of the two jugs containing mango juice is 7; jug 1 doesn't contain banana flavor.

4. Each of the two jugs containing lemon juice is immediately right of a jug containing pineapple juice.

Juices: banana; lemon; mango; orange; pineapple

Starting tip: Place the two jugs with the mango flavor.

Sign In

Each row and column is to contain the digits 1-6. The given signs tell you if a digit in a cell is plus 1 (+) or minus 1 (-) the digit next to it. Signs between consecutive digits always work from left to right or top to bottom.

Examples: $\boxed{3}$ + $\boxed{4}$ or $\boxed{2}$

ALL occurrences of consecutive digits have been marked by a sign.

$\boxed{}$
$\boxed{1}$

Sudoku

Complete this grid so that each column, each row, and each marked 3 X 3 square contains each of the numbers 1 to 9.

				6	2		
8						5	3	7
		1	2					
			9		7		1	
		4	5		2	9		
	5		1		8			
					1	4		
7	3	9						2
		6	8					

Domino Search

A standard set of dominoes has been laid out, using numbers instead of dots for clarity. Using a sharp pencil and a keen brain, can you draw in the lines to show where each domino has been placed? You may find the check grid useful—crossing off each domino as you find it.

2	1	1	3	6	2	3	0
6	6	6	4	0	5	1	3
4	5	1	5	6	3	5	3
2	4	2	0	0	1	4	4
2	6	3	4	5	5	0	2
5	0	0	1	2	4	4	1
1	6	2	3	0	6	3	5

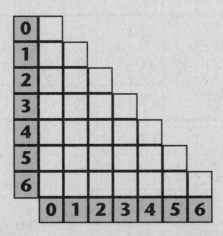

Candy Crush

Mrs. Candy is a kindly, white-haired old lady who runs an old-fashioned candy shop in Stonekeigh and has done so for as long as anyone can remember. Her jars of candy have been a draw for children on their way home from St. Saccharine's primary school for generations, and at the moment she has four eager customers. Can you name each customer, say what each is asking for, and work out in what order their requests are satisfied? (Lefts and rights in the clues are from our point of view.)

Clues

1. None of the boys was served in the order of their number in the diagram (i.e., no. 1 wasn't served first).

2. The third boy to be served was standing next to the boy who wanted aniseed balls; the boy served second was separated at the counter by at least one other boy from Sidney, who didn't want gobstoppers.

3. The last boy served was standing immediately right of the boy who wanted a bag of pear drops.

4. The boy in position 3 was served immediately before Wesley, who wasn't in position 4; the boy in position 4 was later than Rodney.

Customers: Barney; Rodney; Sidney; Wesley
Sweets: aniseed balls; gobstoppers; pear drops; sherbet fountain
Order: first; second; third; fourth

Starting tip: Work out the position of the boy who was served fourth.

On Your Bikes

The four riders on the front row of the Keighshire Motorbike Grand Prix have completed their formation lap and are revving their engines waiting for the start. Before they drop their clutches and start scraping their knees around the corners, can you name each numbered rider, the make of his or her bike, and the number of races he or she has won so far this season? (Lefts and rights are from our point of view.)

Clues

1. Theresa Twist is somewhere to the left of the revving Rapide MkIII and somewhere to the right of the rider who has a single win so far this season; the rider with one win isn't riding the Dash 50 bike.

2. Graham Gere rides a Scuttle Buzz and has won more races so far this season than has the rider of bike 2.

3. The rider revving the engine of bike 3 is hoping to follow up last week's win with another impressive performance this week.

4. The Flite XXR is somewhere to the left of the bike on which Colin Crouch is perched and somewhere to the right of the rider who has notched up two wins so far this season.

Riders: Colin Crouch; Graham Gere; Lorinda Leane; Theresa Twist
Bikes: Dash 50; Flite XXR; Rapide MkIII; Scuttle Buzz
Wins: no wins; 1 win; 2 wins; 3 wins

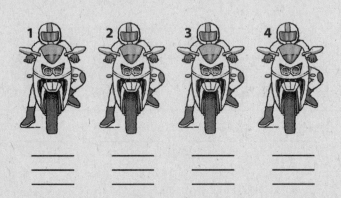

Starting tip: Begin by working out how many wins the rider of bike 3 has so far.

Battleships

Do you remember the old game of battleships? These puzzles are based on that idea. Your task is to find the vessels in the diagram. Some parts of boats or sea squares have already been filled in, and a number next to a row or column refers to the number of occupied squares in that row or column. The boats may be positioned horizontally or vertically, but no two boats or parts of boats are in adjacent squares—horizontally, vertically, or diagonally.

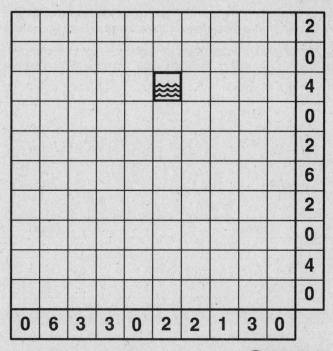

Aircraft carrier:

Battleship:

Cruiser:

Destroyer:

										2
										0
				≈						4
										0
										2
										6
										2
										0
										4
										0
0	6	3	3	0	2	2	1	3	0	

Summer Shows

Andrew Brown, also known professionally as Andy Brett and Austin Barry, is in show business; he sings, dances, plays the piano, tells jokes, and juggles, but none of them particularly well. These days, his main work is in summer seasons at run-down seaside theaters. From the clues, can you work out which resort he worked at in each of the listed years (he spent the summer of 2011 "resting" after a disagreement with his then agent), and the name of the theater and the show in which he worked there?

Clues

1. At Brightbourne, Andrew appeared as a song-and-dance man in *Fun in the Sun!* (not much fun and performed indoors); this was the year before he was one of the *Summer Stars!* (not a recognizable star in sight) at the decrepit fleapit known as the Galleon Theater.

2. Andrew was at the Neptune Theater in Swanmouth the year before he performed at the awkwardly-named (and poorly-maintained) Marine Pier Theater.

3. Neither the theater at which he performed in the year 2012 nor the one in Havensands mentions a pier in its name.

4. Dingle-on-Sea, which wasn't where Andrew spent the summer of 2010, wasn't where he performed in the completely unsensational *Seaside Sensation!*

5. *Hooray for Vacations!* ("Hooray, it's over" might have been closer) was the show in which Andrew appeared (as pianist, juggler, and target for the knife thrower) in 2014.

Year	Resort

	Brightbourne	Dingle-on-Sea	Havensands	Marlcliff	Swanmouth	Anchorage	Galleon	Marine Pier	Neptune	Pierhead	Fun in the Sun!	Hooray for Vacations!	Seaside Sensation!	Song of Summer!	Summer Stars!
2010															
2012															
2013															
2014															
2015															
Fun in the Sun!															
Hooray for Vacations!															
Seaside Sensation!															
Song of Summer!															
Summer Stars!															
Anchorage															
Galleon															
Marine Pier															
Neptune															
Pierhead															

Theater	Show

Cool Cats

Dee Haybee, Radio Keighshire's breakfast show host, also has a once-a-month show on a Saturday evening in which she plays the newest offerings from the world of jazz. Tonight she has five new albums to play, each featuring a current star who is a virtuoso on two instruments. From the clues, can you name each star's new album and the two instruments he or she plays?

Clues

1. "Good evening," began Dee. "We'll begin with the piano virtuoso Fizzy Gillespie tinkling her ivories for us and later we'll play the new album *Bop and Hop* featuring the greatest washboard player of our age."

2. Tammy Dorsey, whose first instrument is something she blows but whose second instrument isn't the kazoo, has released the album *Far Out*; Charlie Barker isn't the performer on *Kinda Cool*.

3. The oddly named *Bluer than Green* features the tenor sax player; the alto sax player only ever used spoons to eat soup, or perhaps stir tea.

4. Giles Davis is a skilled hand at the castanets.

5. The jazz star who is a virtuoso on both the guitar and the Andean pan pipes isn't Jet Baker.

Musician	Album

	Bluer than Green	Bop and Hop	Far Out	Kinda Cool	Mellow Mood	Alto sax	Guitar	Piano	Tenor sax	Trumpet	Castanets	Kazoo	Pan pipes	Spoons	Washboard
Charlie Barker															
Fizzy Gillespie															
Giles Davis															
Jet Baker															
Tammy Dorsey															
Castanets															
Kazoo															
Pan pipes															
Spoons															
Washboard															
Alto sax															
Guitar															
Piano															
Tenor sax															
Trumpet															

Instrument 1	Instrument 2

Party Animals

Miranda is five today and has invited as many party guests as there are candles on her cake. From the clues, can you work out which present each party-goer has brought, which game they won, and in what way they disgraced themselves?

Clues

1. The girl whose mother was keen on healthy eating, who presented Miranda with a basket of homegrown fruit, was later discovered to have disgraced herself by eating two thirds of Miranda's birthday cake before the candles had even been lit.

2. One of the boys refused to hand over his present; Dylan brought shame on himself by tipping a jug of orange juice into a bowl of potato chips.

3. The boy who felt he had been cheated when Daisy, who did not give the crayons, won the game of hide the thimble (which indeed he had been, because he had already triumphed at musical chairs and Miranda's mom wanted to be fair to everyone), got his revenge by stamping on one of Miranda's new toys until it broke. This was not Frankie, whose gift was the model dinosaur.

4. Neither the child who gave the jigsaw puzzle and won the game of blind man's buff nor the one who presented the toy automobile was the little horror who punched Miranda in a fit of jealousy.

5. Betty was not the winner of the pin the tail on the donkey game.

Child	Gift

	Car	Crayons	Dinosaur	Jigsaw puzzle	Fruit	Blind man's buff	Hide the thimble	Musical chairs	Pass the package	Pin tail on donkey	Ate cake	Broke toy	Juice on chips	Punched Miranda	Wouldn't give gift
Betty															
Daisy															
Dylan															
Frankie															
Jackson															
Ate cake															
Broke toy															
Juice on chips															
Punched Miranda															
Wouldn't give gift															
Blind man's buff															
Hide the thimble															
Musical chairs															
Pass the package															
Pin tail on donkey															

Game	Disgrace

What a Scorcher

Half an hour ago, five men who are neighbors along Charcoal Avenue in Netherlipp cleaned their old barbecues, filled them with combustible stuff, and set them alight. They are now in the process of proving to their loved ones that their barbecuing skills have not diminished by gently burning morsels of food to unrecognizable blackened blobs. From the clues, can you name each man and say what it is he is currently cooking?

Clues

1. The man who is burning sausages is the immediate neighbor of both Mr. Sinder and Mr. Krisp.

2. The man at 6 Charcoal Avenue is carefully charring a couple of pork chops.

3. Mr. Sere's wife is a vegetarian, but he hates to see her missing out on all the fun, so he's helpfully cremating a corn on the cob for her.

4. Neither Mr. Krisp nor Mr. Chard, who lives with his family at 2 Charcoal Avenue, is allowed to cook chicken—ever again.

Men: Mr. Chard; Mr. Krisp; Mr. Sere; Mr. Sinder; Mr. Synge
Food: chicken drumsticks; pork chops; sausage; steak; sweet corn

No.2   No.4   No.6   No.8   No.10

———— ———— ———— ———— ————
———— ———— ———— ———— ————

Starting tip: Work out where the man who is burning sausages lives.

USA TODAY

Battleships

Do you remember the old game of battleships? These puzzles are based on that idea. Your task is to find the vessels in the diagram. Some parts of boats or sea squares have already been filled in, and a number next to a row or column refers to the number of occupied squares in that row or column. The boats may be positioned horizontally or vertically, but no two boats or parts of boats are in adjacent squares—horizontally, vertically, or diagonally.

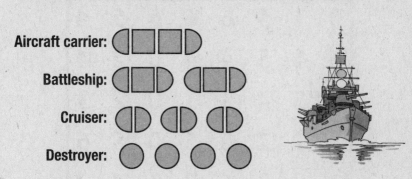

Aircraft carrier:

Battleship:

Cruiser:

Destroyer:

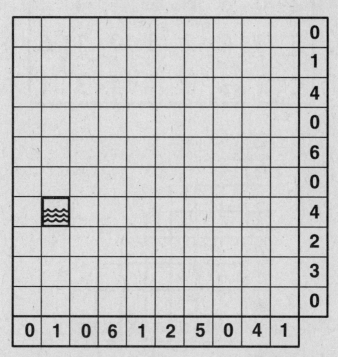

Domino Search

A standard set of dominoes has been laid out, using numbers instead of dots for clarity. Using a sharp pencil and a keen brain, can you draw in the lines to show where each domino has been placed? You may find the check grid useful—crossing off each domino as you find it.

0	1	5	6	6	6	5	4
6	1	5	4	4	0	2	4
6	5	4	3	1	0	2	3
3	2	2	0	5	0	5	6
2	0	3	6	2	1	4	2
5	3	0	2	5	0	1	6
4	1	3	3	1	4	3	1

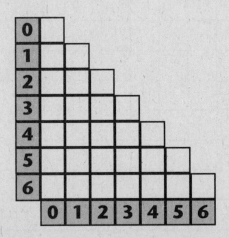

Cyber Caves

Observing a spider in its natural habitat, just before he absent-mindedly picked it off and ate it, one of our cavemen friends had the idea of linking their five caves with vines and designating each to a specific function to inform or entertain the cave community. From the clues, can you discover which cave each caveman uses to maintain which web site?

Clues

1. Egg nominated his cave as a search engine, as by standing at the entrance and "goggling," he could see what was going on in all the other caves. He was next counter clockwise from the social network, where the cavepeople could leave messages by drawing on the walls.

2. One cavemen acquired a flock of birds, which could alert the cavepeople to news of visitors or predators with their alarm calls or otherwise entertain them with their songs; Tweeter, as he called it, was numbered one higher than Agg's abode.

3. Igg's web site was adjacent to Flicker, where the cavepeople could stare into a fire and see pictures in the flames. This was not Ogg's site.

4. Cave 5 was the web log—a large piece of wood on which the occupant would stand and recount his daily doings (he also sometimes did pod casts—throwing seed husks around to express his emotions). It was not adjacent to Egg's site, which was not cave 3.

Cavemen: Agg; Egg; Igg; Ogg; Ugg
Web sites: Flicker; search engine; social network; Tweeter; web log

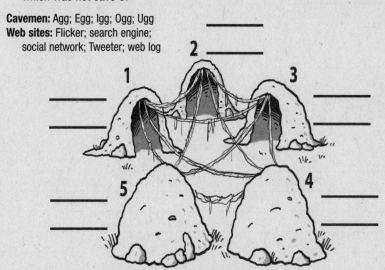

Starting tip: Search for the search engine.

Martial Arts

Stonekeigh Sports Arena last week held a one-day martial arts demonstration to promote the different clubs that it regularly supports throughout the year. From the clues, can you work out for each of the martial arts clubs that was represented the duration of its demonstration, the name of the chief instructor, and how many potential members signed up for its club on the day?

Clues

1. The Thai boxing demonstration lasted 25 mins. and persuaded more than two potential members to sign up; the chief Thai boxing instructor isn't Matthew, who was delighted that his own club attracted eight new members.

2. After a display of flowing movements, break falls, wrist locks and skilful immobilization techniques, the aikido club signed up 11 new members; the chief instructor isn't Bridget, whose demonstration with her club members lasted for only 20 mins.

3. Callum is the chief instructor of the ju jitsu club; its demonstration was five minutes shorter than the one delivered by the kendo club.

4. After demonstrating its martial art moves for 35 mins., one club signed up five new members.

5. Lizzie isn't involved with the martial art that attracted nine new members.

Martial art	Duration

	20 minutes	25 minutes	30 minutes	35 minutes	40 minutes	Andy	Bridget	Callum	Lizzie	Matthew	2 members	5 members	8 members	9 members	11 members
Aikido															
Ju jitsu															
Kendo															
Tae kwon do															
Thai boxing															
2 members															
5 members															
8 members															
9 members															
11 members															
Andy															
Bridget															
Callum															
Lizzie															
Matthew															

Name	New members

Fancy That!

It's the morning after the Grand Keighshire Summer Fancy Dress Ball, and six sore-headed party-goers are waking up in the cells at Netherlipp Jail. They had all come attired as characters familiar to most of us, and something about their dress or behavior had aroused the suspicions of the police. It's easy to guess from their costumes or characters what offenses they may have committed, but from the clues, can you work out the inhabitant of each cell and the outfit that led to their arrest?

Clues

1. When a lady invited the chap in the caveman costume, who introduced himself as Ugg, to go clubbing, he took her at her word and bopped her with his bludgeon. Luckily it was made of cardboard so she wasn't hurt, but he still ended up in the cell opposite the man disguised as St. Keigh's schoolboy Hamish Hazel.

2. Andy Anagram, Chris Conundrum, and Terry Teaser were all in the same row of cells. None of them was the man dressed as Miss Raffles, sister of the famous Amateur Cracksman, whom one sharp-eyed copper had recognized from a sepia-tinted WANTED poster on the police station wall, whose cell was numbered half that of the one occupied by Percy Puzzle.

3. Sir Coward de Custarde with his tinfoil sword and Beau Tighe with his polythene pistols were both arrested for carrying offensive weapons. The Beau, who compounded his offense by challenging the arresting officer to a duel, was in a lower-numbered cell directly opposite the Knight, who made things worse for himself by trying to run away. Neither of these costumes was worn by Chris Conundrum, whose cell was numbered one higher than that of Quentin Quiz.

4. The man disguised as Drone about Town Montague Ffolliott, who was not Andy Anagram, was not directly opposite the Beau Tighe impersonator, whose cell was not adjacent to that of the extremely hungover middle-aged man in the St. Keigh's School uniform.

Names: Andy Anagram; Chris Conundrum; Eddie Enigma; Percy Puzzle; Quentin Quiz; Terry Teaser

Costumes: Beau Tighe; Hamish Hazel; Miss Raffles; Montague Ffolliot; Sir Coward de Custarde; Ugg

Starting tip: Pin down Miss Raffles's cell.

Rocket Full of PIE

Helios 1, the spaceship developed by PIE, the Primary Interplanetary Expedition, which is carrying the first humans to Mars, has been on its way for six months. But for most of that time its seven-strong crew has been asleep—not suspended animation, just a deep sleep—under the control of the ship's computer ZOOK:D. From the clues, can you name the slumbering occupant of each numbered pod, his or her role within the crew, and the order in which Zooky Dee, as she is known, will wake them up over the next few hours?

Clues

1. PIE member Bruce Bean is gently snoring in sleeping pod number 5.

2. Ship's engineer Amanda Armstrong is in one of the three pods immediately adjacent to Zooky Dee's panel.

3. Shelia Shepard is in the pod immediately above the one containing the crew member responsible for communications and immediately below the PIE member who will be the last to be roused from their deep sleep.

4. The first PIE member to be woken will be the doctor, who shares a horizontal level of pods with Andrea Aldrin, who won't be the seventh crew member to be awoken and isn't in pod 7.

5. The commander of Helios 1 is fast asleep in pod 3 but won't be the second person woken up by Zooky Dee's alarm clock.

6. The biologist is sleeping in the same vertical column of pods as the one containing his or her crewmate Sidney Scott, who will be woken from slumber immediately before the occupant of pod number 7.

7. Caroline Conrad will be the sixth crew member to get a wake-up call from Zooky Dee; the geologist is sleeping in an even-numbered pod.

8. The sleeper in pod 4 will be woken fourth by Zooky Dee; pod 1 isn't the sleeping place of the ship's physicist.

PIE crew: Amanda Armstrong; Andrea Aldrin; Bruce Bean; Caroline Conrad; Marcus Mitchell; Sidney Scott; Sheila Shepard

Crew roles: biologist; commander; communications; doctor; engineer; geologist; physicist

Order of waking: first; second; third; fourth; fifth; sixth; seventh

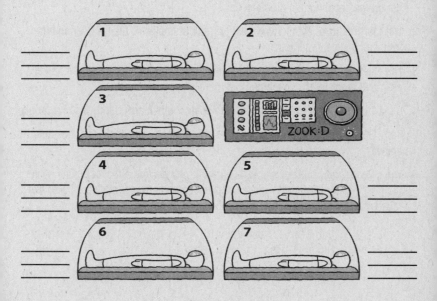

Starting tip: Begin by positioning Amanda Armstrong.

Cut It Out!

The latest edition of Netherlipp TV's *Cut it Out!* presented by Joan Ryss-Griffin was broadcast last night, featuring hilarious outtakes from a variety of TV programs. From the clues, can you discover the celebrities involved in each of the first five clips shown, the type of show each is an outtake from, and the mishap that required a retake?

Clues

1. The second clip involved Charlie Wright and was immediately followed by a clip showing a well-known person tripping and falling into a muddy ditch, but not during the shooting of a drama serial.

2. The fourth outtake didn't involve either Betty Stumbles or Gladys Over and the fifth was a sitcom extract.

3. The clip from the drama series didn't involve a collapse of scenery or a broken prop and the celebrity concerned was not Gladys Over.

4. Doris Tuckfast, who isn't an actress in a soap opera, inadvertently broke a prop.

5. Betty Stumbles isn't a news reporter and didn't forget her lines—not this time, anyway.

6. The celebrity quiz outtake showed Laura Murphy making a fool of herself, while the poor news reporter was unable to pronounce the word "statistics" over five takes and eventually replaced it with the word "numbers."

Order	Celebrity

	Laura Murphy	Gladys Over	Betty Stumbles	Doris Tuckfast	Charlie Wright	Drama	News	Quiz	Sitcom	Soap	Broke prop	Forgot lines	Scenery collapsed	Statistics stumble	Tripped and fell
1															
2															
3															
4															
5															
Broke prop															
Forgot lines															
Scenery collapsed															
Statistics stumble															
Tripped and fell															
Drama															
News															
Quiz															
Sitcom															
Soap															

Type of show	Mishap

Kings of the Castle

The annual end-of-season sandcastle-building competition on Brightbourne Beach has evolved over the years into something rather more complicated and competitive. These days, the only way to catch the judges' eye is to produce a spectacular sand-sculpture, the more eye-popping, the better. From the clues, can you assign this year's finalists' tours-de-force to their correct parent and child creators and say in which position they finished?

Clues

1. Polly Clytus and her offspring produced a scale model of the Willis Tower.

2. Paula's third place prize was not won with help from Michael Angelo.

3. Bernie Knee and his daughter Shelley were judged one place higher than the award given to the sculpture of a snarling T Rex.

4. The sandy automobile (practically full scale), which won second prize, wasn't carved by Robbie and his parent—although they did have a turn sitting in it.

5. Claire helped to produce a model of a roller coaster, around which model cars could actually run, complete with a water-splash feature provided by a rock pool.

6. The winner of the competition was Donna Tellow; Rho Danne was the first to admit that it was only thanks to her son that they didn't finish last.

Parent	Child

	Claire	James	Paula	Robbie	Shelley	1st	2nd	3rd	4th	5th	Willis Tower	Mermaid	Roller coaster	Automobile	T Rex
Bernie Knee															
Donna Tellow															
Michael Angelo															
Polly Clytus															
Rho Danne															
Willis Tower															
Mermaid															
Roller coaster															
Automobile															
T Rex															
1st															
2nd															
3rd															
4th															
5th															

I'm entering it in the "Affordable Housing" category

Position	Sculpture

Ones Who Got Away

A breakfast bar situated in the glorious Appalachian Mountains is a particular hit with vacationers from all over the world. As a business it does very well, but the waiters and waitresses often grumble that tourists for one reason or another don't always leave a tip. From the clues, can you work out which waiter or waitress served which table last week, on which day of the week a customer or customers left without leaving a suitable tip, and the name of the "guilty" party in each case?

Clues

1. Ellie served the customers at table 4.

2. Daniel, who doesn't work on Sundays, served breakfast to the Artois family who sneaked off after discovering they didn't have any more cash—they had an even-numbered table.

3. Amy served a family with bacon, scrambled eggs, and pancakes on Wednesday; this wasn't the Dale family, who was served at table 2 but left in a hurry when they realized they were going to be late to the airport.

4. The customers who left without leaving the requisite 20% tip were served at table 7 on Tuesday; this wasn't the Curtis family who, unfamiliar with American ways, didn't realize they were creating a trouble.

5. On Saturday, the Harris family waited until the serving staff disappeared into the kitchen then made their hasty getaway—Mr. Harris says he was making a stand against low wages for restaurant workers; Mrs. Harris knows he's just mean.

6. Clare didn't serve the Talbot family, who left the sort of minimal tip you might be expected to leave in a greasy spoon diner in Netherlipp.

Server	Table

	2	4	5	7	8	Sunday	Tuesday	Wednesday	Thursday	Saturday	Artois family	Curtis family	Dale family	Harris family	Talbot family
Amy															
Blake															
Clare															
Daniel															
Ellie															
Artois family															
Curtis family															
Dale family															
Harris family															
Talbot family															
Sunday															
Tuesday															
Wednesday															
Thursday															
Saturday															

Day	Customer

Vacation Park

During the school summer vacation our country parks across Keighshire are organizing fun activity sessions to keep the children amused, giving frantic parents an hour or two off, and have sent each house a leaflet explaining what's on offer. From the clues, can you work out which park is organizing which event on which day of the month and the name of the ranger leading each activity?

Clues

1. From the leaflet I can see that Becky Brook will be leading the activity on the 11th, but not at Littletoft Country Park between Churchminster and Netherlipp, where the event is later in the month than the Pond Dipping, whatever that is.

2. The Pond Dipping is not taking place at Grangelands Country Park, just outside Stonekeigh.

3. Dale Moore is organizing the Kingfisher Watch (watching kingfishers, probably), which is more than seven days earlier than the Minibeast Day (hopefully butterflies and ladybirds rather than mosquitoes and scorpions) at Manorfield Hills on the moors just north of Crispin Parva.

4. The event at Hawthorn Chase takes place after the 13th; it isn't the Adventure Trail.

5. Hazel Coppis is not in charge of the Teddy Bears' Picnic—she doesn't have a bear.

6. Flora Forrest is a ranger at Ferndale Woods Country Park.

Date	Country park

	Ferndale Woods	Grangelands	Hawthorn Chase	Littletoft	Manorfield Hills	Adventure Trail	Kingfisher Watch	Minibeast Day	Pond Dipping	Teddy Bears' Picnic	Becky Brook	Hazel Coppis	Will Denness	Flora Forrest	Dale Moore
5th															
11th															
13th															
20th															
22nd															
Becky Brook															
Hazel Coppis															
Will Denness															
Flora Forrest															
Dale Moore															
Adventure Trail											
Kingfisher Watch											
Minibeast Day											
Pond Dipping											
Teddy Bears' Picnic											

No, it's a teddy BEAR'S picnic

Activity	Ranger

Seaside On Air

As a feature for her show *Up Your Road* on Radio Netherlipp, Dee Haybee spent time each day last week with a woman whose work is closely connected with vacations and tourism in one of the region's seaside resorts. From the clues, can you work out the name of the woman Dee talked to each day, her occupation, and the resort where she works?

Clues

1. Dee went out with tourist guide Denise Ellis, who works in a historic town with a one-word name, the day before visiting a resort with a two-word name.

2. Dee's day with Sandra Trent was earlier in the week than her broadcast from Kingswell.

3. On Monday, Dee was in the coastal town of Saxham Market, where the famous 18th-century Admiral Lord Kitson lived.

4. Louise Moor, whom Dee accompanied and talked to on Thursday, wasn't the housekeeper from the Marine Hotel.

5. On Tuesday, Dee spent time with a police officer assigned to patrolling the promenade at one resort.

6. Dee's time with the Parking Enforcement Officer—that's traffic warden to you and me—in Mundham was later in the week than the time she spent with Jill Keely, whose job has no connection with law enforcement.

Day	Name

	Denise Ellis	Jill Keely	Louise Moor	Patsy Quinn	Sandra Trent	Diner waitress	Hotel housekeeper	Police officer	Tourist guide	Parking Enforcement Officer	Kingswell	Mundham	North Allingham	Saxham Market	Wanstoft
Monday															
Tuesday															
Wednesday															
Thursday															
Friday															
Kingswell															
Mundham															
North Allingham															
Saxham Market															
Wanstoft															
Diner waitress															
Hotel housekeeper															
Police officer															
Tourist guide															
Parking Enforcement Officer															

Job	Resort

Hat'll Do

Earl O'Malley, of O'Malley's bar in the southern California town of San Angelo, is fed up with customers looking like they are about to leave or have just popped in to use the phone and so has instigated a no-hat rule. As coincidence would have it, the five private eyes from that city into whose live we regularly peek are all in the bar at the moment, each meeting a prospective female client, who also came in wearing a hat but who is now bare headed (Earl is an equal opportunity authoritarian). Can you work out which of the fedoras (hats 1, 3, 7, 8, and 10) belongs to each private eye, which of the straw bonnets (hats 2, 4, 5, 6, and 9) belongs to which lady, who has come to O'Malley's to meet whom, and what each of them is drinking as they talk?

Clues

1. Mike Mallet, who is drinking an alcoholic beverage, has put his hat immediately to the right of that of his prospective client; this is the only incidence of private eye and client having their hats next to each other on the shelves.

2. The lady who has left her hat in position 5, who isn't Becky Garcia, is settling her nerves with a cognac (a double; she's really very nervous); bonnet 6 belongs to Cassie Harrison, who has not come to O'Malley's to meet Ricky Wrench but is talking to one of the private eyes whose hat is also on the lower shelf.

3. Dolly Ingles' hat is numbered higher than that of the private eye to whom she is talking; Dolly has asked for a glass of cherryade and Earl, being the top barman that he is, has provided her with one.

4. The lady who owns hat 9 is currently telling her story to Spike Spanner; the private eye who has left his hat in position 10 isn't drinking lemonade.

5. The private eye whose hat is in position 8 has come to meet Ellie Johnson, who has a non-alcoholic drink in her hand; the owner of hat 7 is drinking water.

6. The slightly shabby fedora in position 1 belongs to the equally shabby Nicky Nail; he is talking to a woman who has an alcoholic drink.

7. The private eye talking to Addie Foster is drinking a whisky sour; the woman talking to Ricky Wrench is sipping a lime soda.

8. The person drinking cola has left their hat on the top shelf; the person drinking a martini has left their hat on the lower shelf; the gin and tonic drinker is a woman.

Private eyes: Dick Drill; Mike Mallet; Nicky Nail; Ricky Wrench; Spike Spanner
Prospective clients: Addie Foster; Becky Garcia; Cassie Harrison; Dolly Ingles; Ellie Johnson
Drinks: bourbon; cherryade; cognac; cola; gin and tonic; lemonade; lime soda; martini; water; whisky sour

Starting tip: Work out which hat belongs to Mike Mallet.

Logi-5

Each line, across and down, is to have each of the letters A, B, C, D, and E, appearing once. Also, every shape—shown by the thick lines—must also have each of the letters in it. Can you fill in the grid?

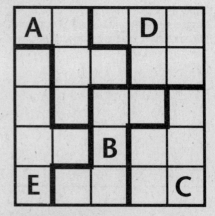

Killer Sudoku

The normal rules of Sudoku apply. In addition, the digits in each inner shape (marked by dots) must add up to the number in the top corner of that box.

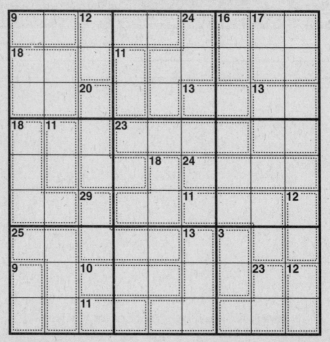

Battleships

Do you remember the old game of battleships? These puzzles are based on that idea. Your task is to find the vessels in the diagram. Some parts of boats or sea squares have already been filled in, and a number next to a row or column refers to the number of occupied squares in that row or column. The boats may be positioned horizontally or vertically, but no two boats or parts of boats are in adjacent squares—horizontally, vertically, or diagonally.

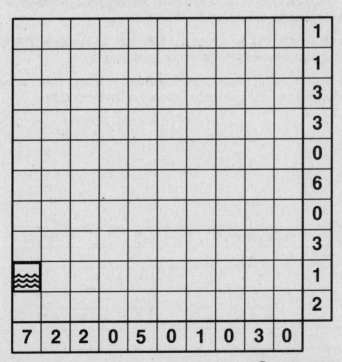

Not in Service

In the 24th century, the Confederated Planets' Star Force operates a large fleet of starships. But there is, naturally, a certain amount of wastage as ships get older or damaged, and on one particular day, five ships have been reported "no longer available for service." From the clues, can you work out the registration number and name of each ship, the reason why it's no longer available, and the name of the space station which has reported its demise?

Clues

1. Both the starship which has been damaged beyond repair by a meteor strike and one of the two whose loss has been reported from a SOL-system space station have registration numbers above 1000, but the *CPSS Mary Rose* does not.

2. The *CPSS Hesperus*, whose Certificate of Spaceworthiness has been revoked after a routine examination, has an odd registration number.

3. The starship NRC-846 has been destroyed in an antimatter explosion; the NRC-973's non-availability for service has been reported by a space station in the SOL system, which was known until the 22nd century as the Solar System.

4. The loss of the *CPSS Titanic*, which has an odd registration number under 1000, has been reported by space station POLARIS2C.

5. The *CPSS Vasa*'s registration number is NRC-1293; the loss of the CPSS *Waratah* has not been reported by the interstellar space station ISD40.

6. The loss of the odd-numbered starship destroyed by an alien attack has been reported by space station SOL4C, in orbit around the planet Mars.

Registration	Starship

	Hesperus	Mary Rose	Titanic	Vasa	Waratah	Alien attack	Antimatter explosion	Certificate revoked	Meteor strike	Withdrawn for scrap	DELOS1C	ISD40	POLARIS2C	SOL3C	SOL4C
NRC-571															
NRC-846															
NRC-973															
NRC-1124															
NRC-1293															
DELOS1C															
ISD40															
POLARIS2C															
SOL3C															
SOL4C															
Alien attack															
Antimatter explosion															
Certificate revoked															
Meteor strike															
Withdrawn for scrap															

Reason	Space station

Drawn Together

Publishers Grimm, Brothers and Andersen have just announced five lavishly illustrated new books, described as "fairy tales for the 21st century." The books are collaborations between a male author and a female illustrator who are familiarly related in some way. From the clues, can you work out the title of each book, the names of the writer and illustrator, and their relationship?

Clues

1. The pictures in *Oak and Ash*, featuring two squirrels of those names, aren't the work of either Linda Naylor or Theresa Vealy; Theresa Vealy, who is an only child, didn't illustrate Robin Trotter's book.

2. Robin Trotter's book was illustrated by his cousin; Gerald Irving, whose book does not have pictures by Linda Naylor, has no children and neither do any of his siblings.

3. *Magic Words*, about a basketball player called Morris "Magic" Words, which isn't by Gerald Irving, has been illustrated by the author's mother, who is professionally known by her maiden name.

4. Judy Liddle is the daughter of the man whose book she illustrated, who is not Ian Keiller.

5. One of the books was written by Clive Escott and illustrated by Maxine Ovett.

6. Daniel Frame is the author of *Warren Hill,* based in a colony of rabbits, while Amanda Clark drew the pictures for the science-fiction adventure *Sunhunters*.

Title	Writer

	Clive Escott	Daniel Frame	Gerald Irving	Ian Keiller	Robin Trotter	Amanda Clark	Judy Liddle	Linda Naylor	Maxine Ovett	Theresa Vealy	Brother/sister	Cousins	Father/daughter	Son/mother	Uncle/niece
Black Roses															
Magic Words															
Oak and Ash															
Sunhunters															
Warren Hill															
Brother/sister															
Cousins															
Father/daughter															
Son/mother															
Uncle/niece															
Amanda Clark															
Judy Liddle															
Linda Naylor															
Maxine Ovett															
Theresa Vealy															

Illustrator	Relationship

I Won't Keep You . . .

Maggie set aside each day this week for an important visit or journey. However, her schedule was thrown into disarray when the phone rang just as she was about to leave the house on each occasion, causing a delay that wrecked her well-laid plans. Can you say who called her each day, where she was about to go, and the reason the trip then had to be aborted?

Clues

1. Maggie's trip to the Passport Office was ruined the day after the long call from her boyfriend, which ran on into a pre-scheduled power outage she'd been warned to avoid, but the day before her plans were curtailed by the arrival of a massive thunderstorm.

2. "I wanted you to be the first to know!" gushed Maggie's tennis partner, just as she was halfway out of the door to visit her aunt; this happened the day before she reached the garden center only to find that the item for which she'd kept the magazine coupon had just sold out, but it didn't cause her to miss her bus.

3. The panic call from Maggie's boss came later in the week than the day she rushed into the station just in time to see her train pull out and hear the announcement of the cancellation of all other trains.

4. Monday's visit was for an important meeting with her mortgage adviser at the bank; this was not the day that her cousin had called to sort out vacation arrangements.

5. "Have you just got a few seconds to discuss your dental X-rays?" said the voice on the end of the phone on Friday; fortunately this was indeed the dentist.

Day	Caller

	Boss	Boyfriend	Cousin	Dentist	Tennis partner	Bank	Garden Center	Passport Office	Post Office	Visit aunt	Item sold out	Missed bus	Power outage	Thunderstorm	Trains canceled
Monday															
Tuesday															
Wednesday															
Thursday															
Friday															
Item sold out										
Missed bus										
Power outage										
Thunderstorm										
Trains canceled										
Bank					
Garden Center					
Passport Office					
Post Office					
Visit aunt					

Destination	Reason

Roommates

The new comedy drama series created for TV features four young women sharing an apartment. Quite a lot of the comedy scenarios are based around the coincidence that each of the women's first names is also one of the other women's surnames. Can you name each of the characters in the promotional poster and give their line of work?

Clues

1. The lady with the surname Carol is somewhere left of the lady with the first name Carol.

2. One Tracy is directly above the scientist and the other Tracy directly above the woman with the surname Hannah.

3. Hannah Tracy doesn't work in marketing; the roommate with the first name Lesley works in finance.

4. Picture 1 doesn't show the advertising executive.

First names: Carol; Hannah; Lesley; Tracy
Surnames: Carol; Hannah; Lesley; Tracy
Professions: Advertising; Finance; Marketing; Science

Starting tip: Find the first name of the woman in picture 3.

Men of Straw

Farmer Groam uses scarecrows to keep the birds away from his crops, and he currently has four standing in different fields. From the clues, can you name each scarecrow (Farmer Groam's gruff exterior is a just a veneer; he's an old softie really and always names his scarecrows), determine which crops it is guarding, and say which type of bird is causing it the most trouble? (Lefts and rights are from our point of view.)

Clues

1. Stalky is between the scarecrow whose main problem is a flock of starlings and the one who is guarding the field of barley, who isn't in position 3.

2. Despite its name, Strawbry isn't the scarecrow in the field of strawberries, which is in position 4.

3. Bailer is immediately left of the scarecrow struggling with some tenacious blackbirds, who aren't attacking the field of rapeseed and who aren't battling a scarecrow immediately adjacent to the even-numbered man of straw who is having trouble with some crows.

4. The wheat field scarecrow isn't immediately next to the one who is doing his best to get rid of a few gulls.

Scarecrows: Bailer; Hayman; Stalky; Strawbry
Crops: barley; rapeseed; strawberries; wheat
Birds: blackbirds; crows; gulls; starlings

Starting tip: Begin by naming scarecrow 4.

The Small Five

The Kubwa Tano Safari Park in the Central African Republic of Kenzango is, according to its brochure, the best place in the world to see the Big Five—the set of large dangerous animals that is a must-see on every tourist's bucket list. What the brochure doesn't tell you is that Kubwa Tano also harbors a fabulous selection of stinging, biting, and generally irritating pests, and while there are guards to protect visitors from the large creatures, the small ones will get you regardless. From the clues, can you find out which area of the park we visited on each day, which of the Big Five we encountered there, and which tiny beasties made our lives a living hell?

Clues

1. When we saw the lions we were bitten by fleas. This was the day after our trip to the swamp where we did not spot any elephants.

2. The valley was infested by swarms of mosquitoes that bit us to blazes the day before we encountered the elephants, which were not accompanied by ravening tsetse flies.

3. On Monday we got ants in our pants, shirts, socks, and everything else but did not see the magnificent herd of buffaloes which were not in the valley.

4. We came across the leopards in the depths of the forest.

5. On Thursday we saw the rhinoceroses, on Friday we visited the mountains, and on Saturday we traveled to the nearest town to buy remedies for all our stings, bites, and itchy bumps.

Day	Habitat

	Forest	Grassland	Mountains	Swamp	Valley	Buffaloes	Elephants	Leopards	Lions	Rhinoceroses	Ants	Bees	Fleas	Mosquitoes	Tsetse flies
Monday															
Tuesday															
Wednesday															
Thursday															
Friday															
Ants															
Bees															
Fleas															
Mosquitoes															
Tsetse flies															
Buffaloes															
Elephants															
Leopards															
Lions															
Rhinoceroses															

Animal	Pest

Chase the Lady

Seven people are playing a sort of chase the lady card game and have each chosen a different one of the seven cards placed on the table on which to place their small bets. From the clues, can you say who gambled on which card and who won by choosing the Queen of Spades?

Clues

1. Ann's chosen card, which wasn't next to the Queen of Spades, was somewhere to the left of the one picked by Dan and somewhere right of the ones selected by Cyd and by Eve; Dan's card had a lower number than Fay's; Eve's card was not number 1 and wasn't immediately right of the Queen of Spades.

2. Bob chose an even-numbered card.

3. Guy's card is two places right of Fay's and somewhere right of the Queen of Spades, which wasn't two places left of Fay's card or two places right of Dan's card.

Players: Ann; Bob; Cyd; Dan; Eve; Fay; Guy

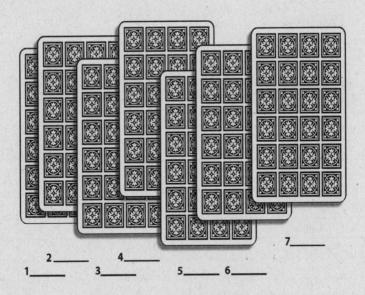

2 _____   4 _____
1 _____   3 _____   5 _____ 6 _____   7 _____

Starting tip: Work out who gambled on card 7.

Battleships

Do you remember the old game of battleships? These puzzles are based on that idea. Your task is to find the vessels in the diagram. Some parts of boats or sea squares have already been filled in, and a number next to a row or column refers to the number of occupied squares in that row or column. The boats may be positioned horizontally or vertically, but no two boats or parts of boats are in adjacent squares—horizontally, vertically, or diagonally.

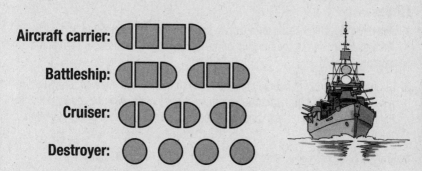

Aircraft carrier:

Battleship:

Cruiser:

Destroyer:

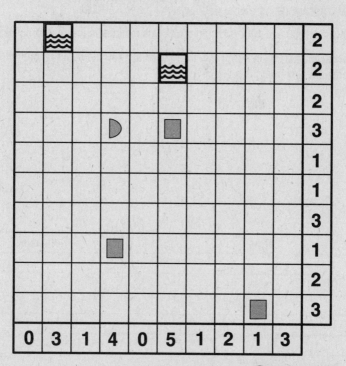

Stake Out

Keighshire Constabulary's undercover anti-vice division is staking out the apartment of a suspected drug smuggling syndicate, observing and recording events from an upper-floor room opposite. Every few hours a new detective takes over the surveillance duties. From the clues, can you discover when each new detective came on duty, and the arrivals, departures, and other events each recorded during his stint?

Clues

1. Detective Moynihan came on duty two hours before the shift when two men were seen arriving at the building opposite; he himself recorded a man and a woman leaving.

2. During one period of observation, one man left and something was thrown from a rear window, but the detective recording these events was not Lewis; Detective Palmer, who took over next, had recorded that loud music was being played in the apartment.

3. The grocery boy delivered to the apartment during the 0600 shift.

4. The detective taking over at 0900 was not Detective Tucker.

5. Between 1200 and 1400, an automobile was recorded cruising past suspiciously.

6. Detective Stockley took over the observation at 1400 but didn't record the bag of garbage being brought out.

Time	Detective

	Lewis	Moynihan	Palmer	Stockley	Tucker	Man and woman left	Grocery boy delivered	One man left	Two men arrived	Woman arrived	Argument heard	Loud music played	Garbage brought out	Suspicious car	Thrown from window
0400															
0600															
0900															
1200															
1400															
Argument heard															
Loud music played															
Garbage brought out															
Suspicious car															
Thrown from window															
Man and woman left															
Grocery boy delivered															
One man left															
Two men arrived															
Woman arrived															

11:19 am. He's looking out of the window with his binoculars again

Movements	Other event

Math Phobia

The new year at Stonekeigh High School is only a week old and Sam already has homework for almost every subject. He decided to try the homework club at lunchtime run by teaching assistants (TAs) but encountered difficulties getting help with his algebra. Each TA made some excuse for not helping with math but then offered to help him with any other subject. From the clues, can you work out the order in which Sam asked each TA for help with his algebra, what excuse was given not to help, and what other subject was each TA more able to give advice about?

Clues

1. Kevin offered to demonstrate some shading techniques needed for Sam's art homework.

2. Brad, who wasn't the first TA to be asked, claimed to have mislaid his glasses; he doesn't really have any expertise in music or history and so didn't suggest helping with those; the third TA Sam approached, who offered help with his history essay, wasn't the one who pointed a finger at another TA, claiming them to be "pretty nifty at sums."

3. The fourth TA to be asked, who wasn't Sonia, confessed to having difficulties with math.

4. The TA who was about to go to lunch said they could offer help on Sam's food technology homework at another time; this wasn't Abbi or Jill, who was the second teaching assistant to be asked.

Order	Name

	Abbi	Brad	Jill	Kevin	Sonia	Helping other pupil	Mislaid glasses	Not good at math	Off to lunch	Suggests another TA	Art	Food technology	French	History	Music
First															
Second															
Third															
Fourth															
Fifth															
Art															
Food technology															
French															
History															
Music															
Helping other pupil															
Mislaid glasses															
Not good at math															
Off to lunch															
Suggests another TA															

Dad, I need some help — what's 4x4?

That's easy A Range Rover

Excuse	Alternative

Marked Men

Yehudi Albert Twerp, known to all by his initials YA, sheriff of Stonekey, USA, had put up posters of five wanted men at large in the main town square. Each man's head carried a bounty for the various crimes committed. From the clues, can you work out the nickname by which each outlaw was known, the crime he was notorious for, the reward offered for his capture "dead or alive," and his visible distinguishing mark?

Clues

1. Slim had a large birthmark on his forehead, not only a problem when trying to melt into a crowd but also a good aiming point for the posse.

2. There was a reward of $1,000 for the capture of Jed Junior; he didn't have a broken nose and wasn't the gunslinger.

3. One poster offered a reward of $5,000 for the cattle rustler.

4. The outlaw with a scar running down the left side of his face had a bounty on his head of $2,000; this wasn't Doc Cassidy, who was wanted after holding up the monthly stagecoach.

5. The outlaw with a broken nose, who wasn't Bronco and who was rather upset that he didn't have the highest reward offered for his capture, was being hunted for his involvement with the recent bank robberies.

6. The arsonist didn't have a large wart on his chin.

Nickname	Crime

	Arson	Bank robbery	Cattle rustling	Gunslinging	Stage robbery	$750	$1,000	$2,000	$5,000	$6,000	Birthmark	Bitten ear	Broken nose	Scar	Wart
Bronco															
Doc Cassidy															
Jed Junior															
Slim															
Wild Willis															
Birthmark																
Bitten ear																
Broken nose																
Scar																
Wart																
$750																
$1,000																
$2,000																
$5,000																
$6,000																

I want something that's absolutely nothing like this

WANTED

Bounty	Mark

Sign In

Each row and column is to contain the digits 1-6. The given signs tell you if a digit in a cell is plus 1 (+) or minus 1 (-) the digit next to it. Signs between consecutive digits always work from left to right or top to bottom.

Examples: $\boxed{3}$ + $\boxed{4}$ or $\boxed{2}$ over $\boxed{1}$ with a minus

ALL occurrences of consecutive digits have been marked by a sign.

Sudoku

Complete this grid so that each column, each row, and each marked 3 X 3 square contains each of the numbers 1 to 9.

			2	9	7			
2				4			8	
		7			4			1
6		5		9	4			8
		3			8		4	6
4				7		2		
5		4			6			
8		1	5		7		9	

Canal Turn

Last weekend the Keighshire Canal Club organized itself into groups to tackle a short stretch of the waterway in Netherlipp that had become unusable. From the clues, can you name the leader of each group, the number of volunteers it contained, the short stretch of canal each team tackled, and the main items they dragged from the canal bottom?

Clues

1. Gary's team spent the morning tidying up the canal at the Old Wharf; Betty's team was surprised to have pulled three bicycles from the canal before 10:30 a.m.

2. The team of seven volunteers spent quite some time dragging shopping carts from the canal; the team working under the bridge wasn't the one pulling automobile tires from the water.

3. Wendy's team included two more volunteers than the group working at the lock.

	3	5	7	Bridge	Lock	Wharf	Bicycles	Automobile tires	Shopping cart
Betty Barge									
Gary Gates									
Wendy Waterman									
Bicycles									
Automobile tires									
Shopping cart									
Bridge									
Lock									
Wharf									

Leader	Volunteers	Stretch	Items

Fussy Cats

My neighbors have five cats and they love them all dearly. The cats have fresh food in the morning and dried food in the evening, but they all have different tastes, and none of them eats the same flavors of fresh and dried food, nor do any of them eat the same combination of flavors. From the clues, can you work out the name and color of each cat and the flavors of fresh and dried food each pampered cat insists on?

Clues

1. Jarvis is a ginger cat who won't eat fish in any form at any time of the day, although that doesn't stop him trying to catch the goldfish.

2. The gray cat likes fresh duck for breakfast but won't go anywhere near dried lamb at dinnertime.

3. Fresh fish and dried duck is the regular dietary regime of one cat.

4. The cat who likes dried beef for its dinner has a name one letter shorter than that of the cat who likes fresh beef to start the day but one letter longer than that of the cat who likes fresh lamb to get the day off to a good start.

5. Neither Ambrose nor the tabby cat will eat poultry in any manifestation, but both Lucy and the black cat will and do.

Name	Color

	Black	Ginger	Gray	Tabby	White	Fresh Beef	Chicken	Duck	Fish	Lamb	Dried Beef	Chicken	Duck	Fish	Lamb
Ambrose															
Jarvis															
Kittycat															
Lucy															
Ninja															
Dried Beef															
Chicken															
Duck															
Fish															
Lamb															
Fresh Beef															
Chicken															
Duck															
Fish															
Lamb															

Fresh food	Dried food

Missed the Boat

Five friends belonging to a local retirement social club had just returned from a two-week Mediterranean cruise together. The voyage started from Valencia Sea Port, with the first port of call being Ibiza, followed by Majorca, Corsica, Sardinia, Sicily, and finally back to Valencia. None of the holidaymakers visited all of the islands, owing to illness or overindulgence. From the clues, can you work out who missed a visit to which particular island, the reason they couldn't make it, and the number of hours that was allocated to the visit?

Clues

1. Ken missed the visit to Majorca; the vacation makers spent two hours longer there than on Corsica.

2. Tom missed a five-hour stay at one of the islands; he wasn't the one who overslept, waking to find the liner almost deserted and immediately assuming a mutiny had occurred.

3. Sheila was a little tender, after getting sunburnt the day before; she didn't miss the stopover at Sicily.

4. It wasn't Vikki who had a hangover from a previous night's frivolities and missed the stopover at Sardinia.

5. One person suffered an attack of food poisoning and, preferring to stay within reach of certain facilities, missed visiting the island where other vacation makers stayed for seven hours.

6. Grace didn't miss a visit to an island that had only been allocated three hours touring time; the cruisers stayed on Ibiza for nine hours—they hadn't meant to stay so long but their coach broke down.

Name	Island

	Corsica	Ibiza	Majorca	Sardinia	Sicily	Food poisoning	Hangover	Overate	Overslept	Sunburnt	3 hours	5 hours	7 hours	8 hours	9 hours
Grace															
Ken															
Sheila															
Tom															
Vikki															
3 hours															
5 hours															
7 hours															
8 hours															
9 hours															
Food poisoning															
Hangover															
Overate															
Overslept															
Sunburnt															

This cruise may not be going anywhere but the buffet is fantastic

Reason	Hours

No Need to Worry . . .

Five moms have taken a well-earned night off for a spot of relaxation and a touch of pampering at the new Crispin Spa, leaving their husbands in charge of the house and the family. But, perhaps unsurprisingly, the stress-free evening is punctuated with a text message to each of the moms which begins, "There's no need to worry but . . ." Can you work out at what time each mom received her "no need to worry . . ." text, the name of her husband who sent it, and what it was about?

Clues

1. Emma's phone buzzed at 7:30 p.m. to indicate she had received a text; Richard's "no need to worry . . ." text arrived fifteen minutes later.

2. Quentin's text read, "There's no need to worry, but when was the last time you saw the dog?"

3. Melanie looked up from her shoulder massage to read her text. "There's no need to worry," it began, "but do we have a fire extinguisher?"; this was half an hour before one lady received a text that read "There's no need to worry, but is the large screen TV still under warranty?"

4. Oliver texted his relaxing wife, who isn't Laura, later in the evening than one lady read, "There's no need to worry, but do we know a good plumber?"; Laura's text was neither the last to arrive nor the next after Oliver's.

5. Kathyrn's husband, Norman, texted her half an hour before one lady read, "There's no need to worry, but do we have the number of an emergency HVAC tech?"

Time	Mom

	Emma	Jane	Kathryn	Laura	Melanie	Norman	Oliver	Patrick	Quentin	Richard	Dog	Fire extinguisher	HVAC tech	Plumber	Television
7 p.m.															
7:15 p.m.															
7:30 p.m.															
7:45 p.m.															
8 p.m.															
Dog															
Fire extinguisher															
HVAC tech															
Plumber															
Television															
Norman															
Oliver															
Patrick															
Quentin															
Richard															

Husband	Text subject

Background Check

Many writers of whodunits and crime thrillers have backgrounds largely unconnected with deeds or with the worlds inhabited by their detective creations and the felons they pursue. From the clues, can you work out the major profession of each of the first-time thriller writers listed below and the name and profession of their detective hero?

Clues

1. James Knight's detective character is a successful mystery-story writer who is involved in a real-life case through a letter from one of his fans.

2. Martin Norman is not the creator of detective Liz Kirk.

3. The consular officer, whose detective is a veterinary surgeon dragged into solving crime by pet owners, is not Gail Hilbert, whose detective is male.

4. Donald Elgin, creator of detective Isaac Hunter, is not the solicitor.

5. Anita Bixby is a partner in her family's firm of funeral directors.

6. The accountant's detective creation, Charles Barbet, is neither the 18th-century physician who has joined the Royal Navy as a surgeon to avoid his gambling debts nor the Professor of math from a redbrick university, who uses his or her knowledge of numbers to solve crimes.

7. Russell Quinn is a restaurateur, owner of the exclusive Saxton's, who only becomes a detective when somebody adds poison to a diner's *homard à la Normande*.

Writer	Occupation

	Accountant	Consular officer	Dentist	Funeral director	Solicitor	Charles Barbet	Isaac Hunter	Liz Kirk	Olive Norbert	Russell Quinn	Mystery writer	Naval surgeon	Professor of math	Restaurateur	Vet
Anita Bixby															
Donald Elgin															
Gail Hilbert															
James Knight															
Martin Norman															
Mystery writer															
Naval surgeon															
Professor of math															
Restaurateur															
Vet															
Charles Barbet															
Isaac Hunter															
Liz Kirk															
Olive Norbert															
Russell Quinn															

Detective	Occupation

Back to School

Trash Can Pictures is making one of those action pictures which won't win any Oscars but will give satisfaction to people who like to see a really creepy bad guy go down in flames. The plot deals with a school in a poor area of New York City which is having trouble with teenage gangs controlled by a drug dealer, and five former pupils who come back from different parts of the USA to help out their old headmaster. Can you work out the full name of each of these five graduates of the school, where they fly in from, and what they've become since they left school?

Clues

1. Melinda, who now lives and works in Miami, is not the ex-pupil named Van Der Byl who has become a top martial arts instructor.

2. The army officer now based at Fort Bragg is not just any army officer but a Major in the Green Berets.

3. Tony's surname isn't Kruger.

4. Piretta has become a citizen of Chicago.

5. Patrick Reilly is, as his name might lead you to suspect, an Irish-American.

6. The bank robber, who has stolen over $10 million in the last five years, uses his brains rather than violence and never even carries a loaded gun on a job; the explosives expert's surname isn't Kruger.

7. Billy is a senior CIA agent, in charge of a special training facility; Faith isn't in the army and doesn't live in Denver.

First name	Surname

	Kruger	La France	Piretta	Reilly	Van Der Byl	Chicago	Denver	Fort Bragg	Miami	San Diego	Army officer	Bank robber	CIA agent	Explosives expert	Martial arts instructor
Billy															
Faith															
Melinda															
Patrick															
Tony															
Army officer															
Bank robber															
CIA agent															
Explosives expert															
Martial arts instructor															
Chicago															
Denver															
Fort Bragg															
Miami															
San Diego															

Flew in from	Occupation

Piece of Cake

After winning Netherlipp TV's *Cake Off* series last year, Madeleine Baker has become known to all in Crispin Parva as the Queen of Cakes and is continually called upon to produce cakes for some event or other, and this week was no exception. From the clues, can you work out what type of cake she baked on each day, which organization it was for, and what the event was in each case?

Clues

1. Monday's contribution to the bring and buy sale wasn't the rock cakes.

2. Madeleine baked for the summer fair the day after she made the tea loaf and the day before she baked for the British Legion.

3. The St. Barnabas Sunday School cake was baked on Wednesday.

4. The Dundee cake for the old people's home was baked the day after the one destined for the coach trip.

5. The Madeira cake was to be sold at the yard sale, which was nothing to do with the church.

6. One of the cakes was enjoyed at the Playgroup tea party.

Day	Type of cake

	Dundee cake	Madeira cake	Rock cakes	Tea loaf	Victoria sponge	British Legion	Church	Old people's home	Playgroup	Sunday School	Bring and buy sale	Yard sale	Coach trip	Summer fair	Tea party
Monday															
Tuesday															
Wednesday															
Thursday															
Friday															
Bring and buy sale															
Yard sale															
Coach trip															
Summer fair															
Tea party															
British Legion															
Church															
Old people's home															
Playgroup															
Sunday School															

Organization	Event

Just Browsing

A sudden cloudburst over Netherlipp High Street had sent shoppers scurrying for cover, and five rain dodgers had ended up in The Stationery Station stationery store and newsstand. Shaking off the rain, they each spent a few minutes browsing a couple of different sections while waiting for the rain to ease off. From the clues, can you work out who browsed which two sections of goods and how long they spent in the store before slinking off out of the door without buying anything?

Clues

1. Loretta Linger, who lingered for longer than six minutes, spent her first few minutes in the shop browsing the DVDs; Imelda Idol, who didn't look at the DVDs at all, spent two minutes longer in the shop than the person who looked first at the reference book section (looking up the answer to a crossword clue in that morning's paper) but left the shop two minutes before the person who first stood in front of the pens and paper section.

2. Brian Brows' second browsing area was the cookbooks where he flicked through a large recipe book trying to discover why his soufflés fell apart the night before.

3. Larry Loyter browsed one section of the shop for seven minutes before moving to the section that had first attracted Wendy Waite when she dodged in out of the rain.

4. The man who first browsed the greeting card section trying to remember if there was an imminent occasion for which he should be buying one of those things was still in the shop when the other four had left; this wasn't the same man who perused the reference books after moving to that section from elsewhere in the shop.

5. The rain dodger who began their rain dodging among the cookbooks didn't move on to the greeting card section.

6. The person who looked at the pens and paper section second didn't spend exactly ten minutes in The Stationery Station that morning.

Rain dodger	Section 1

	Cookbooks	DVDs	Greeting cards	Paper and pens	Reference books	Cookbooks	DVDs	Greeting cards	Paper and pens	Reference books	6 minutes	8 minutes	10 minutes	12 minutes	14 minutes
Brian Brows															
Imelda Idol															
Larry Loyter															
Loretta Linger															
Wendy Waite															
6 minutes															
8 minutes															
10 minutes															
12 minutes															
14 minutes															
Cookbooks															
DVDs															
Greeting cards															
Paper and pens															
Reference books															

Section 2	Time

Bad Form

Households across the country are full of people shuffling around filled with gloom and depression at the arrival of the new school year—and that's just the teachers. Can you match the five apprehensive staff members below with the subject they teach, the particularly uncooperative class they'd been hoping to avoid this year— and the day of the week they've just found out they're down to teach them after all?

Clues

1. Senora Escuela is supposed to be teaching her class some Spanish—but it might as well be Double Dutch.

2. The Technology class, which is not taught by Mrs. Boord or Mr. Markham, takes place on a Wednesday, but not to one of the 2nd forms; Mr. Markham's bête noire is class IJ.

3. The teacher attempting, but failing miserably, to give instruction to Form 2E will be seeing them the day before the Physics lesson, but not on Monday.

4. Miss Graydes is relieved—slightly—to find that her dreaded lesson will be over before the middle of the week, unlike the poor lady "in charge" of Form 3C.

5. Form 2M's chance to torment their Biology teacher does not fall on a Tuesday.

Teacher	Subject

	Biology	History	Physics	Spanish	Technology	1J	2E	2M	3C	4B	Monday	Tuesday	Wednesday	Thursday	Friday
Mrs. Boord															
Senora Escuela															
Miss Graydes															
Mr. Kane															
Mr. Markham															
Monday															
Tuesday															
Wednesday															
Thursday															
Friday															
1J															
2E															
2M															
3C															
4B															

Class	Day

Enforced Stoppages

Each of the Keighshire Canal Club teams worked hard all morning clearing their section of the waterway, but just about lunchtime each found something in the canal that forced them to stop as they called in the professionals. Can you say at what time each team had to stop, what they had found, and to which nearby pub they retired?

Clues

1. The team that was horrified when they spotted a floating body retired to the The Towpath for a stiff drink or two while the police investigated (it turned out to be a mannequin).

2. Betty's team found a number of large but very dead rats, and she thought it prudent to call in the environmental safety officers; they retired to the bar 15 minutes after Wendy's team, who didn't patronize The Old Barge.

3. One team watched a barrel bob to the surface, pop open, and begin oozing a luminous yellow chemical into the canal and, at 12:45 p.m., retired to the bar.

	12:30 p.m.	12:45 p.m.	1:00 p.m.	Body	Chemical spill	Dead rats	The Lighterman	The Old Barge	The Towpath
Betty Barge									
Gary Gates									
Wendy Waterman									
The Lighterman									
The Old Barge									
The Towpath									
Body									
Chemical spill									
Dead rats									

Leader	Time	Item found	Bar

Domino Search

A standard set of dominoes has been laid out, using numbers instead of dots for clarity. Using a sharp pencil and a keen brain, can you draw in the lines to show where each domino has been placed? You may find the check grid useful—crossing off each domino as you find it.

1	6	0	4	5	1	2	4
3	6	0	6	3	5	6	5
0	3	2	2	0	1	4	3
5	3	5	1	4	4	2	0
6	6	5	1	2	3	2	3
1	1	3	0	4	2	4	1
4	5	2	6	0	5	0	6

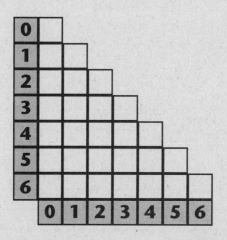

Selling Point

Five Storbury residents received pleasant surprises when they took some junk along to the Albion TV auction show *Peddle It!* and managed to sell it at the auction. From the clues below, can you work out what each of the lucky five took along to the show, where they had been keeping it at home, and how much they got for it?

Clues

1. The elderly gentleman who took along an old book (which turned out to be a first edition) was offered less than the man who went along with a large old vase he'd found in his garden shed (an unusual example of early Ballingdon ware).

2. Mrs. Inman received $85 for her item, which hadn't come from the cupboard under her stairs.

3. Mr. Owen found his item in his basement, where it had been gathering dust for at least ten years.

4. One of the lucky five picked up $100 for an item which had been acting as a spider's adventure playground in the garage.

5. Mrs. Wells' teapot (yellow ceramic, and regarded by her as "a horror" ever since she was given it as a wedding present) didn't sell for $70.

6. The plate—a rare example of the Chinese P'ing dynasty, apparently— was bought by local dealer Will Patten for $55.

7. Mr. Shaw's item didn't sell for $55 or $115.

Name	Item

	Book	Music box	Plate	Teapot	Vase	Attic	Basement	Garage	Garden shed	Under stairs	$55	$70	$85	$100	$115
Mr. Clark															
Mrs. Inman															
Mr. Owen															
Mr. Shaw															
Mrs. Wells															
$55															
$70															
$85															
$100															
$115															
Attic															
Basement															
Garage															
Garden shed															
Under stairs															

TELEVISION MATH

SCRAPHEAP CHALLENGE + **TIME** = **ANTIQUES ROADSHOW**

Storage	Price

Emergency Roster

The five tenants (previously students) who live in a large house together now all have jobs in the same town since graduating last summer. In their undergraduate days they organized household activities according to duty rosters and have recently invented another one. Begrudgingly, they have been forced to take it in turns to take a day off work to deal with household emergencies. From the clues, can you work out in which month each recent graduate took a day off work this year, for which tradesperson they waited, and how he or she occupied themselves during that day?

Clues

1. Danny waited for the glazier to arrive after a vigorous game of tabletop pool got out of hand, which wasn't in June or October.

2. Fran, who didn't wait for the locksmith, occupied her time by playing the guitar most of the day; she had nothing to do with the roofer who came to do a job in August after a sudden downpour exposed a distinct lack of watertightness.

3. The tenant who stayed at home waiting and waiting on one day in September read a novel from cover to cover by the time the tradesperson turned up.

4. The roommate who waited for the electrician to arrive to wire in a new external security light played video games; this wasn't Liam or Millie, who was quite miffed at having to wait around on a glorious day in July; she didn't spend her day watching TV.

5. The plumber arrived later in the year than the day Alicia had to take her day off work.

Name	Tradesperson

	Electrician	Glazier	Locksmith	Plumber	Roofer	June	July	Aug	Sept	Oct	Listened to radio	Played guitar	Played video games	Read book	Watched TV
Alicia															
Danny															
Fran															
Liam															
Millie															
Listened to radio															
Played guitar															
Played video games															
Read book															
Watched TV															
June															
July															
Aug															
Sept															
Oct															

Month	Activity

Lone Star Rangers

Back in the days of the Wild West, law enforcement in most of the huge state of Texas was the responsibility of the Texas Rangers. Working in ones and twos with minimal support from their central organization, by the standards of the period, they did a pretty good job. We feature five such lawmen here. From the clues, can you work out where—in or outside Texas—each Ranger had been born, the job he had been doing immediately before joining the law enforcers, and the most distinctive thing about his appearance?

Clues

1. The former horse breaker, recognizable by his heavy mustache, wasn't one of the two Rangers who was known by the name of Red or Dutchy.

2. The man born in the Texas town of Brownsville, who favored a Mexican-style sombrero as headwear over the usual Stetson, had been christened Bartholomew but had always, from his childhood, been known by a nickname; he had never worked as a cowhand.

3. The former trail boss had been born in El Paso, on the Mexican border.

4. Ben Cooper, who had been a Corporal in the US 7th Cavalry before joining the Rangers, wasn't the man who always wore a buckskin jacket and hadn't been born in San Antonio.

5. Mike Nealey had been born in New York, of Irish immigrant parents, and gradually drifted west; it wasn't Red Samson who had been a railroad laborer before joining the Texas Rangers.

6. Jed Kinsman, known for always wearing a red shirt, wasn't the one-time trail boss.

Name	Born in

	Brownsville	El Paso	New York	Phoenix	San Antonio	Cowhand	Horse breaker	Laborer	Soldier	Trail boss	Buckskin jacket	Mustache	Red shirt	Scar on cheek	Sombrero
Ben Cooper															
Dutchy Ernst															
Jed Kinsman															
Mike Nealy															
Red Samson															
Buckskin jacket															
Mustache															
Red shirt															
Scar on cheek															
Sombrero															
Cowhand															
Horse breaker															
Laborer															
Soldier															
Trail boss															

Former job	Feature

A Haunting We Will Go

On October 31, Keighshire Scouts held an event in the Netherlipp Woodlands, a small copse on the edge of the Keighshire Moors. With the aid of candlelit pumpkins and previously hidden sweets and tricks, the scouts had a whale of a time hunting for the treats among the leaves, under logs and hanging from the branches of trees. Only one treat could be had by each scout and five of the quickest found the best ones. From the clues, can you work out the costume each youngster wore, the treat he or she found, and what their unexpected surprise was?

Clues

1. Ben dressed as a vampire, complete with flowing cape and bloodstained fangs.

2. Hannah was suddenly covered in a blanket of dropped wet leaves as she approached a tree; she wasn't dressed as a devil or ghost; the ghost found the bag of licorice.

3. Courtney discovered the can of assorted toffees; she wasn't the scout who put a hand into a hollow part of a trunk, thinking there might have been a treat there but instead came away with a hand covered in sticky maple syrup.

4. The youngster who was hit by a flour bomb was lucky enough to find the packet of chocolate cookies.

5. The scout dressed as a skeleton, who wasn't Joseph, was alarmed when a large, very realistic looking spider appeared from nowhere; they didn't get the toffees.

6. Daniel didn't find the fudge.

Name	Costume

	Devil	Ghost	Skeleton	Vampire	Zombie	Assorted candy bars	Choc cookies	Fudge	Licorice	Toffee	Flour bomb	Leaves	Maple syrup	Spider	Water
Ben															
Courtney															
Daniel															
Hannah															
Joseph															
Flour bomb															
Leaves															
Maple syrup															
Spider															
Water															
Assorted candy bars															
Choc cookies															
Fudge															
Licorice															
Toffee															

Treat	Trick

Bring to Book

Five people are lining up to have their books issued at the Stonekeigh Central Public Lending Library. From the clues, can you discover the title of the book each is borrowing, the name of its author, and the section from which it has been taken?

Clues

1. Mrs. Wordley is borrowing neither *Midnight Hags* nor *The Temple Gates*—she read those last week!

2. *Midnight Hags* is neither by Naomi Franklin nor is it a travel book; *The Temple Gates* is not by D. R. Goodman, who is also not a historian or a biographer.

3. *Looking Back* is from the biography section (the story of Olympic rower Walter Ryder, who spent all of his sporting career, well, looking back), but its author is not Gareth Morgan.

4. Naomi Franklin writes romantic fiction; Mr. Tomes's detective novel is not by D. R. Goodman.

5. Mr. Paige is borrowing *Touch the Hills*, and Miss Plott a book by Alexander Shaw.

6. *After the Storm* is by Arthur Brewer.

Borrower	Title

	After the Storm	Looking Back	Midnight Hags	The Temple Gates	Touch the Hills	Arthur Brewer	Naomi Franklin	D. R. Goodman	Gareth Morgan	Alexander Shaw	Biography	Detective fiction	History	Romantic fiction	Travel
Mr. Paige															
Miss Plott															
Mrs. Reade															
Mr. Tomes															
Mrs. Wordley															
Biography															
Detective fiction															
History															
Romantic fiction															
Travel															
Arthur Brewer															
Naomi Franklin															
D. R. Goodman															
Gareth Morgan															
Alexander Shaw															

Author	Section

Borrowed Heroes

In his latest volume of short crime stories, Dick Carter-Johnson includes five in which the detective is actually the hero of a famous novel, acting outside the role in which he was originally depicted. From the clues, can you identify the title of each of these stories, the profession of the murder victim, the way in which he is killed, and the name of the borrowed hero who acts as detective?

Clues

1. In one story, the victim is clubbed to death and dumped into the sea, but the criminal is brought to justice by the man who discovers the body—the one-legged Captain Ahab of the whaling ship *Pequod*.

2. The story in which the victim is killed with a knife has a shorter title than the one in which the detective is no-longer-little Lord Fauntleroy, now grown up and, as a Lieutenant in the military, investigating the killing of a brother officer.

3. In one story, a smuggler is poisoned with arsenic; the murder victim in *Swansong* is not a physician.

4. It's not the killer of the wine merchant in *Manslayer* who is exposed by Bilbo Baggins, the well-known Hobbit.

5. The killer in *Fratricide* who is trapped by Sir Percy Blakeney, better known as The Scarlet Pimpernel, does not poison his victim with snake venom.

6. The victim in *Deathwatch*, who is poisoned with cyanide, is not a physician.

7. The Lilliputian killer detected by Lemuel Gulliver kills his victim with poison; Gulliver does not appear in *Breathless*.

Title	Victim

	Army officer	Musician	Physician	Smuggler	Wine merchant	Arsenic	Club	Cyanide	Knife	Snake venom	Bilbo Baggins	Captain Ahab	Lemuel Gulliver	Lord Fauntleroy	Sir Percy Blakeney
Breathless															
Deathwatch															
Fratricide															
Manslayer															
Swansong															
Bilbo Baggins															
Captain Ahab															
Lemuel Gulliver															
Lord Fauntleroy															
Sir Percy Blakeney															
Arsenic															
Club															
Cyanide															
Knife															
Snake venom															

Weapon	Detective

Hits for Six

The Six Nightingales have had a string of hits over the last ten years, but only five reached the heights of the Top Ten. From the clues, can you work out the month and year of release of each, its title, and the highest position it reached on the charts?

Clues

1. The Six Nightingales' 2010 Top Ten hit was *See My Heart*, while their 2011 release did better in the charts than *Lost and Gone*.

2. *Whisper Goodbye* was a September release, later in the year than the 2014 single was released, which reached number 3.

3. Both the January release and *Always Sometimes* were hits before 2013, and both did better than the 2016 single.

4. The 2016 single was released in a month listed one place before the 2012 musical offering.

5. Their only chart-topper was released in August.

6. *Don't You Understand* was the least successful of the five.

Month	Year

	2010	2011	2012	2014	2016	Always Sometimes	Don't You Understand	Lost and Gone	See My Heart	Whisper Goodbye	1	3	4	7	9
January															
May															
August															
September															
November															
1															
3															
4															
7															
9															
Always Sometimes															
Don't You Understand															
Lost and Gone															
See My Heart															
Whisper Goodbye															

Title	Highest position

Skiffit

Hugh Heffaugh is an avid science fiction fan and subscribes to *SciFi Times* magazine, which lists forthcoming movie releases in that genre, together with information on the running time, director, and writer. This month's edition of "Skiffit," as it's known to its readers, has landed on Hugh's doormat. Can you work out the running time, director, and scriptwriter of each of these five eagerly awaited movies?

Clues

1. The superhero action adventure *Red Moon*, which isn't directed by Leigh Kinnison, is longer than the movie directed by Hank Graeme but not as long as the one scripted by Moses Lytton, which doesn't run for 133 minutes.

2. The film directed by Benny Atreides, which is neither futuristic war drama *Iron Range* nor the one scripted by Cheryl Bronte, runs for 128 minutes.

3. *Zero Zone*, which is the work of a male scriptwriter and is supposed to be based on "ideas from the works of Mark Twain," runs for an odd number of minutes.

4. The film directed by Walt Van Rijn runs three minutes longer than the apocalyptic *Night Wind*—though he is rumored to be working on a special director's cut approximately twice as long.

5. *Cold Dragon*, based on a comic book which was based on a 1960s TV show adapted from a Japanese feature film of 1957, is exactly one minute longer than the movie directed by Leigh Kinnison.

6. The film scripted by Earl Dickens (an American, not an aristocrat) is shorter than the film that is the work of Cheryl Bronte.

Title	Running time

	126 minutes	127 minutes	128 minutes	130 minutes	133 minutes	Benny Atreides	Damien Carter	Hank Graeme	Leigh Kinnison	Walt Van Rijn	Becky Austen	Cheryl Bronte	Darren Chaucer	Earl Dickens	Moses Lytton
Cold Dragon															
Iron Range															
Night Wind															
Red Moon															
Zero Zone															
Becky Austen											
Cheryl Bronte											
Darren Chaucer											
Earl Dickens											
Moses Lytton											
Benny Atreides						
Damien Carter						
Hank Graeme						
Leigh Kinnison						
Walt Van Rijn						

Director	Scriptwriter

Select Committee

Payper, Bach and Pulp is a small publishing company in Churchminster established many years ago by Mr. Payper, Mr. Bach, and Mr. Pulp and which is run to this day by descendents of the founders. This morning, five members of the board met to discuss a few potential novels, starting with *Scandal on High*. From the clues, can you work out in what order each spoke, their one-word description of the novel, and their forecast for its publishing outcome?

Clues

1. "Let me begin," said the first person to speak. "I cannot express how disgraceful I think this book is, but I'll have a go." Pandora Pulp watched from across the table and nodded.

2. "It's just appalling," said another board member sometime later. "I've never read anything quite so . . . appalling. It'll be a publishing sensation." "I agree," added Bertram Bach speaking next. "It'll make a fortune."

3. "Shameful," said Percival Pulp, pushing the manuscript further away and wiping his hand. "Shameful, shameful, shameful."

4. The board member who said *Scandal on High* would be a big hit, who wasn't Petula Payper, wasn't the one who had used the word outrageous—quite a number of times.

5. "But having said that," said the fourth board member to make their feelings public, "I have no doubt it will be at the top of the sales charts."

6. "So, if I may sum up," said Peregrine Payper speaking last and after using a number of words to describe the book, only one of which we feel able to include here, "we all dislike *Scandal on High* intensely but are keen to add it to our list." Everyone nodded sagely.

Order	Board member

	Bertram Bach	Pandora Pulp	Percival Pulp	Peregrine Payper	Petula Payper	Appalling	Disgraceful	Outrageous	Shameful	Shocking	Big hit	Chart topper	Make a fortune	Publishing sensation	Sell millions
First															
Second															
Third															
Fourth															
Fifth															
Big hit															
Chart topper															
Make a fortune															
Publishing sensation															
Sell millions															
Appalling															
Disgraceful															
Outrageous															
Shameful															
Shocking															

Description	Forecast

Logi-5

Each line, across and down, is to have each of the letters A, B, C, D, and E, appearing once. Also, every shape—shown by the thick lines—must also have each of the letters in it. Can you fill in the grid?

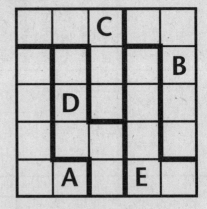

Killer Sudoku

The normal rules of Sudoku apply. In addition, the digits in each inner shape (marked by dots) must add up to the number in the top corner of that box.

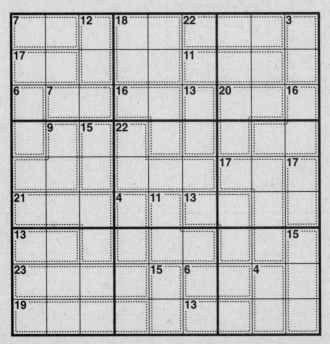

Grounded

On Monday morning, Santa's flying practice preparations for the 24th have been disrupted, as three of his reindeer have reported sick with minor ailments and have been told not to fly for a short while. Can you work out which reindeer has which ailment and for how long they have to stay on the ground?

Clues

1. One of the reindeer has been to see the North Pole Medical Elf with a nasty case of nose rash.

2. Comet, who has a problem with a hoof, has been grounded for one day shorter than the reindeer who told the Medical Elf of an acute ache.

3. The reindeer with a problematic antler has been told to avoid flying for longer than Prancer.

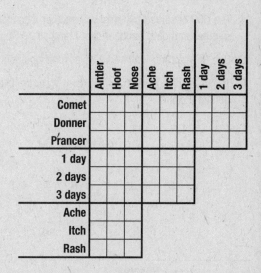

Reindeer	Body part	Ailment	Grounded

Lights in the Sky

Ever since a research balloon fell out of the sky near Greenman Hill on the Eastshire Downs, a growing number of reports have been received of sighting of spaceships from other parts of the universe by the police, TV, newspapers, and frankly anyone who'll listen. From the clues, can you discover where each of these Eastshire folk saw the alleged craft, what it looked like, and how many minutes it stayed within view?

Clues

1. Clare's UFO, which was of a silver appearance, was not seen above Marsham, while Ray saw his in the sky over Little Green, but not for the longest time of the five.

2. Joe saw three bright lights in the sky, but Terry's sighting was not of a spinning globe.

3. One of the supposed extra-terrestrial craft hovered above Oddleigh for four minutes, but neither it nor the one seen over Marsham appeared as a red glow.

4. The UFO observed by Harry was neither a spinning globe nor watched for two minutes and didn't appear over Marsham.

5. One UFO-spotter watched a silver tube zip about the sky for three minutes.

6. The silver disc hung in the sky over Weardon like a . . . well, like the Moon behind a cloud.

Observer	Location

	Fenomenham	Little Green	Marsham	Oddleigh	Weardon	Red glow	Silver disc	Silver tube	Spinning globe	Three lights	1 minute	2 minutes	3 minutes	4 minutes	5 minutes
Clare															
Harry															
Joe															
Ray															
Terry															
1 minute															
2 minutes															
3 minutes															
4 minutes															
5 minutes															
Red glow															
Silver disc															
Silver tube															
Spinning globe															
Three lights															

Appearance	Duration

Action Wedding

Nathan is a wedding photographer, and during the latter part of last year he has managed to combine his job with a spot of travel and adventure. In order to capture the perfect wedding photos, he took part in some of the daredevil activities that the happy couples were keen to be involved with during their off-the-wall wedding ceremonies. From the clues, can you name the bride and groom in each case, work out what activity they engaged in, and say in which country each wedding ceremony took place?

Clues

1. Belinda is Gavin's new wife.

2. Gareth and his bride, who wasn't Bridget, went water skiing in their wedding outfits at their chosen resort, which wasn't in the Bahamas; Bridget traveled with her husband-to-be, who wasn't George, to the Maldives.

3. A bride, groom, vicar, one guest, and Nathan all crammed beside the pilot into the basket of a hot air balloon and took to the skies above New Zealand.

4. Glen and his bride, who aren't the couple who persuaded Nathan to don a parachute and leap out of a plane to capture their sky diving ceremony, recited their wedding vows in Thailand; Glen's bride wasn't Bonnie, who left these shores with her then fiancé to enjoy a scuba diving vacation and an underwater wedding.

5. Beth didn't go with her fiancé to the Seychelles.

Bride	Groom

	Gareth	Gavin	George	Glen	Greg	Bungee jump	Hot-air balloon	Scuba dive	Sky dive	Water skiing	Bahamas	Maldives	New Zealand	Seychelles	Thailand
Beatrice															
Belinda															
Beth															
Bonnie															
Bridget															
Bahamas															
Maldives															
New Zealand															
Seychelles															
Thailand															
Bungee jump															
Hot-air balloon															
Scuba dive															
Sky dive															
Water skiing															

Modern Proverbs №26: If at first you don't succeed, don't try skydiving

PROVERBS

Activity	Country

Music Makers

The National Concert Center has five major classical and popular music concerts next month, details of which are given below; from that information can you discover the date on which each concert is to take place, the name of the promoter, and the normal ticket price?

Clues

1. GBP is the promoter of the concert on the 22nd, which is later in the month than the Royal London Orchestra's concert, for which ticket prices are $50.

2. Neither the event on the 4th nor that being staged by Wildwood involved orchestras, and the tickets for both are cheaper than for the Norwich Symphony Orchestra concert.

3. The Norwich Symphony Orchestra is the event immediately before Jennifer Earle.

4. Tickets for the Hugo Lindsay event are more expensive than for Barney and the Farmers in concert.

5. Tickets for the Posh Frock Promotions event are the most expensive, while those for the event on the 17th are the least expensive.

6. Jeff Barclay is being presented by Green House Productions.

Date	Event

	Barney and . . .	Jeff Barclay	Jennifer Earle	Norwich Sym Orch	Royal London Orch	GBP	Green House Prod	Hugo Lindsay	Posh Frock Prom	Wildwood	$45	$50	$55	$60	$65
4th															
12th															
17th															
22nd															
29th															
$45															
$50															
$55															
$60															
$65															
GBP															
Green House Prod															
Hugo Lindsay															
Posh Frock Prom															
Wildwood															

Ah yes, I know this bit...
It's from the ad

Promoter	Ticket price

On the Buses

Five different bus routes use a stop in London's Oxford Street, and thirty prospective passengers are waiting there. From the clues, can you discover how many of them are waiting for each bus, the number of minutes they've been waiting, and the destination of each bus?

Clues

1. Four passengers are waiting for the bus for Tower Bridge, which isn't the No. 14.

2. The group that has been waiting for the No. 42 for 9 minutes is one person larger than the group waiting for the Marylebone bus.

3. The group waiting for the Islington bus has one more person in it than the group waiting for the No. 98 and one person fewer than the group that has been waiting 7 minutes.

4. Some people have been waiting 4 minutes for the Chelsea bus.

5. The No. 6 bus goes toward Bank, but the last one called at the stop less than 10 minutes ago.

6. The group of six passengers has been waiting the longest.

Passengers	Bus

	No. 6	No. 14	No. 42	No. 98	No. 207	4 minutes	7 minutes	9 minutes	11 minutes	12 minutes	Bank	Chelsea	Islington	Marylebone	Tower Bridge
4 passengers															
5 passengers															
6 passengers															
7 passengers															
8 passengers															
Bank															
Chelsea															
Islington															
Marylebone															
Tower Bridge															
4 minutes															
7 minutes															
9 minutes															
11 minutes															
12 minutes															

London's 'bendy buses' reveal their secret.

Wait	Destination

Rescue Dogs

At Canine Cove, Southern Australia, Mandy and Mitch work as lifeguards patrolling the beach and saving bathers in daring rescues. But last week was quite different from any other they had ever known. On five occasions, instead of rescuing people, they rescued dogs from the surf, going to the pooches before the owners thought about doing the same thing. From the clues, can you work out the owner and breed of each dog, what day of the week the rescue happened, and the reason the dog got into difficulties?

Clues

1. The poodle, which wasn't rescued on the weekend, was brought to Canine Cove by Dom.

2. Bruce's dog fell from a speedboat after barking overenthusiastically at the waterskier being towed along behind.

3. The incident involving Ellen's dog, which wasn't a Jack Russell, happened on Wednesday; it didn't slip off a surfboard.

4. The German shepherd was rescued on Friday.

5. It was on Sunday when the lifeguard noticed a dog chasing a stick that had been thrown quite some way into the sea by its owner. The Labrador got into difficulties after playing with another dog when both had swam out to sea; its owner isn't female.

Owner	Breed

	Border collie	German shepherd	Jack Russell	Labrador	Poodle	Sunday	Tuesday	Wednesday	Friday	Saturday	Chased stick	Fell from boat	Jumped off jetty	Played with dog	Slipped off surfboard
Bruce															
Corrine															
Dom															
Ellen															
Freddie															
Chased stick															
Fell from boat															
Jumped off jetty															
Played with dog															
Slipped off surfboard															
Sunday															
Tuesday															
Wednesday															
Friday															
Saturday															

You can't call me a mongrel anymore. It's not PC... these days I'm a hybrid.

Day	Incident

Paintball

The five roommates from Goatsferry whom we have followed from student life to working life are having a day off. They have arranged a day out to play a fun game of paintball and were adamant about playing on the same side against another team. They lost the first game in short order, as just one hit eliminated a player and each member of the team had been quickly targeted and forced to sit on the sidelines. From the clues, can you work out whereabouts on the playing area each one was caught, the body part that was hit, and how many minutes it was into the game that each was eliminated?

Clues

1. Alicia was hit as she made a dash for the tower to grab the opposition flag; she was eliminated sometime before the player who was hit on the shoulder.

2. The game was just twelve minutes old when Fran was hit.

3. Liam noticed yellow paint on his arm after he had been hit; he hadn't been hiding under a hedge or behind the oak tree, and the oak tree isn't where Millie had been hiding when she was hit.

4. A player was hit on the side of the head (on the helmet) after being spotted behind a wall by an opposing player; this wasn't Danny, who also wasn't the last player to get hit, eventually getting their back covered in paintball paint.

5. After twenty minutes of game time, one of our five players opened the door of the hut and was immediately hit.

Name	Area

	Hedge	Hut	Oak tree	Tower	Wall	Arm	Back	Head	Shoulder	Thigh	10 minutes	12 minutes	17 minutes	20 minutes	24 minutes
Alicia															
Danny															
Fran															
Liam															
Millie															
10 minutes															
12 minutes															
17 minutes															
20 minutes															
24 minutes															
Arm															
Back															
Head															
Shoulder															
Thigh															

Body part	Time

Tunnel Trouble

Hold-ups, hiccups, and delays on the Paris underground are often put down to the Metro Gnome, a mischievous imp who inhabits the tunnels and who amuses himself with the discomfort of the commuting Parisians. Last week, the Gnome was particularly active, causing various problems on successive days of the week. From the clues given below, can you work out all the details, saying who was inconvenienced on which day by which mishap at which Metro station?

Clues

1. Alain's beret fell on to the track just as his train was approaching the day after the Gnome was wreaking havoc at Les Invalides.

2. It was at Concorde station that Sylvie was inconvenienced.

3. Marcel's unlucky day was Thursday.

4. Henri fell victim to the Metro Gnome's wiles earlier in the week than the passenger who failed to beat the barrier entrance when already late for an appointment.

5. The passenger who tripped on the stairs at Champ de Mars station was a victim later in the week than Jacqueline.

6. The incident at the Etoile did not occur on Tuesday or Friday.

7. It was on Wednesday that someone accidentally boarded a train heading in the wrong direction.

8. The Gare du Nord station was not the scene of the incident the day after someone trapped their foot in the train door just as it was setting off.

Day	Passenger

	Alain	Henri	Jacqueline	Marcel	Sylvie	Beret on track	Caught wrong train	Failed to beat barrier	Trapped foot	Tripped down stairs	Champ de Mars	Concorde	Etoile	Gare du Nord	Invalides
Monday															
Tuesday															
Wednesday															
Thursday															
Friday															
Champ de Mars															
Concorde															
Etoile															
Gare du Nord															
Invalides															
Beret on track															
Caught wrong train															
Failed to beat barrier															
Trapped foot															
Tripped down stairs															

It was originally built for fracking but the tourist thing seems to be working out OK

Mishap	Station

Bagging a Bargain

Our family loves browsing in thrift stores and usually comes away with some fantastic bargains! Below are details of five recent visits to various shops; from the information given, can you work out which clothes item and which other item we purchased at each and the bargain price paid?

Clues

1. We bought some lovely wineglasses at Scope, but they were not part of the $25 purchase.

2. We bought the shirt and a vinyl LP in one shop, which wasn't Age UK, and they cost less than half of what we spent at Oxfam.

3. Our Salvation Army purchases, which included a very nice sweater, cost less than we spent at Mind.

4. We didn't buy the lamp at Age UK.

5. The suit wasn't part of the most expensive purchase.

6. The tie and at least one other item cost only $7, while the purchase including some good books came to only $12.

Shop	Clothes item

	Dress	Sweater	Shirt	Suit	Tie	Books	Jigsaw puzzle	Lamp	LP	Wineglasses	$7	$12	$13	$25	$36
Age UK															
Mind															
Oxfam															
Salvation Army															
Scope															
$7															
$12															
$13															
$25															
$36															
Books															
Jigsaw puzzle															
Lamp															
LP															
Wineglasses															

Other item	Total paid

Curious Couriers

Awaiting the delivery of an online order being fulfilled by nationwide couriers Dawdel, Phil has been trying to keep abreast of its progress via their web-tracking facility—to find his package being considerably better-traveled than he expected. From the clues, can you work out where Phil's package was on each occasion he looked, what its status was, and at what time that day it was updated?

Clues

1. Phil typed the reference code in on Tuesday of the first week to see that his order was being processed—an encouraging start.

2. On one day in the second week, Phil might have been pleased to see that his package had been delivered to his correct street address in Dorchester, Dorset, except that Phil himself was sitting waiting for it in Dorchester-on-Thames, Oxfordshire.

3. A glance at the tracking information one evening revealed that it had reached Exeter at 6 p.m., but not on a Tuesday.

4. A morning visit to the website showed that at 5am it had arrived "at the hub"—whatever that meant—but not in Croydon, where it had been the last time he looked.

5. The package's visit to Norwich took place after it was reported somewhere at 3 p.m., but the occasion before the Item was declared to be "in transit."

6. For some reason Phil's package began the second week with a trip to Manchester, arriving there sometime in the afternoon.

Day	Venue

	Croydon	Dorchester	Exeter	Manchester	Norwich	5 a.m.	8 a.m.	1 p.m.	3 p.m.	6 p.m.	At depot	At hub	Courier in transit	Order being processed	Package delivered
Tues. week 1															
Thurs. week 1															
Mon. week 2															
Tues. week 2															
Thurs. week 2															
At depot															
At hub															
Courier in transit															
Order being processed															
Package delivered															
5 a.m.															
8 a.m.															
1 p.m.															
3 p.m.															
6 p.m.															

Time	Status

Find the Lady

Special Agent Rick Carton is pursuing the trail of sultry villainess Mata Hartburn all over the world, but each time he thinks that he's caught her, he discovers he has arrived just too late to prevent her latest crime—and the fact that she always leaves him a mocking reminder of her presence makes his blood boil all the more. From the clues, can you piece together which city Mata has visited in each recent month, what crime she had come to commit, and what little keepsake she left for Rick to fume over?

Clues

1. Mata traveled to Cairo to steal the sacred scarab brooch of Queen Haphketshup, but not in July, when a silk scarf monogrammed with Mata's initials was Rick's reward for "allowing" her to escape.

2. The March operation was an arson attack to destroy some incriminating memoirs penned by one of Mata's many cast-off lovers; the November escapade was not the occasion she left Rick a beautiful white orchid for his pains.

3. Mata's parting gift to Rick in Florence was a locket containing a few strands of his nemesis' hair.

4. The fact that the ruby ring Mata left behind in one city was probably worth more than the bejeweled dagger Rick had failed to prevent her stealing just made it even more galling.

5. In September, Mata's crime did not involve the theft of any precious item; in May, her nefarious schemes took her to St. Petersburg.

6. Mata's successful attempt on the life of a visiting ambassador took place sometime before she traveled to Singapore.

Month	City

	Cairo	Florence	New York	Singapore	St. Petersburg	Destroy memoirs	Intercept plans	Murder ambassador	Steal dagger	Steal scarab	Handkerchief	Locket of hair	Ruby ring	Silk scarf	White orchid
March															
May															
July															
September															
November															
Handkerchief															
Locket of hair															
Ruby ring															
Silk scarf															
White orchid															
Destroy memoirs															
Intercept plans															
Murder ambassador															
Steal dagger															
Steal scarab															

Crime	Keepsake

Battleships

Do you remember the old game of battleships? These puzzles are based on that idea. Your task is to find the vessels in the diagram. Some parts of boats or sea squares have already been filled in, and a number next to a row or column refers to the number of occupied squares in that row or column. The boats may be positioned horizontally or vertically, but no two boats or parts of boats are in adjacent squares—horizontally, vertically, or diagonally.

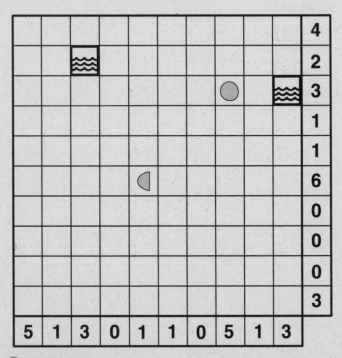

Aircraft carrier:

Battleship:

Cruiser:

Destroyer:

Training Days

Santa's team may be banned from flying until Thursday but earthbound training can continue. Can you work out in what part of the process Santa drills his team on each of the three grounded days and say which member of the crew had what accident during final practice, leaving Santa with his head in his hands?

Clues

1. During the emergency harnessing drill one reindeer caught his hocks in the straps.

2. Zachary, who is one of Santa's elves, had a problem during rapid loading practice.

3. On Tuesday Santa and his team practiced reversing around a chimney.

4. The day that Blitzen slipped over on the icy surface, pulling the rest of the team to the ground, was later in the week than when Cupid had a small accident.

	Harnessing	Reversing	Loading	Blitzen	Cupid	Zachary	Hocks caught	Slipped over	Tipped sleigh
Monday									
Tuesday									
Wednesday									
Hocks caught									
Slipped over									
Tipped sleigh									
Blitzen									
Cupid									
Zachary									

Day	Practice	Crew member	Accident

Band on the Run

One Saturday during the festive shopping period at Netherlipp Mall, the Keighshire Marching Band has been marching up and down between the shops playing carols and festive songs. To be honest, there's not really enough room and the music tends to echo a bit, but it's the thought that counts. On one pass along the Mall the band suffered five hiccups after five players were distracted for a moment. Can you work out each distracted player's instrument, what distracted them, and the problem it caused?

Clues

1. Joanna was distracted from the job in hand as the band marched by the We Am Phones mobile phone shop spotting the new yFone in the window; she isn't the bass drum player who, surprised by what they saw, bashed the drum so hard the skin split.

2. Gareth, who wasn't the player distracted by the sight of Santa Claus being lowered from the roof on his sleigh, returned from his moment's reverie and leapt into the chorus of *Frosty the Snowman* while the rest of the band was playing *Silent Night*.

3. Isabella is a cornet player; the musician who was distracted after spotting that the toy shop was stocking the toy they wanted to get for their child has never played the clarinet.

4. The woman who plays the piccolo in the Keighshire Marching Band and who was distracted by the wafting smell of the sweet chestnut-filled cream doughnuts wasn't the musician who tripped and found themselves splayed across the polished tiles while the rest of the band marched on.

5. The musician who spotted their aunt among the shoppers and was distracted enough to keep marching when the rest of the band came to a halt wasn't Kenny.

Musician	Instrument

	Clarinet	Cornet	Drum	Flute	Piccolo	Food stall	Phone shop	Santa Claus	Spotted aunt	Toy shop	Didn't stop	Split drum	Tripped	Wrong key	Wrong song
Gareth															
Heather															
Isabella															
Joanna															
Kenny															
Didn't stop															
Split drum															
Tripped															
Wrong key															
Wrong song															
Food stall															
Phone shop															
Santa Claus															
Spotted aunt															
Toy shop															

Distraction	Accident

Band of Sisters

Five women, inspired by the recent movie *The Vigilante Sisterhood* from the Ivywood Studios in Netherlipp, decided to band together to fight injustice by means not necessarily restricted by the letter of the law. Naming themselves the Band of Sisters, they used a double security system, referring to each other by either a code number or a code name when communicating. Can you match each member of the group with her profession in the world outside the Band and her number and code name within it?

Clues

1. The toxicologist has chosen the code name Lucrezia, hinting at the somewhat sinister manner in which she occasionally carries out her vigilante assignments.

2. Susan has a higher code number within the organization than the judge, but a lower one than the member known as Juno.

3. The real identity of number 5, also known as Aurora, is not Katherine.

4. Professor Harriet is much respected by her colleagues in the senior common room; her Band code number is lower than that of the attorney.

5. The name Nemesis, which perhaps surprisingly was not chosen by the judge, is accompanied by an odd code number.

6. The Band of Sisters member referred to as number 3 is a noted psychologist.

7. Angela has the code number 2, but is not code-named Medusa.

Name	Profession

	Attorney	Judge	Psychologist	Toxicologist	University professor	1	2	3	4	5	Aurora	Juno	Lucrezia	Medusa	Nemesis
Angela															
Harriet															
Katherine															
Lorna															
Susan															
Aurora															
Juno															
Lucrezia															
Medusa															
Nemesis															
1															
2															
3															
4															
5															

Code-number	Code-name

Needles and Tinsel

The five households below have been getting themselves in a festive mood by spending the afternoon setting up the family Christmas tree. From the clues, can you work out what sort of tree each family has, what traditional ornament is sitting on its top, and how many presents there are currently stacked up beneath its branches?

Clues

1. One family spent a happy hour straightening out the branches of their well-loved old silver tinsel tree before putting four presents underneath it.

2. The Scots never tire of the light show produced by their little fiber-optic tree; they are not the couple looking contently at the star glowing over the single present they have laid for each other under their tree in its familiar corner.

3. The alternative tree—a few triangular lumps of MDF nailed to a bit of wood and painted green—has a rather more mainstream robin sitting on top of it.

4. The Douglas family currently has six presents sitting enticingly beneath their tree, but are expecting a lot more.

5. There is a tinsel snowflake crowning the Furghs' tree, which has one more present under it than the one in the Forrests' sitting room but fewer than are under the traditional real tree, which isn't topped with a fairy.

Family	Tree

	Alternative	Fiber-optic	Green plastic	Silver tinsel	Traditional real	Angel	Fairy	Robin	Snowflake	Star	2 packages	3 packages	4 packages	5 packages	6 packages
Douglas															
Forrest															
Furgh															
Pigne															
Scot															
2 packages															
3 packages															
4 packages															
5 packages															
6 packages															
Angel															
Fairy															
Robin															
Snowflake															
Star															

It takes all the stress out of it

PRE-NEEDLE-DROPPED TREES

Top spot	Presents

Christmas Mass

On Christmas Day, the little snow-covered town of Beaver Lake, in Massachusetts, shuts down almost completely—but not quite; members of certain uniformed organizations have to be on duty in case of emergency. Can you work out where each of the five uniformed Beaver Lakers listed is spending Christmas Day, what he's doing while waiting for the phone to ring (and hoping it won't), and why he's been selected for Christmas duty?

Clues

1. Elmer Rogers is on duty at the Beaver Lake armory of the Massachusetts National Guard; Chuck Palowski isn't at the Forestry Service or at the town's firehouse, where they don't have a TV.

2. The man at Forestry Service HQ isn't the one who volunteered to spend Christmas Day playing solitaire because all his pals have families and he doesn't, nor the one who was just told it was his turn on the rotation.

3. Anson Nader volunteers to work every Christmas because he belongs to a denomination which doesn't celebrate it; he never watches TV.

4. The man who's watching TV didn't volunteer for Christmas duty because it pays triple overtime, nor is he working as a punishment for what was described by his boss as "goofing off."

5. The cop who took duty at Police HQ for the overtime isn't the one who's spending the day on the phone (his own cell, of course) to friends and relations.

6. Ben Overton is passing the time reading, while the cop in the patrol car is parked and listening to his collection of country music CDs on his mobile player.

Name	Place

	Fire house	Forest Service HQ	National Guard armory	Police HQ	Police patrol car	Listening to CDs	On phone	Playing solitaire	Reading book	Watching TV	No family	Overtime	Punishment	Religion	Rotation
Anson Nader															
Ben Overton															
Chuck Palowski															
Dennis Quinn															
Elmer Rogers															
No family															
Overtime															
Punishment															
Religion															
Rotation															
Listening to CDs															
On phone															
Playing solitaire															
Reading book															
Watching TV															

Pastime	Reason

Hit the Right Note

Four boys are trying to learn musical instruments. Sadly for each of them their less than tuneful training annoyed a passing teacher, and they found their "instrument" confiscated. Can you say who was playing what, which teacher relieved them of their music-maker, and how they replied to the question "When do you think I might get it back, sir?"

Clues

1. "What are you doing with that old paintbrush and that pencil?" asked Mr. Grimm. "They're my drumsticks, sir. Wizard aren't they?" replied one lad. "No they're not. Hand them over," said Mr. Grimm; it wasn't Martin Masters who fell foul of a grumpy Mr. Stern.

2. "What is that awful noise?" asked one teacher looking around. "It's my old harmonica, sir," replied Ben Barton, " I know it's not great yet, but only two of the notes work. What do you think, sir?" "Give it here," said the teacher.

3. "When do you think I might get my panpipes back, sir?" asked one lad. "When you've learned not to play them in the library," replied the teacher.

4. "You can have it back," said Mr. Stoney, taking possession of an "instrument," "when you can be trusted not to make such an awful noise right next to my ear."

5. Chris Cockroft, whose question about his item's repatriation was met with "When the time is right," wasn't the boy trying to get more than a high-pitched shriek out of an old and battered tin whistle.

6. "Give it to me, Hazel," said Mr. Gaunt; he wasn't the teacher who said the boy could have his instrument back "When I say so."

Boy	Instrument

	Drumsticks	Harmonica	Panpipes	Tin whistle	Mr. Gaunt	Mr. Grimm	Mr. Stern	Mr. Stoney	When I say	When the time . . .	When you can be . . .	When you've learned . . .
Ben Barton												
Chris Cockroft												
Hamish Hazel												
Martin Masters												
When I say												
When the time . . .												
When you can be . . .												
When you've learned . . .												
Mr. Gaunt												
Mr. Grimm												
Mr. Stern												
Mr. Stoney												

Teacher	Reply

Battleships

Do you remember the old game of battleships? These puzzles are based on that idea. Your task is to find the vessels in the diagram. Some parts of boats or sea squares have already been filled in, and a number next to a row or column refers to the number of occupied squares in that row or column. The boats may be positioned horizontally or vertically, but no two boats or parts of boats are in adjacent squares—horizontally, vertically, or diagonally.

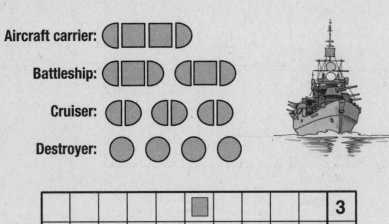

Aircraft carrier:

Battleship:

Cruiser:

Destroyer:

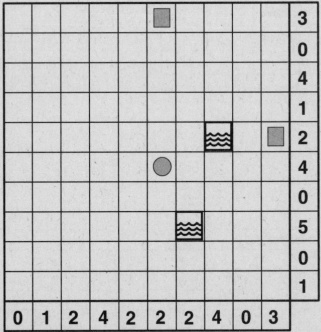

Domino Search

A standard set of dominoes has been laid out, using numbers instead of dots for clarity. Using a sharp pencil and a keen brain, can you draw in the lines to show where each domino has been placed? You may find the check grid useful— crossing off each domino as you find it.

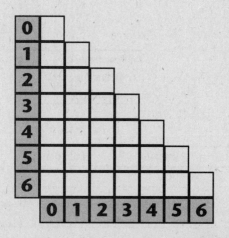

1	0	6	1	3	1	5	6
5	1	4	0	2	3	6	1
5	2	4	6	5	0	0	6
5	1	4	2	0	4	2	6
3	1	0	4	6	5	1	4
4	2	3	2	2	3	3	0
5	6	0	3	4	3	5	2

Teacher

Phillipa Thyme has a busy life. She's a qualified personal trainer and, in addition to her private clients, three evenings a week she teaches an exercise session at one of the local towns. Can you work out which type of exercise session she teaches where and on which day, and how many attended each session last week?

Clues

1. Last Wednesday there were two more attendees at Phillipa's session at the Netherlipp Arena than there were at her aerobics class.

2. More people turned up for Phillipa's Monday class than braved the rain and the wind to get to Churchminster Sports Hall later in the week.

3. Phillipa's Pilates class, which isn't on Friday, attracted two fewer people than attended her session at the Stonekeigh Leisure Center.

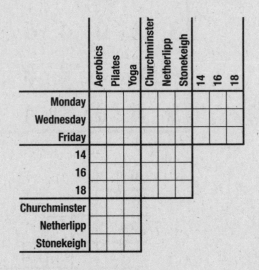

Day	Session	Location	Number

Student

On three of the evenings that Phillipa Thyme isn't busy teaching exercise classes, she attends lessons at The Keighshire Technical College to expand both her mind and her practical skills. Can you work out on which day Phillipa takes which course, who teaches it, and for how many weeks it will run?

Clues

1. Professor Alice Sonne teaches her Egyptology course, The Road to Cleopatra, which lasts two fewer weeks than the pottery lessons.

2. On Tuesday nights, Phillipa gets her hands oily at the automobile mechanics class.

3. Saturday night's course will run for fourteen weeks; May Lern's lessons will last for twelve weeks.

	Car mechanics	Egyptology	Pottery	Alice Sonne	May Lern	Will Preach	12 weeks	14 weeks	16 weeks
Tuesday									
Thursday									
Saturday									
12 weeks									
14 weeks									
16 weeks									
Alice Sonne									
May Lern									
Will Preach									

Evening	Course	Teacher	Length

A, B, Seeds

Three people have visited the Home and Garden superstore on the outskirts of Stonekeigh. Each customer has begun their visit in the garden area and, by coincidence, has bought three packs of seeds to grow crops of vegetables beginning with A, B, and C. Can you work out who has bought what?

Clues

1. Brian bought a pack of broccoli seeds—he's not keen on it but it's good for his kids; Amanda bought a pack of seeds to grow aubergines because she likes the color.

2. Chris has a pet rabbit and has bought some carrot seeds.

3. One shopper bought seeds for both cabbages and broad beans, but the person who bought a pack of celery seeds didn't buy a pack of asparagus seeds.

	Artichoke	Asparagus	Aubergine	Beets	Broad beans	Broccoli	Cabbage	Carrots	Celery
Amanda									
Brian									
Chris									
Cabbage							
Carrots							
Celery							
Beets			
Broad beans			
Broccoli			

Customer	A seeds	B seeds	C seeds

A, B, C, DIY

After selecting their seeds in the puzzle above, the three customers moved to the DIY section of the store, and by further coincidence, each placed three items in their shopping baskets beginning with A, B, and C. Can you say what each bought?

Clues

1. Amanda is a woman, Brian is a man; Chris, who didn't buy the auger, is the same sex as the person who did.

2. A woman bought an axe and a clamp; a man bought a bolt cutter and a chisel.

3. One shopper bought a set of Allen keys and a wire brush.

	Allen keys	Auger	Axe	Blowtorch	Bolt cutter	Brush	Chisel	Clamp	Crowbar
Amanda									
Brian									
Chris									
Chisel									
Clamp									
Crowbar									
Blowtorch									
Bolt cutter									
Brush									

Customer	A tools	B tools	C tools

Pier of the Realm

Brightbourne Pier, jutting out into the calm of Eastshire Bay, opens for business in the middle of May. On the left-hand side as you start your promenade out across the water are four small kiosks selling sweet things and each has a promotion to start the season. From the clues, can you say who owns and runs each of the kiosks, numbered 1 to 4 from the shore seawards, what the kiosk sells, and its current promotion?

Clues

1. The owner of the pick'n'mix stall offers patrons their last scoop free—taken with the special "last scoop" scoop—small and missing its scoopy sides.

2. The Brightbourne Rock Emporium, owned and run by Sheryl Schilling, is further out to sea than the kiosk offering a "buy one get one free" promotion.

3. Kiosk number 3 is owned and run by Tommy Tanner; kiosk number 2, which doesn't sell cotton candy, is offering a free pack of postcards with every purchase over $5.

4. The first kiosk promenaders encounter is the slightly overnamed Brightbourne Pier Ice Cream and Cone Minimart; it's not run by Fenella Farthing, who isn't offering 50 cents off the standard price.

Kiosk number	Owner

	Fenella Farthing	Pete Penney	Sheryl Schilling	Tommy Tanner	Cotton candy	Ice cream	Pick'n'mix	Rock	Buy one get one free	50p off	Free postcards	Free scoop
Kiosk 1												
Kiosk 2												
Kiosk 3												
Kiosk 4												
Buy one get one free												
50 cent off												
Free postcards												
Free scoop												
Cotton candy												
Ice cream												
Pick'n'mix												
Rock												

Wares	Promotion

Key Bay Selling

KeyBay is an on-line auction site that covers the length and breadth of Keighshire, and four KeyBay enthusiasts have decided to sell one of their products to raise a little cash. Can you work out what each seller has polished and photographed for posting on the site, on what day they have decided the auction will end, and the method of transport to the winning bidder they have specified?

Clues

1. Delilah has bought a new automobile and so has decided to sell the after-market digital radio from her old one.

2. One item description originally read: "Electric guitar—pick-up only" but had to be changed to explain that it wasn't just the guitar pick up for sale but that it had to be picked up.

3. Arnold decided to close his auction the day after the sale of the games console concluded and the day before the item whose seller had offered a personal delivery service in the hope of achieving a higher price.

4. The sale of the lawn mower, which isn't being sold by Colin, will run until Sunday (which is more than you can say for the lawn mower.)

5. Belinda's sale item, which will be delivered by a local courier, won't be the first to be sold.

Seller	Item

	Digital automobile radio	Electric guitar	Games console	Lawn mower	Thursday	Friday	Saturday	Sunday	Courier	Package post	Personal delivery	Pick-up
Arnold												
Belinda												
Colin												
Delilah												
Courier								
Package post								
Personal delivery								
Pick-up								
Thursday				
Friday				
Saturday				
Sunday				

Closing day	Delivery

USA TODAY   301

Key Bay Buying

While the four KeyBay sellers from the previous puzzle were posting their own items for sale, they each noticed something they'd like to have in their own homes. From the clues, work out what each seller decided to buy, on what day the auction is set to end, and how much each buyer has keyed into KeyBay as their maximum bid.

Clues

1. Colin spotted a porcelain vase he thought might look nice on his mantelpiece; Arnold will discover if he is the new owner of an item on Monday.

2. The auction on which Belinda has placed a bid will close one day after the one for the large wall clock; the person bidding on the wall clock has set their maximum bid at $10 less than Belinda's maximum.

3. The person hoping to buy the large mirror has keyed in $40 as their maximum bid.

4. The person waiting until Tuesday to see if their maximum bid of $20 will be enough isn't Delilah.

Buyer	Item

	Mirror	Painting	Porcelain vase	Wall clock	Monday	Tuesday	Wednesday	Thursday	$20	$30	$40	$50
Arnold												
Belinda												
Colin												
Delilah												
$20								
$30								
$40								
$50								
Monday				
Tuesday				
Wednesday				
Thursday				

Out of Order

Closing	Maximum bid

Keigh Bay Sellers

Four erstwhile sailors who have given up the dream of a life on the open sea have decided to part with their small sailing dinghies and have towed their small vessels to the quay at Keigh Bay to meet a potential buyer. But before the viewers arrive, there's a little painting that needs to be done. Can you work out the type of dinghy each seller is selling, its name, and the color he or she is dabbing on to the parts that need a little touching up?

Clues

1. Graham is selling the *Spicy Sal* after his girlfriend, the eponymous Sally, dumped him to be spicy with someone else.

2. The Heron type dinghy is being touched up with a dab of bright red.

3. Felicity, who had plans to sail round the world but found that she got bored sailing round the bay, isn't the owner of the Minto type dinghy the *Dainty Dot*.

4. Eric, who, try as he might, just can't get his sea legs and gets nauseous just looking at his Wayfarer dinghy, isn't the current owner of *Zesty Zoe*, who is having her stern painted in a very fetching shade of zesty lemon.

5. The *Briny Bess* is having her keel spruced up, but not with a dab of green.

Seller	Dinghy type

	Heron	Minto	Mirror	Wayfarer	Briny Bess	Dainty Dot	Spicy Sal	Zesty Zoe	Navy blue	Green	Red	Yellow
Eric												
Felicity												
Graham												
Hazel												
Navy blue												
Green												
Red												
Yellow												
Briny Bess												
Dainty Dot												
Spicy Sal												
Zesty Zoe												

Name	Color

Keigh Bay Buyers

With their boats spruced up, the nautical sellers from the previous puzzle were ready to meet their potential buyers. From these clues, and the information discovered in the previous puzzle, can you work out the name of each seller's buyer, the time of the appointment, and the rather disappointing remark with which they departed after viewing the vessel?

Clues

1. One seller introduced prospective buyer Karen to the Heron type dinghy later in the day than one buyer left with, "Hmm, I'll be in touch."

2. The potential buyer of the *Briny Bess* gave a her a quick look over and said, "OK, I'll let you know," as they walked, a little too quickly, back along the quay; this was earlier in the day than the seller of the green boat met their buyer but later than one seller shook Jerry's hand.

3. One of the women sellers had arranged to meet Leonard on the quay.

4. The prospective purchaser with the 12 p.m. appointment, who wasn't Isabel, wasn't the one who left with the, frankly a little dismissive, "I'll get back to you."

Seller	Buyer

	Isabel	Jerry	Karen	Leonard	11 a.m.	12 p.m.	1 p.m.	2 p.m.	Be in touch	Get back to you	Let you know	Think about it
Eric												
Felicity												
Graham												
Hazel												
Be in touch												
Get back to you												
Let you know												
Think about it												
11 a.m.												
12 p.m.												
1 p.m.												
2 p.m.												

No, I said I like sales

Appointment	Parting phrase

Driving for Perfection

As usual the Driving Test Center in Netherlipp has been very busy this morning with some students passing but five failing to reach the required standard. From the following information, can you discover the time of each unprepared candidate's test, the botched maneuver that contributed most to his or her failure, and where that maneuver took place?

Clues

1. Helen Weales messed up her reversing ("Oh you mean reverse round this corner without going on the pavement. Honestly! You should have said"), while Ron Gear came to grief in Hawthorn Way.

2. Roland Brake's test was at 9:00, but his examiner didn't take him along Mill Road.

3. Rex Chance's test was an hour before that of the candidate who made a poor maneuver in Market Street, while Vera Swerve's began half an hour after the one that was failed on the emergency stop.

4. The test failed on the parking maneuver began at 10:30.

5. The 9:30 candidate made a mistake in Balmoral Close.

6. The failed hill start was halfway up Church Hill, a quarter of the way up Church Hill, and then again near the bottom of Church Hill.

Time	Candidate

	Roland Brake	Rex Chance	Ron Gear	Vera Swerve	Helen Weales	Emergency stop	Hill start	Parking	Reversing	Signaling	Balmoral Close	Church Hill	Hawthorn Way	Market Street	Mill Road
9:00															
9:30															
10:30															
11:00															
11:30															
Balmoral Close															
Church Hill															
Hawthorn Way															
Market Street															
Mill Road															
Emergency stop															
Hill start															
Parking															
Reversing															
Signaling															

No, it's probably my fault. I should've explained what I meant by parallel parking

DRIVING SCHOOL

Maneuver	Location

Minor Injuries

The life of a student contains periods of hard academic study, of deep thought, and of contemplative discussion and debate punctuated with periods of ill-considered pursuits and overconfident activity. Five students are being treated in Goatsferry Medical Center for injuries caused by their own stupidity, carelessness, or clumsiness. From the clues, can you work out what each student is studying, what they did to themselves, and how they did it?

Clues

1. A female student came to grief at the college disco when she caught her fashionable high-heeled shoe in her fashionable wide-leg pants and sprained her ankle. A male student injured himself while attempting to balance a bucket on the head of the imposing statue of the college founder.

2. The chemistry student was working on a chemistry experiment when injury struck—that they were trying to juggle two conical flasks and a test tube at the time is beside the point. This was neither Andrew nor the student who turned up with a bleeding nose.

3. Simon arrived cradling a burnt arm. He was not the male history student who injured his knee, but not while trying to ride a skateboard down the steps of a lecture theater.

4. Greg is studying geology, when he can find the time. The student who damaged an upper part of their body when the cooking got out of control wasn't any of the trio of Greg, Delia, and the English student.

Student	Studying

	Chemistry	English	Geology	History	Physics	Bruised knee	Burnt arm	Cut hand	Nosebleed	Sprained ankle	Climbing statue	Cooking	Dancing	Experimenting	Skateboarding
Andrew															
Delia															
Greg															
Pauline															
Simon															
Climbing statue															
Cooking															
Dancing															
Experimenting															
Skateboarding															
Bruised knee															
Burnt arm															
Cut hand															
Nosebleed															
Sprained ankle															

And here we see Newton's Law of Gravitation in action

Injury	Cause

Sales and Returns

Jane is laid up with one of the winter viruses (cat flu or man flu or something) but is determined not to miss the sales and has asked some of her friends to search out a bargain or two on her behalf. Sadly each item has turned out to be unsuitable in some way, meaning a trip back to the stores when Jane has recovered, to see if she can persuade them to take it back. From the clues, can you sort out who bought what from which store, and what was wrong with it?

Clues

1. Jane's co-worker Susan produced an offering which Jane should manage to get changed on the grounds that it is badly frayed.

2. The blouse came from Supergirl, but will soon be on its way back.

3. Jane's boyfriend, Colin, found her an item in Tripark; this wasn't the scarf—which does have a valid reason for its return, being torn.

4. The item Jane was hoping to return because it was too small wasn't bought at G & J's—a store Jane's cousin Amanda wouldn't be seen dead in, even on someone else's behalf; her cousin's bargain was not the hat.

5. It was Jane's brother Scott who found her a cut-price sweater; this was neither the item bought at Sharks & Denser, which turned out to be too big, nor the one featuring the logo of Jane's favorite football team's greatest rivals, Netherlipp United.

Sale item	Shopper

	Aunt	Boyfriend	Brother	Cousin	Co-worker	Bodenham's	G & J's	Sharks & Denser	Supergirl	Tripark	Frayed	Has tear	Too big	Too small	Wrong logo
Blouse															
Hat															
Sweater															
Scarf															
Slippers															
Frayed															
Has tear															
Too big															
Too small															
Wrong logo															
Bodenham's															
G & J's															
Sharks & Denser															
Supergirl															
Tripark															

Store	Problem

Jammy Winners

The Eastshire Jam and Preserve Society is a small but keen group of people fascinated with forcing fruit and sugar into jars. Last fall they held their usual competition to find the Preservation President. From the clues, can you discover how many jars of different fruit jams each competitor made and his or her home village?

Clues

1. Dorothy is noted for the excellence of her raspberry jam; she made the next lowest number of jars below the number of blackberry and apple.

2. Rosalind, from Much Picking, made the next lowest number of jars below the number of strawberry.

3. The strawberry jam wasn't made by Barnaby, and he didn't make 30 jars.

4. The Canefield jam-maker produced 37 jars this year; his or her name is longer than that of the competitor from Fullhedge.

5. Thirty-three jars of plum jam were produced, while the Bottleham jam-maker produced more than 25 jars of gooseberry jam.

6. Larry doesn't live in Brambleigh.

Jars	Type of jam

	Blackberry and apple	Gooseberry	Plum	Raspberry	Strawberry	Barnaby	Dorothy	Elizabeth	Larry	Rosalind	Bottleham	Brambleigh	Canefield	Fullhedge	Much Picking
25															
30															
33															
37															
42															
Bottleham															
Brambleigh															
Canefield															
Fullhedge															
Much Picking															
Barnaby															
Dorothy															
Elizabeth															
Larry															
Rosalind															

Maker	Village

Collision Course

The new Hollywood blockbuster *Last January* isn't about the first month of the year—it's about the last January of mankind, when, a few years in the future, a giant and unstoppable meteorite is discovered to be about to hit Earth on or about the 28th of the month. It features five major stars, whose characters view the impending disaster from various parts of the USA and from outer space. From the clues, can you work out the name and occupation of each star's character and the place from which they view their impending doom?

Clues

1. The astronaut, played by a female movie star, is orbiting Earth in a space station watching as panic ensues.

2. Sam Gomez, who's in a small town in Southern California, isn't played by hunky Brad Peat.

3. J P Burke and the ecologist are played by stars of the same gender.

4. Tom Hooks plays Mike McLaine, who is not the character in Florida.

5. Kate Winett's character isn't Nic Leroy, and Al Pinici's isn't the police officer.

6. Demi Meare's character spends the whole of the film in Wyoming, complaining (in fact *Whining in Wyoming* was considered as a possible title, for a short while anyway).

7. Red Weber is a ginger-haired reporter for a newspaper called *USA Tomorrow.*

Star	Name

	J P Burke	Mike McLaine	Nic Leroy	Red Weber	Sam Gomez	Astronaut	Astronomer	Ecologist	Police officer	Reporter	California	Florida	New York	Space station	Wyoming
Al Pinici															
Brad Peat															
Demi Meare															
Kate Winett															
Tom Hooks															
California															
Florida															
New York															
Space station															
Wyoming															
Astronaut															
Astronomer															
Ecologist															
Police officer															
Reporter															

Occupation	Location

Sign In

Each row and column is to contain the digits 1-6. The given signs tell you if a digit in a cell is plus 1 (+) or minus 1 (-) the digit next to it. Signs between consecutive digits always work from left to right or top to bottom.

Examples: 3 + 4 or 2
-
1

ALL occurrences of consecutive digits have been marked by a sign.

Sudoku

Complete this grid so that each column, each row, and each marked 3 X 3 square contains each of the numbers 1 to 9.

			3					
		9					6	5
	8		7			4	3	
2		4	9	1		5		7
			2			1	9	
								2
		6	8	4				
	3	1		7				4
	4		1		2		5	8

Answers

Battleships, p. 1

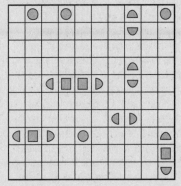

Acceptance . . ., p. 2

Barry Barman won an award for *Sinnin' in the Rain* (clue 3), so the winner of best extra in *Hound of Music*, who wasn't Jenny Jenman (clue 1), must have been Rick Rickman, leaving Jenny Jenman winning the award for the park scene in *Lizard of Oz* (clue 2). Rick Rickman's best extra award wasn't for the street scene, which won the best cut-out (clue 2), so he must have won it for the stadium scene. By elimination, Barry Barman must have won the best cut-out award for the street scene in *Sinnin' in the Rain*, leaving Jenny Jenman winning the best outtake for the park scene in *Lizard of Oz*.

Best cut-out, Barry Barman, street, *Sinnin' in the Rain*.
Best extra, Rick Rickman, stadium, *Hound of Music*.
best outtake, Jenny Jenman, park, *Lizard of Oz*.

. . . Speeches, p. 3

One tearful recipient thanked their hairdresser and their grandma (clue 2), so Jenny Jenman, who thanked her plumber (clue 3), but not her mother (clue 3), must have thanked her neighbor, her plumber and her dad (clue 2). Rick Rickman thanked his newsagent (clue 1), so Barry Barman must have thanked his grocery boy. So he didn't also thank his teacher (clue 2) and must have thanked his grocery boy, his hair dresser, and his grandma, leaving Rick Rickman passing on his gratitude to his newsagent, his teacher, and his mom.

Barry Barman, grocery boy, hair dresser, grandma.
Jenny Jenman, neighbor, plumber, dad.
Rick Rickman, newsagent, teacher, mom.

Drive and Deliver, p. 4

The automobile parts are not being delivered by Terry or Nigel (clue 2), Dean, who is delivering food (clue 6), or Colin, who is carrying either washing-machines or TVs (clue 3), so they must be the load in Sam's Fiat truck (clue 5). They are not destined for Upper Crispin (clue 2), Brandywell (clue 5), Churchminster, where the TVs are bound (clue 4), or Crispin Parva, where the Ford truck is heading (clue 1), so it must be Wallingfen. The load of shoes is not in the Ford or Leyland trucks (clue 1), nor is it in the Fiat, which is carrying the automobile parts, or the Mercedes, carrying the washing-machines (clue 4), so it must be the Renault. As the TVs are bound for Churchminster, the Ford truck with the cargo of food must be on its way to Crispin Parva, with Dean at the wheel. By elimination, the TVs must be loaded in the Leyland truck. Its driver is not Colin (clue 3), so he must be delivering the washing-machines in his Mercedes truck. Terry is not driving the Leyland truck (clue 2), so it must be the Renault with its load of shoes, and as he is not heading for Upper Crispin, it must be

Brandywell. By elimination, the Leyland must be driven by Nigel, and Colin must be taking the washing-machines to Upper Crispin.

Colin, Mercedes, washing-machines, Upper Crispin.
Dean, Ford, food, Crispin Parva.
Nigel, Leyland, TVs, Churchminster.
Sam, Fiat, automobile parts, Wallingfen.
Terry, Renault, shoes, Brandywell.

Leading Ladies, p. 6

Davina is Davina Young (clue 5) and Ms. Vickers has been cast in *Wait Until Dark* (clue 1), so Gloria, whose surname is one letter longer than that of the girl who has been cast in *Pygmalion* (clue 5), can't be Ms. Oliphant or Ms. Keen nor since she is from Storbury (clue 5) can she be Ms. Vickers who isn't from there (clue 1), so she must be Gloria Ervine. So, from clue 5, Davina Young must be starring in *Pygmalion* (clue 5). We know that Gloria Ervine is not starring in *Pygmalion* or *Wait Until Dark*. Maureen has been cast in *An Inspector Calls* (cue 3) and the Churchminster society will be performing *The Lark* (clue 4), so Gloria Ervine must be Juliet in *Romeo and Juliet*. We now know in which plays Davina Young, Gloria Ervine and Maureen will be appearing so Veronica, who isn't from Churchminster (clue 4), must have been cast in *Wait Until Dark* and is therefore Veronica Vickers, leaving Selma as the actress from Churchminster. Her surname isn't Oliphant (clue 2), so she must be Selma Keen and Maureen must be Maureen Oliphant. She is not from Netherlipp (clue 2) or Colnecaster (clue 3), so she must be from Stonekeigh. Finally Davina Young, who is in *Pygmalion*, is not from Netherlipp (clue 5) so she must be in the Colnecaster Society, leaving Veronica Vickers starring in *Wait Until Dark* in Netherlipp.

Davina Young, Colnecaster, *Pygmalion*.
Gloria Ervine, Storbury, *Romeo and Juliet*.
Maureen Oliphant, Stonekeigh, *An Inspector Calls*.

Selma Keen, Churchminster, *The Lark*.
Veronica Vickers, Netherlipp, *Wait Until Dark*.

Give Up the Ghost, p. 8

A transparent ghost of an old woman was seen by one of the women (clue 1), David Ross saw the skull-faced figure (clue 6) and the headless ghost appeared in the Drawing Room (clue 3), so Bruce Oaks, who encountered a ghost in the kitchen (clue 5), which wasn't the one with its throat cut (clue 5), must have seen the ghost covered in blood. We know the transparent old woman wasn't seen in the drawing room or the kitchen while it was the nun who appeared in the conservatory (clue 5). A female ghost hunter saw the old woman (clue 1), so she couldn't have appeared in the entrance hall, where a man saw a ghost (clue 3), and so she must have manifested herself in the library. The woman who saw her wasn't Annie Nash (clue 4) and so must have been Cindy Price. The ghost covered in blood, seen in the kitchen by Bruce Oaks, wasn't the young girl (clue 2), and Eric Stone saw the ghostly Butler (clue 1), so the blood-covered apparition must have been that of the soldier. The nun who appeared in the conservatory wasn't the one with the cut throat (clue 5), so she must have been the skull-faced apparition seen by David Ross (clue 6). So, by elimination, the man who saw a ghost in the entrance hall (clue 3) must have been Eric Stone and the ghost must therefore have been the butler (clue 1). By elimination, it must have had its throat cut, leaving Annie Nash as the ghost hunter who saw a headless phantom in the drawing room which must have been that of the young girl.

Annie Nash, drawing room, young girl, headless.
Bruce Oaks, kitchen, soldier, covered in blood.

Cindy Price, library, old woman, transparent.
David Ross, conservatory, nun, skull-faced.
Eric Stone, entrance hall, butler, throat cut.

An Actor's Life, p. 10

Ms. Hayes wanted to be a pianist (clue 2), and Ms. Miller's a chorus dancer (clue 6), so the would-be actress who's become an usherette, who isn't Ms. Edison or Ms. Oates (clue 3), must be Ms. Smith. Judy, who wanted to be a pop singer, isn't the chorus dancer or the stooge (clue 1). The producer has an odd number of letters in her first name (clue 4), so Judy must be the barmaid. Her ambition or actual job rule out three surnames and Ms. Edison's first name is Paula (clue 5), so Judy must be Judy Oates. From clue 4, the producer can't be Ms. Hayes, so she must be Paula Edison and Ms. Hayes must be the stooge. Paula Edison didn't want to be a ballerina (clue 5), so her ambition must have been to be a comedian, leaving the would-be ballerina as Ms. Miller, the chorus dancer. From clue 6, she must be Denise Miller, Ms. Hayes the stooge must be Anita Hayes and Ms. Smith the usherette must be Gillian Smith.

Anita Hayes, pianist, stooge.
Denise Miller, ballerina, chorus dancer.
Gillian Smith, actress, usherette.
Judy Oates, pop singer, barmaid.
Paula Edison, comedian, producer.

Sign-In, p. 12

1	3	6	5	4	2
2	1	3	4	5	6
4	6	2	3	1	5
3	2	5	1	6	4
6	5	4	2	3	1
5	4	1	6	2	3

Sudoku, p. 12

1	5	4	6	9	3	2	8	7
9	6	7	8	2	5	1	4	3
2	8	3	7	1	4	5	9	6
7	4	1	3	5	2	8	6	9
5	9	8	1	4	6	7	3	2
3	2	6	9	8	7	4	5	1
4	7	9	5	6	1	3	2	8
8	3	5	2	7	9	6	1	4
6	1	2	4	3	8	9	7	5

Uke Can Do, p. 13

Alec spent less than two other customers (clue 3), so the man who bought the $45 instrument for his collection must be Colin. So the ukulele bought to play in a band, which didn't cost $35 or $40 (clue 3) must have been the most expensive. It wasn't bought by Doris, who bought a uke to learn to play (clue 1), or Alec (clue 3), so it must have been bought by Briony. From clue 3, Colin's $45 instrument bound for his collection must be the tenor and Alec must have spent $40 and Doris' learning uke must have cost $35. By elimination, Alec must have bought a uke as a present. It wasn't the baritone (clue 4) or the concert (clue 2), so it must have been the soprano. So, from clue 4, Doris must have bought the concert uke for $35 and Briony's $50 instrument must be the baritone.

Soprano, Alex, present, $40.
Concert, Doris, learn to play, $35.
Tenor, Colin, collection, $45.
Baritone, Briony, play in band, $50.

Withdrawal Symptoms, p. 14

Mrs. Bradley is a Bank of East Anglia customer (clue 4) and the Lancashire Bank's customer has keyed in 3162 (clue 3), so Mr. Mclean, whose personal number is 4630, and who is not a Westshire customer (clue 1), and can't be the Mercia customer withdrawing $160 (clues 1 and 5), must bank with the Midminster. So he is not withdrawing $80 (clue 1), $20, for which the number 6757 is being used (clue 6), or $10 (clue 5), so it must be $40. The $80 must therefore be the amount being withdrawn from the Westshire Bank (clue 1). As the Lancashire Bank's customer's personal number is 3162, the $20 must be Mrs. Bradley's withdrawal from the Bank of East Anglia, and, by elimination, the withdrawal from the Lancashire Bank must be $10. The number used by the Westshire customer is not 4061 (clue 1), so it must be 3989, leaving 4061 as the number entered by the Mercia Bank customer. The Lancashire customer is not Mr. Doyle (clue 3) or Miss Hanson (clue 2), as the amount being withdrawn is $10, so it must be Mrs. Kerr, whose number is 3162. As Miss Hanson's number is not 3989 (clue 2), she must be the person using number 4061 to withdraw $160 from the Mercia cash machine, leaving the Westshire customer entering 3989 to withdraw $80 as Mr. Doyle.

Bank of East Anglia, Mrs. Bradley, 6757, $20.
Lancashire, Mrs. Kerr, 3162, $10.
Mercia, Miss Hanson, 4061, $160.
Midminster, Mr. Mclean, 4630, $40.
Westshire, Mr. Doyle, 3989, $80.

Gun Running, p. 16

In 1917 Henri was in Oslo (clue 5), and in Brussels he posed as Axel Carlsen (clue 4), so the European capital in which he lived as Vasco Carmona in 1909 (clue 2) must have been Paris. The city in which he posed as Sean Daley the priest wasn't Oslo (clue 5) or New York, where he posed as an engineer (clue 4), so it must have been Montevideo. We now know the years or the occupations for four of the cities, so in 1913, when Henri was posing as a chemist (clue 3), he must have been in Brussels living under the name of Axel Carlsen (clue 4). The city

in which Henri was living in 1905 wasn't Montevideo (clue 1), so he must have been there in 1917. By elimination, in 1905 Henri must have been in New York posing as an engineer. The name he used there wasn't Diego Palotra (clue 1), so he must have been Erich Korner, leaving Diego Palotra as the name he used in Oslo in 1917. At that time he did not claim to be a journalist (clue 1), so he must have pretended to be a rifle maker, leaving journalism as the cover occupation he used when he lived as Vasco Carmona in Paris in 1909.

1905, Erich Korner, engineer, New York.
1909, Vasco Carmona, journalist, Paris.
1913, Axel Carlsen, chemist, Brussels.
1917, Diego Palotra, rifle maker, Oslo.
1921, Sean Daley, priest, Montevideo.

Great Sheikhs, p. 18

10,000 gushas were paid out in 2011 (clue 4), and 15,000 was the reward for defending the oasis (clue 2), so, from clue 5, the sheikh who won the camel derby in the year 2013 must have been rewarded with 5,000 gushas. This was not Sheikh Yahand (clue 5), nor can it be Sheikh Hays-el-rod, who found water in the desert (clue 1), Sheikh Ratl-en-rol, who received 12,500 gushas (clue 3), or Sheikh Adu-bel-sichs, who won the 2014 gratuity (clue 6), so it must have been Sheikh Mahfist. We now know the 2015 bounty was not 5,000 or 10,000 gushas, nor can it have been 15,000 (clue 1), and we know from his achievement that Sheikh Hays-el-rod did not receive 15,000 gushas either, so clue 1 also rules out 12,500 for the year 2015. Therefore 7,500 gushas must have been paid out last year. So, from clue 1, Sheikh Hays-el-rod was given 10,000 in 2011 for finding water in the desert. We have now matched four amounts with a year or a sheikh, so the amount awarded to Sheikh Adu-bel-sichs in 2014 must have been 15,000 gushas, and he therefore defended the oasis. Now, by elimination, 2012 must have been the year Sheikh Ratl-en-rol was rewarded, and it must be Sheikh Yahand who was given a gratuity in 2014. The former was not the trainer of the Sheikh's racehorses (clue 3), so he must have sunk a new oil well, and Sheikh Yahand must be the racehorse trainer.

2011, Sheikh Hays-el-rod, 10,000 gushas, finding water.
2012, Sheikh Ratl-en-rol, 12,500 gushas, sinking oil well.
2013, Sheikh Mahfist, 5,000 gushas, winning camel Derby.
2014, Sheikh Adu-bel-sichs, 15,000 gushas, defending oasis.
2015, Sheikh Yahand, 7,500 gushas, training horses.

Stonekeigh Spa, p. 20

The drypool swimming is in position 6 (clue 4). The subject of the ad in position 8 isn't the downhill biking (clue 1), virtual jogging (clue 3), stand in aerobics or weights watching (clue 6), calorie-free lunches or mental sauna (clue 6) or, since cold steam room isn't in position 6 or 9 (clue 5), either cold steam room or finger yoga (clue 5), so it must be the clean mud wrap. So, from clue 2, Douglas must run the session in position 7. Position 9 doesn't show the downhill biking (clue 1), the virtual jogging (clue 3), the cold steam room or the finger yoga (clue 5), the stand-in aerobics (clue 6) or the mental sauna and the calorie-free lunch (clue 7), so it must be the weights watching. It's run by a woman (clue 6), but not by Eleanor (clue 3), Claire (clue 4), or Bridget (clue 7). Isobel's session is shown in position 5 (clue 5) and Fiona runs the finger aerobics (clue 5), so Gillian must run the weights watching in position 9. Virtual jogging is immediately above Archie's session and below Eleanor's (clue 3), so it can't be in either position 5 or 7 and must be in position 4, with Eleanor in position 1 and Archie organizing the drypool swimming in position 6. The staff member in position 2 isn't

Hector (clue 2), Fiona (clue 5), Jeffrey (clue 6), or Bridget (clue 7), so must be Claire. The stand-in aerobics is run by a man (clue 6), so can't be shown in positions 1, 2, or 5. It's immediately above Jeffrey's session (clue 6), so can't be in position 3 or 10, and so must be in position 7, run by Douglas, with Jeffrey organizing whatever is advertised in position 10. So, Fiona's finger yoga corner location can now only be position 3. Since virtual jogging is in position 4, from clue 7, calorie-free lunches can't be in position 5 and so Bridget can't organize the clean mud wrap sessions in position 8. So Bridget must organize the virtual jogging, Eleanor, in position 1, must do the calorie-free lunches and Claire, in position 2, must provide the mental sauna. By elimination, Hector must organize the clean mud warp in position 8. Finally, from clue 5, Isobel's activity in position 5 must be the cold steam room, leaving Jeffrey running the downhill exercise bike sessions shown in position 10.

1, calorie-free lunches, Eleanor; 2, mental sauna, Claire; 3, finger yoga, Fiona.
4, virtual jogging, Bridget; 5, cold steam room, Isobel.
6, drypool swimming, Archie; 7, stand-in aerobics, Douglas.
8, Clean mud wrap, Hector; 9, weights watching, Gillian; 10, Downhill exercise bike, Jeffrey.

An American Cousin, p. 22

Annabelle's March victim wasn't Gus Stewart (clue 4) or Buck Wayne from Santa Fe (clue 2). Rusty Cooper was robbed in either June or August (clue 1) and it wasn't March when Annabelle posed as a widow to rob Sam Autry (clue 5), so her March victim must have been Mason Hart. He wasn't the victim in Cheyenne, where she posed as an actress (clue 3), and nor, as we know, was that Buck Wayne or Sam Autry; Rusty Cooper's town had a two-word name (clue 1), so the Cheyenne victim must have been

Gus Stewart. This must have been in either June or September (clue 4), but wasn't in June (clue 3), so must have been in September and Annabelle must have posed as a detective in August (clue 4). She didn't pose as a singer when in Santa Fe robbing Buck Wayne (clue 2) or when robbing Rusty Cooper (clue 1), so must have done so when robbing Mason Hart in March. So, from clue 2, she must have robbed Buck Wayne in Santa Fe in May. We now know the month or the victim to go with four of Annabelle's roles, so for the May crime in Santa Fe when Buck Wayne was the victim she must have posed as an heiress. By elimination, she must have posed as a widow to rob Sam Autry in June. Therefore, from clue 1, Rusty Cooper must have been robbed in August. This wasn't in Dodge City (clue 6), nor, from the victim's name, in Tombstone (clue 1), so it must have been in El Paso. Finally, Tombstone wasn't where Annabelle robbed Sam Autry in June (clue 5), so must have been the location of the March crime, leaving June, when she posed as a widow to rob Sam Autry, as the month she was in Dodge City.

March, Tombstone, singer, Mason Hart.
May, Santa Fe, heiress, Buck Wayne.
June, Dodge City, widow, Sam Autry.
August, El Paso, detective, Rusty Cooper.
September, Cheyenne, actress, Gus Stewart.

Housey-Housey, p. 24

Greengates is for sale through Norman's (clue 1) and the Howards' house sale is being handled by Acme (clue 2), so the Millers' house, Larksnest, which isn't being sold by J and P (clue 4), must be for sale through Gilmore's. Acme aren't handling the sale of number 4, Oakland (clue 2), so must be selling Rosebank, leaving J and P selling Oakland. Since Oakland is number 4, from clue 1, the Johnsons can't have decided to buy number 2 or number 8, nor did they choose the Colemans' home, number 6, so they must have gone for number 4. So, from clue 1, Greengates must be number 6 and Norman's were selling it for the Colemans. So, the Stone family must be selling Oakland through J and P, and the Johnsons must have decided to buy it. So, from clue 3, Rosebank can't be number 2 and must be number 8, leaving number 2 as Larksnest.

No. 2, Larksnest, Millers, Gilmore's.
No. 4, Oakland, Stones, J and P.
No. 6, Greengates, Colemans, Norman's.
No. 8, Rosebank, Howards, Acme.

Domino Search, p. 25

4	5	4	1	2	1	5	2
3	0	6	1	3	4	3	0
2	5	4	4	1	4	5	5
6	6	0	6	0	0	1	2
3	3	4	1	5	3	6	2
6	2	1	3	5	2	0	4
3	5	6	6	0	2	0	1

The Front Line, p. 26

The man in position 3 cannot be the infantry sergeant (clue 1), the paratrooper (clue 3), the marine, who is Francisco Lorca (clue 4), the rifleman (clue 6), or the infantry private, who works for Luigi Carcano (clue 8), so must be the gunner. The man in position 1 can't be Miguel Gomez (clue 7), Juan Hernandez (clue 1), Francisco Lorca (clue 4), Matteo Costa who works for the CIA (clue 5), or Antonio Rojas (clue 8), so must be Fidel Perez. He does not work for Red Dawn (clue 1), for the *New York Gazette*, the CIA (clue 5), WCNN (clue 2), or Luigi Carcano, so must work for Ivan Kozenko. From clue 2, the WCNN's employee must be in position 2. Fidel Perez cannot be the paratrooper (clue 3) or the rifleman (clue 6), so he must be the infantry sergeant. From clue 1, Juan

Hernandez must be in position 2. He cannot be the paratrooper (clue 3) nor, since he works for WCNN, the infantry private whose employer is Luigi Carcarno, so he must be the rifleman. The gunner in position 3 cannot work for Red Dawn (clue 1) or the CIA (clue 5), so he must work for the *New York Gazette*. We now know the name or rank of the men working for Luigi Carcarno and the CIA, so Francisco Lorca the marine (clue 4) must work for Red Dawn, leaving Matteo Costa as the paratrooper. The infantry private is not Antonio Rojas (clue 8), so he must be Miguel Gomez, leaving Antonio Rojas as the gunner in position 3. The man in position 5 is not Miguel Gomez (clue 7) or Francisco Lorca (clue 4), so must be Matteo Costa the paratrooper also in the pay of the CIA. Francisco Lorca, marine and Red Dawn operative, can't be in foxhole 6, so he must be in foxhole 4, leaving Miguel Gomez, infantry private and Luigi Carcano employee, in foxhole 6.

1, Fidel Perez, sergeant (infantry), Ivan Kozenko.
2, Juan Hernandez, rifleman, WCNN.
3, Antonio Rojas, gunner, *New York Gazette*.
4, Francisco Lorca, marine, Red Dawn.
5, Matteo Costa, paratrooper, CIA.
6, Miguel Gomez, private (infantry), Luigi Carcano.

Holding On, p. 28

The automobile insurance call involved 5 menus (clue 1), the 3-menu call included *Robert De Niro's Waiting* (clue 4) and the 26-minute hold involved 6 menus (clue 3), so the call to the bank which involved listening to *24 Hours from Tulsa* and which was neither the one with the fewest menus or the one that lasted longest (all clue 2) must have had 4 menus. It didn't last 18 or 26 minutes (clue 2) or 22 minutes (clue 1). The call to the travel agent had a 20-minute hold (clue 4), so the bank call must have

had the 24-minute hold. So, from clue 2, the 6-menu, 26-minute hold must have been accompanied by *We Have All the Time in the World*. It wasn't to the energy company (clue 2), and we know from its number of menus that it wasn't to the automobile insurance company and from its length that it wasn't to the travel agent, so it must have been to the phone company. The call to the travel agent didn't have 3 menus and *Robert De Niro's Waiting* (clue 4), so that must have been the set up at the energy company, leaving the 18-minute karaoke to *I'm Still Waiting* (clue 5) as the call to the 5-menu automobile insurance call center. By elimination, the travel agent must have a 2-menu system and must play *Hanging on the Telephone* while Anna was doing just that for 20 minutes and the energy company must have 3 menus, play *Robert De Niro's Waiting*, and keep Anna waiting for 22 minutes.

Bank, 4 menus, *24 Hours from Tulsa*, 24 minutes.
Phone company, 6 menus, *We Have All the Time in the World*, 26 minutes.
Car insurance, 5 menus, *I'm Still Waiting*, 18 minutes.
Energy company, 3 menus, *Robert De Niro's Waiting*, 22 minutes.
Travel Agent, 2 menus, *Hanging on the Telephone*, 20 minutes.

Back Home, p. 30

Sheilah lives in Australia (clue 4). The Caseys living in the USA and Brazil are both male (clues 2 and 3), so Bridget, who doesn't live in Britain (clue 7), must live in Spain. The man in Brazil is a builder (clue 3), so can't be Declan, who's a priest (clue 6), nor is the builder Niall (clue 3), so he must be Kevin. We now know the occupations of Declan and Kevin, so the soldier, who's also male (clue 5), must be Niall. The police officer giving the jewelry isn't Bridget (clue 7), so must be Sheilah and, by elimination, Bridget must be a folk-singer. The wine isn't being given by

Kevin or Niall (clue 3) or Declan (clue 6), so must be Bridget's gift. The American-based donor of the painting (clue 2) isn't Niall (clue 5), so must be Declan the priest, and, by elimination, Niall must live in Britain. Finally, from clue 1, Niall's gift isn't the tea set, so it must be the candlesticks, leaving the tea set as the gift of Kevin the builder from Brazil.

Bridget, folk-singer, Spain, wine.
Declan, priest, USA, painting.
Kevin, builder, Brazil, tea set.
Niall, soldier, Britain, candlesticks.
Sheilah, police officer, Australia, jewelry.

Money for Old . . . , p. 32

Tuesday's buyers were the Fujitas (clue 1). Mrs. Hofmann bought the tallboy (clue 5), and the Bergs were in the shop later than the buyers of the mirror (clue 2), so the wife who bought the lamp on Monday, who wasn't Mrs. Yurkowitz, must have been Mrs. McAndrew, whose husband bought the musket (clue 3). So the music box, which was bought the day after the loving cup (clue 2), wasn't sold on Tuesday or Thursday and the telescope was sold on Thursday (clue 4), so the music box wasn't sold on Friday and must have been sold on Saturday. The loving cup was therefore sold on Friday. As one couple bought the clock and the bust (clue 6), they weren't purchased on Thursday or Friday, so they must have been bought on Tuesday, by the Fujitas. Mrs. Berg didn't buy the mirror (clue 2), so she must have bought the music box on Saturday and the mirror must have been chosen by Mrs. Yurkowitz, and they must have been the Thursday buyers, with Mr. Yurkowitz buying the telescope (clue 4). The man who bought the loving cup on Friday must have been Mr. Hofmann, whose wife bought the tallboy, leaving Mr. Berg, the Saturday shopper whose wife bought the music box, as the purchaser of the tantalus.

Monday, musket, lamp, McAndrew.
Tuesday, clock, bust, Fujita.
Thursday, telescope, mirror, Yurkowitz.
Friday, loving cup, tallboy, Hofmann.
Saturday, tantalus, music box, Berg.

Great Expectations, p. 34

Aunt Constance went out on Tuesday (clue 8). Montague was the Thursday escort (clue 6), so, from clue 2, Aunt Victoria cannot have been out on Friday, nor can that be the day Gerald and his Aunt Euphemia had an outing (clue 1). From clue 5, the tapestry exhibition was not attended by Aunt Priscilla on Friday, so it must have been Aunt Millicent who went out that day. Her escort was not Archie (clue 4), and we know he was not Gerald or Montague, and clue 2 rules out Friday for Rupert, so it must have been Edward who escorted Aunt Millicent, who therefore went to the art exhibition (clue 3). Since Aunt Constance was escorted on Tuesday, clue 2 rules out Rupert for Monday escort duty, and clue 4 rules out Archie, so it must have been on Monday that Gerald escorted his Aunt Euphemia. This was not to the flower show (clue 1), and the opera outing was on Wednesday (clue 7), so Gerald and Aunt Euphemia must have gone to the ballet. By elimination, Priscilla's tapestry exhibition must have been attended by her and Montague on Thursday, Aunt Constance must have gone to the flower show on Tuesday, and it must be Aunt Victoria who was escorted to the opera on Wednesday. So, from clue 2, Rupert took his Aunt Constance to the flower show on Tuesday, leaving Archie as Aunt Victoria's companion to the opera.

Monday, Gerald Huntington, Aunt Euphemia, ballet.
Tuesday, Rupert de Grey, Aunt Constance, flower show.
Wednesday, Archie Fotheringhay, Aunt Victoria, opera.
Thursday, Montague Ffolliott, Aunt Priscilla, tapestry exhibition.
Friday, Edward Tanqueray, Aunt Millicent, art exhibition.

Logi-5, p. 36

C	A	B	E	D
D	E	C	B	A
B	D	A	C	E
A	C	E	D	B
E	B	D	A	C

Killer Sudoku, p. 36

2	6	9	5	7	1	3	4	8
3	4	8	6	2	9	5	7	1
5	1	7	8	4	3	2	9	6
8	3	5	1	9	7	6	2	4
6	7	2	4	8	5	1	3	9
1	9	4	2	3	6	7	8	5
4	8	6	7	5	2	9	1	3
9	2	1	3	6	4	8	5	7
7	5	3	9	1	8	4	6	2

Battleships, p. 37

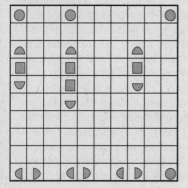

Marriage Knot, p. 38

Nigel married Carol (clue 2). David's bride wasn't Julie or Sarah (clue 1), and, since her maiden name was McAlpine (clue 1), she can't have been Tessa, who was Haines (clue 3), so she must have been Karen McAlpine. Peter's surname is Cammack (clue 3), so, from clue 4, Keith, who married David's sister, can't have been Mr. Purchan who married Miss Cammack, who wasn't Simon either (clue 5). We know Purchan wasn't David or Peter, so he must have been Nigel Purchan and the former Miss Cammack was therefore Carol Cammack. We now know that neither David nor Nigel married Miss Purchan, and since Nigel is her brother, clue 4 rules out Keith. Nigel Purchan married Carol Cammack, so Peter Cammack can't have married Miss Purchan (intro), and it must have been Simon who did. We now know that Tessa Haines didn't marry David, Nigel, or Simon, nor did she marry Peter Cammack (clue 3), so her husband must be Keith. So, from clue 4, David, who married Karen McAlpine, must be David Haines and, by elimination, Peter Cammack married Miss Tweedale. She wasn't Sarah, who married Mr. McAlpine (clue 1), so must have been Julie, and Sarah's Mr. McAlpine must have been Simon. By elimination, it must have been Keith Tweedale who married Tessa Haines.

David Haines, Karen McAlpine.
Keith Tweedale, Tessa Haines.
Nigel Purchan, Carol Cammack.
Peter Cammack, Julie Tweedale.
Simon McAlpine, Sarah Purchan.

An Expert Writes, p. 40

Eddie Gordon is the former marathon runner (clue 1) and the boxer now writes for the *Sun Times* (clue 2), so Nick Pauly, who writes for the *World of Sports* (clue 3) but wasn't an ice hockey player or a golfer (clue 2), must be the former decathlete who lives and works in London (clue 4). The *Miami Record* doesn't employ marathon runner Eddie Gordon (clue 1) or the ice hockey player (clue 5), and we know it's not the decathlete or the boxer, so it must be the former golfer. We now know either the writer or the city for three sports, so Tom Zalewski, who writes for a publication in Toronto (clue 2) but who doesn't write about boxing for the *Sun Times* (clue 2) must write about ice hockey. Randy Spring doesn't write for a San Diego publication, so he must write in Adelaide. So we know he doesn't write on golf, marathon running, decathlon or ice hockey, so he must be the boxer who writes for the *Adelaide Sun Times*, leaving Bernard Corrio as the former golfer whose words appear in the *Miami Record*. By elimination, Eddie Gordon's publication must be based in San Diego. It's not the *Journal* (clue 6), so it must be the *San Diego Sports News*, leaving Tom Zalewski writing about ice hockey for the *Toronto Journal*.

Bernard Corrio, golf, *Miami Record*.
Eddie Gordon, marathon, *San Diego Sports News*.
Nick Pauly, decathlon, *London World of Sports*.
Randy Spring, boxing, *Adelaide Sun Times*.
Tom Zalewski, ice hockey, *Toronto Journal*.

Is It Art?, p. 42

Ivan Rippov's stainless steel pyramid must have cost Marston either $10,000 or $20,000 (clue 1). $10,000 was the price paid for the pile of old automobile tires (clue 4), so the Rippov must have cost $20,000. Therefore it must have been the Schamm Gallery from which the automobile tires were purchased (clue 1) and the piece from the Foni Gallery must have been the $5,000 work by Monty Banks (clue 2). This was not the automobile tires, the steel pyramid, the waste basket of cans, which cost more than the broken glass in the frame (clue 3), or the broken glass itself, which was purchased from Fake Modern (clue 5), so it must have been the yellow-painted kettle. As the waste basket cost more than the broken glass (clue 3), the former must have been $25,000 and the latter $15,000. The Ivan Rippov piece was not acquired from the Huddwinker Gallery (clue 1), so it must have been the Pinchbeck,

and, by elimination, the waste basket full of cans must have been the work from the Huddwinker. Artie Fishall's piece was not the automobile tires or the waste basket (clue 4), so it must have been the broken glass from Fake Modern. As the Con Swindell piece cost more than the Esau Hoakes (clue 6), the former must have been the $25,000 waste basket of cans, and the latter the $10,000 pile of old automobile tires.

Fake Modern, Artie Fishall, broken glass in frame, $15,000.
Foni, Monty Banks, yellow-painted kettle, $5,000.
Huddwinker, Con Swindell, waste basket of old cans, $25,000.
Pinchbeck, Ivan Rippov, stainless steel pyramid, $20,000.
Schamm, Esau Hoakes, pile of old automobile tires, $10,000.

Spelling Schools, p. 44

Sowrash is where the pupil is studying fortune-telling (clue 5) and Prof. Squirrel teaches at Gruntpimples, so Prof. Deerkey, who teaches wandwork (clue 1) and is not a fellow of Hamboils or Porkwens Academies (clue 1), must be at Boarpocks. His pupil there is not Lottie Baxter (clue 2), Larry Lester, who attends Porkwens (clue 1), Barry Carter, who is taught by Prof. Tumbledown (clue 3), or Carrie Foster, who is studying potions (clue 4), so it must be Gary Dexter. We know that Larry Lester is not studying wandwork or potions, nor is it invisibility, so Larry must be studying flying there. Therefore his professor is not Deerkey, Tumbledown or Squirrel. Prof. McTavish is not a fellow of Porkwens (clue 2), so Prof. Snoop must be teaching Larry. Lottie Baxter is not being taught by Prof. McTavish (clue 2), so her tutor must be Prof. Squirrel at Gruntpimples Academy. By elimination, Prof. McTavish must be teaching Carrie Foster about potions. They are not at Sowrash Academy, where one of the five is studying fortune-telling, so, by elimination, it must be Hamboils. Therefore the pupil at Sowrash must be Barry Carter, studying under Prof. Tumbledown, and Lottie Baxter must be studying invisibility at Gruntpimples Academy.

Barry Carter, Sowrash, fortune-telling, Prof. Tumbledown.
Carrie Foster, Hamboils, potions, Prof. McTavish.
Gary Dexter, Boarpocks, wandwork, Prof. Deerkey.
Larry Lester, Porkwens, flying, Prof. Snoop.
Lottie Baxter, Gruntpimples, invisibility, Prof Squirrel.

Hounds and Homes, p. 46

The Labrador lives at number 6 (clue 4) and Butch at number 4 (clue 3). Ricky, the Dalmatian, cannot live at number 8 (clue 1), so he must live at number 2 and, from clue 1, the Kennells' house must be number 4 and they own Butch. By elimination, the spaniel owned by the Doggetts (clue 5) must live at number 8, and his name, which is not Simba (clue 5), must be Jack. Now, by elimination, the Labrador at number 6 must be Simba, and Butch must be the bulldog. Clue 2 now tells us the Barkers must live at number 2, which leaves the family at number 6 as the Yapps.

2, Barker, Ricky, Dalmatian.
4, Kennell, Butch, bulldog.
6, Yapp, Simba, Labrador.
8, Doggett, Jack, spaniel.

Domino Search, p. 47

0	0	3	1	2	3	0	6
2	0	5	2	4	4	0	2
6	1	5	3	1	3	5	4
5	2	2	6	2	2	6	1
6	6	4	3	5	0	4	4
0	1	4	6	1	6	3	1
0	1	3	5	4	5	3	5

Logi-5, p. 48

C	E	B	D	A
D	B	C	A	E
B	A	D	E	C
A	C	E	B	D
E	D	A	C	B

Killer Sudoku, p. 48

7	4	6	9	1	5	3	8	2
3	1	8	7	2	6	9	5	4
9	5	2	3	4	8	7	1	6
8	3	4	2	9	7	5	6	1
5	7	1	6	8	3	2	4	9
6	2	9	4	5	1	8	7	3
1	6	3	5	7	9	4	2	8
2	8	7	1	3	4	6	9	5
4	9	5	8	6	2	1	3	7

World View, p. 49

The 10-inch globe is number 4 (clue 4), so the smallest globe, which isn't globe 1 or 2 (clue 3) or globe 3 (clue 4) must be globe 5. The 7-inch globe isn't globe 2 (clue 2), so the 10-inch globe 4 can't have the white seas. The 9-inch globe has the traditional blue seas (clue 1), so the 10-inch globe, which doesn't have a yellow sea (clue 3) or a red sea (clue 4) must have the silver sea.

So, from clue 2, globe 5, the 6-inch world, must have the white seas and globe 3 must be 7 inches across. Now, from clue 3, globe 1 must be 8 inches in diameter and globe 2 must be the 9 incher with the blue sea. Finally, globe 1 doesn't have yellow seas (clue 3), so must have red seas, leaving the 7-inch globe 3 with yellow seas.

1, 8 inches, red.
2, 9 inches, blue.
3, 7 inches, yellow.
4, 10 inches, silver.
5, 6 inches, white.

Student Quarters, p. 50

The gerbil in module 3 is Regina (clue 3) and the student in module 5 drinks fruit teas (clue 1), so Spot's owner who cannot be in module 1, 4, or 5 (clue 3), must be in module 2 and, from clue 3, Lynne Keble must be in module number 1. We know her gerbil is not Spot or Regina. Nor is it Poppy, which is Iona Hertford's pet (clue 2), while clue 4 rules out Darcy, so it must be Princess, and Lynne Keble therefore is a keen woodworker (clue 1). We know that module 2 is where Spot lives, so it is not the woodworker's module nor the fruit tea drinker's; clue 3 tells us that the student in module 2 is not the UFO Investigator and clue 4 rules out the cacti collector, so number 2 must belong to the reader of western novels, Nora Merton (clue 2). Darcy's owner is not Cassie Balliol (clue 4), so she must be Yvonne Wadham, leaving Cassie Balliol in number 3 with Regina her gerbil. She is not the cacti collector (clue 4) and we know that she is not the woodworker or the western reader, while her module number rules out the fruit tea drinker, so she must be the UFO Investigator. Finally, from clue 4, module 4 is not occupied by Yvonne Wadham and Darcy, so it must belong to Poppy's owner, Iona Hertford, who, by elimination, must be the cacti collector, leaving the fruit tea drinker in number 5 as Darcy's owner Yvonne Wadham.

1, Lynne Keble, Princess, woodworker.
2, Nora Merton, Spot, reads westerns.
3, Cassie Balliol, Regina, UFO watcher.
4, Iona Hertford, Poppy, collects cacti.
5, Yvonne Wadham, Darcy, fruit teas.

The Klashers, p. 52

The Klasher who wears the apron does the cooking (clue 2), so the one who wears the top hat, who does not drive or do the laundry (clue 3), and is not Dafi the cleaner (clue 5), must be the gardener. The red Klasher wears the waistcoat (clue 6), so the purple Klasher, who does the laundry but doesn't wear the wellies (clue 4), must sport the sou'wester and is therefore Bati. (clue 6). Luni is yellow (clue 1), so Dipi, who is neither pink nor green (clue 1), must be the red Klasher with the waistcoat. Dipi does not do the cooking, gardening, or laundry, so he must be the driver. By elimination, Dafi must wear the wellies. The green Klasher is not the top-hat-wearing gardener or the one who wears the apron, so it must be welly-wearing Dafi. The Klasher with the top hat is not pink (clue 3), so it must be the yellow Luni, and, by elimination, the pink Klasher must be Gaga, and must wear the apron to do the cooking.

Bati, purple, sou'wester, laundry.
Dafi, green, wellies, cleaning.
Dipi, red, waistcoat, driving.
Gaga, pink, apron, cooking.
Luni, yellow, top hat, gardening.

Great Eastshire Menu, p. 54

The shaven-headed chef, whose restaurant is in Storbury, isn't Jay Hammond-Eggz, Tim Sweet-Bredd or Dirk D'Essert (clue 2) or Perry Rasher, whose restaurant is in Colnecasater (clue 6), so he must be Angus Bannock, the Oriental cookery expert (clue 3). Jay Hammond-Eggz has a pigtail (clue 5), Perry Rasher has distinctive facial hair (clue 3), and Tim Sweet-Bredd doesn't dress in green (clue 1), so the chef who does must be Dirk D'Essert. As the nouvelle cuisine chef has a goatee beard (clue 1), and the fish chef doesn't wear green (clue 1), neither of these can be Dirk D'Essert, nor is he the British traditional chef (clue 2). We know Angus Bannock's the Oriental chef, so Dirk D'Essert must be the vegetarian chef from Brightbourne (clue 4). Jay Hammond-Eggz's restaurant isn't in Meadowland (clue 5), so it must be in Middlehampton, and Tim Sweet-Bredd's must be in Meadowland. Perry Rasher's Colnecaster restaurant doesn't specialize in fish (clue 6), and neither does Tim Sweet-Bredd's in Meadowland (clue 1), so Jay Hammond-Eggz of Middlehampton must be the fish specialist. Tim Sweet-Bredd's specialty isn't British traditional food (clue 7), so he must be the nouvelle cuisine chef with the goatee beard, and, by elimination, Perry Rasher from Colnecaster must cook British traditional food, and must have a walrus mustache.

Angus Bannock, shaven head, Oriental, Storbury.

Dirk D'Essert, dresses in green, vegetarian, Brightbourne.

Jay Hammond-Eggz, pigtail, fish, Middlehampton.

Perry Rasher, walrus mustache, British traditional, Colnecaster.

Tim Sweet-Bredd, goatee beard, nouvelle cuisine, Meadowland

yAbe, p. 56

Penny Pylup collects items by OS Tasker (clue 5) and Sophia Storem collects paperweights (clue 2), so the first edition books by AJ Barclay, which are not wanted by Kate Kerlecht (clue 4) or Stanley Stox (clue 3), must be being sought by Oscar Oared from Dover (clue 1). The Lincoln collector of leaky fountain pens isn't Penny Pylup (clue 6) or Stanley Stox (clue 3) and we know it isn't Oscar Oared or Sophia Storem, so it must be Kate Kerlecht. The items made by KT Latimer are not being advertised for by Sophia Storem (clue 2), so

they must be the items collected by Stanley Stox. Her items are not guitars (clue 2), so Stanley Stox of Penzance must collect KT Latimer copper pots, leaving Penny Pylup collecting guitars by OS Tasker. Penny doesn't live in Carlisle (clue 5), so she must live in Leicester, leaving Sophia Storem as the collector in Carlisle. Finally, the fountain pens collected by Kate Kerlecht of Lincoln aren't made by JP Wilmott (clue 6), so they must be by PB Watchman, leaving Sophia Storem of Carlisle collecting paperweights by JP Wilmott.

Kate Kerlecht, Lincoln, fountain pens, PB Watchman.

Oscar Oared, Dover, first editions, AJ Barclay.

Penny Pylup, Leicester, guitars, OS Tasker.

Sophia Storem, Carlisle, paperweights, JP Wilmott.

Stanley Stox, Penzance, copper pots, KT Latimer.

Detectives Storey, p. 58

Lucy Regan, the IAD officer, wasn't created by any of the police officers from Boston, Miami, or New York (clue 1), and the Diamond Insurance investigator's creation is a Military Police officer (clue 6), so Lucy Regan must be the creation of the Stern Agency investigator, John Kengo (clue 4). Dave Carey created the federal agent (clue 2), so the man who created the police chief (clue 5) must be Saul Rossi. The New York cop is also male (clue 6); we know that he isn't John Kengo, nor is he Saul Rossi (clue 5), so he must be Dave Carey. His federal agent isn't Andy Gomez (clue 5), Patsy-Ann Bowen (clue 2), or Maisie Hovik, who is Wendy Vance's creation (clue 3); we know that John Kengo created Lucy Regan, so the federal agent must be Carl Van Damm. We know the creator's employers to go with three fictional detectives' occupations; the Miami cop's creation isn't a private eye (clue 4), so must be the police chief created by

Saul Rossi, who is therefore the Miami cop, leaving the Boston cop as the creator of the private eye. We now know the employers of three real detectives; the Diamond Insurance investigator isn't Moira Penn (clue 6), so must be Wendy Vance, creator of Maisie Hovik, leaving Moira Penn as the Boston cop who created the private eye. The private eye is female (clue 6), so must be Patsy-Ann Bowen, leaving Andy Gomez as Saul Rossi's creation, the police chief.

Dave Carey, New York police, Carl Van Damm, federal agent.
John Kengo, Stern Agency, Lucy Regan, IAD officer.
Moira Penn, Boston police, Patsy-Ann Bowen, private eye.
Saul Rossi, Miami police, Andy Gomez, police chief.
Wendy Vance, Diamond Insurance, Maisie Hovik, Military Police officer.

Sign-In, p. 60

2	1	6	5	3	4
5	6	1	4	2	3
3	2	5	1	4	6
1	5	4	3	6	2
4	3	2	6	1	5
6	4	3	2	5	1

Sudoku, p. 60

6	1	7	4	2	8	5	3	9
8	4	9	5	1	3	6	2	7
3	5	2	9	7	6	4	8	1
5	6	1	8	4	2	9	7	3
4	9	8	7	3	1	2	5	6
2	7	3	6	9	5	8	1	4
9	2	4	1	5	7	3	6	8
1	8	5	3	6	9	7	4	2
7	3	6	2	8	4	1	9	5

Daily Exercise, p. 61

Prisoner 4 was boss in Tulsa (clue 3) and Tony Sambani is prisoner 1 (clue 4), so Don Bedelio from Providence, who is not prisoner 2 (clue 1), must be prisoner 3. So his nickname was not Pistols (clue 4). Muscles was the St. Louis boss (clue 2) and Spider was the nickname of Frankie Fabiani (clue 3), so Don Bedelio must have been Crazy man. Spider Fabiani is not prisoner 4 (clue 3) so must be prisoner 2, leaving Joey Miliano as prisoner 4. We now know the nickname or city for three mobsters, so Muscles from St. Louis must be Tony Sambani, prisoner 1. By elimination Joey Miliano must have been nicknamed Pistols and Frankie Spider Fabiani must have been gang boss in Detroit.
1, Tony Sambani, Muscles, St. Louis.
2, Frankie Fabiani, Spider, Detroit.
3, Don Bedelio, Crazy man, Providence.
4, Joey Miliano, Pistols, Tulsa.

Roman Vacation, p. 62

The Thomases went to the Trevi Fountain (clue 1) and Mr. Grey lost his item in the diner (clue 5), so the item left on the bus at the Forum (clue 6), which wasn't lost by Mr. Shepherd or Mr. Lewes (clue 6), must have been lost by Mr. Simkin, and so he must have left the sunblock on the bus (clue 4). The item lost at the Spanish Steps wasn't the phrase book or the postcards (clue 7) and the hat was left behind at the Pantheon (clue 3), so it must have been the sunglasses that were lost during the visit to the Spanish Steps. The postcards weren't forgotten at the Colosseum (clue 7), so they must have been lost by Mr. Thomas at the Trevi Fountain, leaving the phrase book being left in the taxi (clue 2) at the Colosseum. Mr. Thomas didn't leave the postcards on a seat (clue 1), so he must have left them at an ice-cream stall. Mr. Shepherd didn't leave the phrase book in the taxi at the Colosseum (clue 6), so that must have been Mr. Lewes. Mr. Shepherd didn't lose his sunglasses (clue 6), so he must have lost his hat at the Pantheon. We know he didn't leave it in the diner, so must have left it on a seat, leaving the Greys visiting the Spanish steps and losing Mr. Grey's sunglasses in a diner.

Grey, Spanish Steps, sunglasses, diner.
Lewes, Colosseum, phrase book, taxi.
Shepherd, Pantheon, hat, seat.
Simkin, Forum, sunblock, bus.
Thomas, Trevi Fountain, postcards, ice-cream stall.

A Book by Its Cover, p. 64

Emma Starr's autobiography is priced at $18.99 (clue 6). The senator, whose book is priced at $15.99 (clue 4), is not Hugh Jeago (clue 3), Ed Biggar (also clue 4), or Caleb Ritty, the soccer player (clue 1), so it must be Guy Fuller, author of *The Fuller Story* (clue 1). *Speaking Personally* is priced at $16.99 (clue 2), so *Talking of Me*, written by the radio presenter (clue 3), must be at least $17.99 and Hugh Jeago's book must be more expensive still. It is not $18.99 (clue 6), so must be $19.99. Hugh Jeago is not the pop singer (clue 2), so he must be the opera singer. *Speaking Personally* is not the autobiography of the opera singer or the pop singer (clue 2), so it must be the soccer player, and is therefore the $16.99 book by Caleb Ritty. By elimination, the $17.99 book must be the one written by Ed Biggar. *Quite a Life* is not the life-story of the pop singer (clue 2), so it must be the opera singer's $19.99 volume. Finally, *I Say!* is not priced at $17.99, so it must be Emma Starr's $18.99 book and, by elimination, she must be the young pop singer. This leaves *Talking of Me* as radio presenter Ed Biggar's autobiography, priced at $17.99.

I Say! by Emma Starr, $18.99, pop singer.
Quite a Life by Hugh Jeago, $19.99, opera singer.
Speaking Personally by Caleb Ritty, $16.99, soccer player.
Talking of Me by Ed Biggar, $17.99, radio presenter.
The Fuller Story by Guy Fuller, $15.99, senator.

Beaux on Board, p. 66

The admiral's daughter on the same cruise as Beau Legges was not Augusta or Caroline (clue 2), while Charlotte was a fellow guest of Beau Streate (clue 4), and Matilda's father is the ambassador (clue 1), so the admiral's daughter must be Sophia, and she and Beau Legges were on the 1817 cruise (clue 5). So, from clue 2, Caroline sailed in 1816, and is therefore the earl's daughter (clue 6). Charlotte's father is not the rich merchant (clue 4), so, by elimination, he must be the baronet, leaving the merchant's daughter as Augusta. Beau Streate and Charlotte were not aboard in 1816 or 1820 (clue 4), so they must have been guests of Beau Spritt in 1819. Clue 1 rules out 1816 for Matilda's voyage, so she must have sailed with Beau Spritt in 1820, leaving Augusta on the 1816 trip. The Beau who sailed with Matilda in 1820 was not Beau Nydel (clue 1), nor can he have been Beau Belles (clue 3), so he must have been Beau Tighe. Beau Belles did not pursue Caroline in 1816 (clue 6), so he must have been Augusta's traveling companion in 1816, leaving Beau Nydel as the man intent on getting to know the earl's daughter, Caroline.

1816, Beau Belles, Augusta, rich merchant.
1817, Beau Legges, Sophia, admiral.
1818, Beau Nydel, Caroline, earl.
1819, Beau Streate, Charlotte, baronet.
1820, Beau Tighe, Matilda, ambassador.

On Report, p. 68

Sophie got a B+ in French (clue 4). The subject awarded a C+ cannot have been Science (clue 2), or history (clue 5), nor was it given by Mr. Fletcher for English (clue 7), so it must have been Sophie's math grade.

Therefore, from clue 5, she received a B for history. This was from Mrs. Jefferson (clue 6). The C+ in math was not awarded by Miss Roberts (clue 5), and we know Sophie's math teacher is not Mr. Fletcher or Mrs. Jefferson, while clue 2 rules out Mr. Dingle as the awarder of the C+, so Mrs. Carter must teach math. Her comment was "a steady worker" (clue 3). Since Mr. Dingle does not teach science (clue 2), he must be Sophie's French teacher, who gave her the B+, and her science teacher must be Miss Roberts. Clue 2 now reveals the comment "intelligent" as the one accompanying the B grade in history, since we know it was not made for math. The A grade was matched by the comment "excellent" (clue 1), so the teacher who awarded the A- must have used either "solid progress" or "works hard." But clue 1 rules out the latter, so "solid progress" must have gone with the A-. Therefore, from clue 7, it must be Mr. Fletcher who gave the A as his English assessment, and that clue also tells us Miss Roberts gave the A- and commented "steady progress" in science, which leaves "works hard" as Mr. Dingle's comment for French.

English, A, Mr. Fletcher, excellent.
French, B+, Mr. Dingle, works hard.
History, B, Mrs. Jefferson, intelligent.
Math, C+, Mrs. Carter, a steady worker.
Science, A-, Miss Roberts, solid progress.

Poster Boys, p. 70

The reward on offer in White River is an even number of hundreds of dollars (clue 3), but $400 is the sum on the Little Pine posters (clue 2), and since the White River reward is $100 less than that for the murderer (also clue 3), it is not $1,000, so it must be $600, and therefore the outlaw concerned must be Link O'Reilly (clue 5). The reward for the murderer must therefore be $700 (clue 3). The reward for Scotty McRae is $300 more than that for the cattle rustler (clue 1), but it is not $1,000, since the reward for the

murderer is $700. Therefore, the reward being offered in Harris Falls for Scotty McRae (clue 1) must be $700. Also therefore, the cattle rustler must be wanted in Little Pine for a reward of $400. The 'Wanted' poster in White River does not bear the likeness of the train robber Zack Monroe (clue 4), or the bank robber, who is wanted in Gibbsville (clue 6), so Link O'Reilly must be wanted in White River for horse stealing. Therefore, by elimination, the Yellow Creek poster must bear the picture of Zack Monroe. As the reward being offered by Gibbsville is not $500 (clue 6), it must be $1,000, leaving the $500 as the reward being offered by Yellow Creek. Finally, the $400 being offered by Little Pine is not for the capture of Hank Gilmore (clue 2), so it must be for Baxter Gould, leaving Hank Gilmore as the bank robber wanted in Gibbsville.

Gibbsville, Hank Gilmore, bank robbery, $1,000.
Harris Falls, Scotty McRae, murder, $700.
Little Pine, Baxter Gould, cattle rustling, $400.
White River, Link O'Reilly, horse stealing, $600.
Yellow Creek, Zack Monroe, train robbery, $500.

Piece of Cake, p. 72

Mrs. Angel's cake was delayed by an tractor-trailer (clue 2) and the tenth birthday cake was held up by a tractor (clue 4). So Mr. Simnel's cake, which wasn't delayed by a backhoe or, since it was delayed for 5 minutes longer than the cake for Mrs. Dundee (clue 1) and a man's delivery was delayed for 10 minutes (clue 3), for 15 minutes (clue 1), must have been delayed for 20 minutes. So, from clue 1, Mrs. Dundee's delivery must have been delayed for 15 minutes by a horse trailer (clue 5) and the cup cake delivery must have been held up for 25 minutes. From either the reason or length of delay, we now know that Mrs. Dundee hadn't ordered the cupcakes, 10th birthday cake or wedding cake. Nor was it the 50th birthday cake (clue 3), so Mrs. Dundee must have ordered the anniversary cake. Mrs. Angel didn't order the 50th birthday cake (clue 4) and the tractor-trailer that got in the way rules out the 10th birthday cake, so she must have ordered the cup cakes delayed by 25 minutes. The delivery of the 50th birthday cake was delayed for 10 minutes (clue 3), so Alice must have been held up on the way to deliver the 10th birthday cake for 5 minutes. So it wasn't delivered to Mr. Eccles (clue 6) and must have been delivered to Mr. Battenburg, leaving Mr. Eccles taking delivery of the 50th birthday cake. Finally, this cake wasn't held up by the truck (clue 3), so it must have been delayed by the backhoe, leaving the drive to deliver Mr. Simnel's daughter's wedding cake delayed by a truck for 20 minutes.

Mrs. Angel, cup cakes, tractor-trailer, 25 minutes.

Mr. Battenburg, birthday cake 10th, tractor, 5 minutes.

Mrs. Dundee, anniversary cake, horse trailer, 15 minutes.

Mr. Eccles, birthday cake 50th, backhoe, 10 minutes.

Mr. Simnel, wedding cake, truck, 20 minutes.

Out of the Game, p. 74

Diane Frost owns a pub (clue1) and both Brian Cooper and Tommy Warton are self-employed (clue 4), so the sports teacher, who isn't Penny Robins (clue 3), must be Jane Martin who punched an umpire (clue 5). She was not the BMX rider (clue 3) or the footballer (clue 5). The squash player was involved in the bribery scandal (clue 5) and Brian Cooper was the javelin thrower (clue 4), so Jane Martin must have played tennis. We know that the person involved in the divorce scandal is not now a sports

teacher. Nor, from clue 1, is he or she the charity worker or the pub owner, and the dog breeder drugged an opponent (clue 2), so the divorce scandal must have led to a sports star becoming a freelance journalist. Penny Robins' sport was not BMX riding (clue 3) or football (clue 5), so she must be the former squash player. We know Penny Robins is not a pub landlady or a sports teacher and the cause of her downfall tells us she is not a dog breeder or a freelance journalist, so she must be the charity worker. The BMX rider did not libel their manager (clue 3) or get involved in the divorce scandal (clue 1) so must have drugged an opponent and so now breeds dogs. We know that this person isn't Jane Martin or Penny Robins. Nor is she Diane Frost (clue 1), so the BMX rider must have been Tommy Warton. By elimination Diane Frost must have played football and the javelin thrower, Brian Cooper, must have become a freelance Journalist after the divorce scandal, leaving Diane Frost as the person who libeled her manager.

Brian Cooper, javelin, divorce scandal, freelance journalist.

Diane Frost, football, libeled manager, pub owner.

Jane Martin, tennis, punched umpire, sports teacher.

Penny Robins, squash, bribery scandal, charity worker.

Tommy Warton, BMX cycling, drugged opponent, dog breeder.

Collection Day, p. 76

The family at No. 9 has donated a box of toys (clue 1), so the Grays, who live next to the shoe donators (clue 2), can't live at No. 11. Nor is No. 11 the home of the Brauns (clue 4) or the Greenes (clue 3), so it must belong to the Whytes, who have donated a bag of pants (clue 4). Since the books are not being donated from No. 9, from clue 3, the sweaters can't be in the bag from No. 5. Nor is that bag full of sweatshirts (clue 4), so it must be the bag of T-shirts. With the pants being donated from No. 11, the books can't be in the box outside No. 7 (clue 3). Nor does it contain shoes (clue 2), so it must have the DVDs. The box next to the bag of T-shirts outside No. 5 doesn't contain books (clue 3), so it must have the shoes, leaving the books being donated by the Whytes at No. 11. Now, from clue 3, the Greenes must live at No. 9 and the bag outside No. 7 must contain sweaters, leaving the Greenes' bag containing the sweatshirts. Finally, from clue 2, the Grays must live at No. 7 donating sweaters and DVDs, leaving the Brauns at No. 5 donating T-shirts and shoes.

No. 5, Braun, T-shirts, shoes.
No. 7, Gray, sweaters, DVDs.
No. 9, Greene, sweatshirts, toys.
No. 11, Whyte, pants, books.

Battleships, p. 77

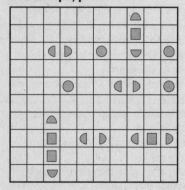

Plane Investigations, p. 78

The Westland Lysander crashed off Mariners Haven (clue 4) and the Junkers JU 52/3M is being investigated by Ulrich Tasman (clue 2), so the plane off Viking Head being investigated by Tom Solomon, which was not the Douglas C47 or the Short Stirling (clue 4), must be the Messerschmitt Bf110. The Douglas C47 crashed in 1945 (clue 1) and the plane at Rocky Point in 1944 (clue 3), while it was in 1943 that the plane being investigated by Don Coral went down (clue 3). The Messerschmitt at Viking Head did not crash in 1942 (clue 3), so it must have crashed in 1941. The Lysander didn't come down in 1943, so it must have been in 1942, leaving Ulrich Tasman working on a Junkers which crashed in 1944 at Rocky Point (clue 3). By elimination, the 1943 crash Don Coral's working on must have been of the Short Stirling. The Douglas C47 is not being investigated by Charlie Beaufort (clue 1), so that must be Owen North's assignment. So it didn't crash at Seal Bay (clue 2) and must have come down at Devil's Rock. Finally, by elimination, the Seal Bay crash must have been of the Short Stirling in 1943 assigned to Don Coral, and the Lysander at Mariners Haven that crashed in 1942 must be Charlie Beaufort's Assignment.

Devil's Rock, Douglas, 1945, Owen North.
Mariners Haven, Westland, 1942, Charlie Beaufort.
Rocky Point, Junkers, 1944, Ulrich Tasman.
Seal Bay, Short Stirling, 1943, Don Coral.
Viking Head, Messerschmitt, 1941, Tom Solomon.

That's the Ticket, p. 80

Ticket 2 was for the circus and ticket 4 is dated September (clue 5), so the November ticket, which was numbered half that of the football game ticket (clue 2) couldn't have been any of tickets 1, 4, 5, 6, 7, 8 or 9. Ticket 3 couldn't have been issued in November (clue 3), so Sylvester must have visited the circus with ticket 2 in November. So, from clue 2, the football game ticket must be ticket 4, the September one. Now, from clue 1, the trio of tickets from the opera, June, and the theme park ticket can't be tickets 5, 2, 4, or, since tickets 3 and 5 are the same shape, tickets 6, 3, or 5. Tickets 6 and 8 are also the same shape, so they can't be tickets 9, 6, 8, and must be 8, opera ticket, 5, June ticket, and 7, theme park ticket. Ticket 3 wasn't for the theater or the movie house (clue 3), the train journey (clue 4), or the art gallery (clue 6), so must be for the museum. Ticket 1 was issued the month after ticket 9 (clue 4), so, since the September ticket is number 4, ticket 9 can't be the August art gallery ticket (clue 6). Nor is that ticket 6 (clue 6), so the art gallery ticket dated August must be ticket 1 and, from clue 4, ticket 9 must be dated July. Since ticket 5 is dated June, ticket 9, dated July, can't be for the movie house, which is dated a month after ticket 3 (clue 3). Nor is ticket 9 for the train journey (clue 4), so it must be for the theater. So, from clue 3, the movie house ticket must be dated in June and is therefore ticket 5, and ticket 3, for the museum, must be dated May. By elimination, the train ticket must be number 6. So it wasn't dated April or October (clue 4) and must be dated March. Finally, the opera ticket wasn't for April (clue 1) and must have been in October, leaving the theme park trip in April, as shown by ticket 7.

1, art gallery, August; 2, circus, November; 3, museum, May;

4, football game, September; 5, movie house, June; 6, train journey, March; 7, theme park, April; 8, opera house, October; 9, theater, July.

Very Special Days, p. 82

Rachel Shaw's reception will cost $6,000 (clue 2), and the $7,200 reception will be for Mark Lewis and his bride (clue 3). From clue 6, the reception for Alison Bell and Simon Ryder can't be costing $4,200 or $4,800, so it must be costing $5,400, and, from the same clue, Nick Murphy's must be costing $4,200. We now know the prices to go with three grooms; the $4,800 reception is for the wedding at the stately home (clue 5), so Jon Ireton's reception at the football ground (clue 1) must be costing $6,000, and his bride is therefore Rachel Shaw. From the same clue, Liz Monk's reception is costing $7,200, and

she is therefore marrying Mark Lewis. By elimination, the stately home wedding and $4,800 reception must be Daniel Clark's. As Clare Dane will be marrying on the lake shore (clue 4), her reception isn't costing $4,800, so it must be costing $4,200, and she's therefore marrying Nick Murphy, leaving Emma Finch as Daniel Clark's bride who's having the $4,800 reception. Finally, Liz Monk and Mark Lewis aren't marrying in a hot-air balloon (clue 3), so they must have booked a Tudor chapel, and the hot-air balloon must be where Alison Bell and Simon Ryder are marrying before their $5,400 reception.

Alison Bell, Simon Ryder, hot-air balloon, $5,400.

Clare Dane, Nick Murphy, lake shore, $4,200.

Emma Finch, Daniel Clark, stately home, $4,800.

Liz Monk, Mark Lewis, Tudor chapel, $7,200.

Rachel Shaw, Jon Ireton, football ground, $6,000.

Sunday Celebs, p. 84

From clue 3, Stan Scribe must have the Friday morning deadline. The Diner Crew had a Thursday deadline (clue 4), Horace Hack was the leader of the Nightclub Sweep (clue 1), and the Home Stalkers were headed by a woman (clue 2), so Stan Scribe, who doesn't lead the Office Stalkers (clue 3), must head the Dumpster Divers. He and his team aren't targeting TV stars (clue 1), politicians (clue 3), or athletes (clue 4). The Home Stalkers are after movie stars (clue 3), so Stan Scribe and his Dumpster Divers must be rummaging through pop stars' dumpsters and delivering their copy on Friday morning. The Wednesday morning deadline wasn't given to Horace Hack or Sally Scoop (clue 1) or to Stella Stringer (clue 5), so it must be Will Wright's deadline. So he doesn't lead the Diner Crew with their Thursday deadline (clue 4) or the Home Stalkers (clue 2), so he must lead the Office Stalkers. Since Stan Scribe has the Friday deadline, Horace Hack's Nightclub Sweep team can't have the Thursday afternoon one (clue 1). Nor is Thursday afternoon the deadline for the Home Stalkers (clue 2), so it must be the deadline for the Diner Crew. From this deadline, the Diner Crew can't be targeting TV stars (clue 1). Nor are the TV stars the target of the Nightclub Sweep (clue 1), so they must be the quarry of Will Wright's Office Stalkers. Stella Stringer doesn't have the Thursday morning deadline (clue 5), so she must be due to deliver on Wednesday afternoon, leaving Horace Hack with the Thursday morning deadline. He wasn't targeting athletes (clue 4), so must have been after politicians, leaving the Diner Crew hunting athletes. Finally, from clue 1, the Diner Crew, with their Thursday afternoon deadline must be led by Sally Scoop, leaving the Home Stalkers, led by Stella Stringer, chasing movie stars and delivering their copy by Wednesday afternoon.

Dumpster Divers, Stan Scribe, pop stars, Friday a.m.
Diner Crew, Sally Scoop, athletes, Thursday p.m.
Home Stalkers, Stella Stringer, movie stars, Wednesday p.m.
Nightclub Sweep, Horace Hack, politicians, Thursday a.m.
Office Stalkers, Will Wright, TV stars, Wednesday a.m.

Van Guard, p. 86

One trailer is the Eldorado Meteor (clue 5). The 6-berth Explorer (clue 1) can't be the Northwest, trailer A (clues 1 and 3), or the Lynewood (clue 1), so must be the Arundel. Clue 1 rules it out as trailer A or B and clue 4 as trailer D, so it must be trailer C. Therefore, from clue 1, the Lynewood must be trailer B, leaving the Eldorado Meteor as trailer D, with 2 berths (clue 4). The Northwest, which isn't

4-berth (clue 3), must be 5-berth, leaving the Lynewood as the 4-berth. So, from clue 2, the Lynewood must be the Olympus and the Northwest the Colorado.

A, Northwest Colorado, 5.
B, Lynewood Olympus, 4.
C, Arundel Explorer, 6.
D, Eldorado Meteor, 2.

Logi-5, p. 87

D	B	A	E	C
A	E	C	B	D
B	C	E	D	A
E	A	D	C	B
C	D	B	A	E

Sudoku, p. 87

4	1	5	3	6	8	2	7	9
3	7	9	4	2	1	8	6	5
6	8	2	7	9	5	4	3	1
2	6	4	9	1	3	5	8	7
7	5	3	2	8	4	1	9	6
1	9	8	6	5	7	3	4	2
5	2	6	8	4	9	7	1	3
8	3	1	5	7	6	9	2	4
9	4	7	1	3	2	6	5	8

Battleships, p. 88

Mixed Drinks, p. 89

The brandy is mixed with custard (clue 2), so the spirit in glass 5 to go along with the chicken stock (clue 3), which isn't rum (clue 1), vodka (clue 2), whisky (clue 3), or gin (clue 4), must be tequila. So, from clue 1, glass 2 must have the ketchup. Glass 3 doesn't contain vinegar (clue 1), custard (clue 2), or mustard (clue 4), so it must have the Worcestershire sauce. From clues 1, 2, and 4, the glasses in the back row contain rum, vodka, and gin, so the whisky, which now can't be in glass 6 (clue 3), must be in glass 4 and the brandy and custard must be in glass 6. So, from clue 2, glass 3 must have vodka and Worcestershire sauce. The rum is directly behind the vinegar (clue 1), so isn't in glass 2, and so glass 1 must contain rum and glass 4, whisky and vinegar. By elimination, the gin must be in glass 2 with the ketchup and the rum in glass 1 must be flavored with mustard.

1, rum and mustard; 2, gin and ketchup; 3, vodka and Worcestershire sauce; 4, whisky and vinegar; 5, tequila and chicken stock; 6, brandy and custard

Read the Signs, p. 90

The Pisces person will miss an appointment (clue 6), so Anne, whose birthday is later in the year than the person whose horoscope includes news of health problems for a pet (clue 2), can't be Pisces or Aries. Cora is a Leo (clue 1) and the Scorpio should expect a windfall (and large bar bill) (clue 6), so Anne, who will meet an old friend (clue 2) must be a Gemini. So, from clue 2, the pet's health problems must be destined for the Aries person. Eric is to expect an unexpected expense (clue 3) and the person who will lose an item will also receive news from overseas (clue 4), so Anne, the Gemini meeting an old friend, must prepare herself for an increased workload. We now know either the name or star sign for four pieces of bad news, so Cora, the Leo, must be the staff member who will lose an item and receive news from abroad. Eric's unexpected expense rules him out as the Pisces or the Aries, so he must be the Scorpio who will have the windfall. From clue 5, the person who will have the romance isn't an Aries, so must be the Pisces, leaving the Aries as the worker with the promise of a career advancement. This isn't Bill (clue 3), so it must be Dawn who is the Aries with an impending career move and a problem with a pet's paw, leaving Bill as the Pisces with the exciting romance and the missed appointment.

Anne, Gemini, meet old friend, increased workload.
Bill, Pisces, romance, miss appointment.
Cora, Leo, overseas news, lose item.
Dawn, Aries, career advance, pet's health.
Eric, Scorpio, windfall, unexpected expense.

Serve You Right, p. 92

Shelley is in 8th grade (clue 2), so Nicky, who is not in 10th or 11th grade (clue 3) or 7th grade, the pupil being served by Mavis (clue 3), must be in 9th grade. The 10th grade child is being served peas (clue 4), so is not Lee, who is having fish sticks (clue 5), or Rosie (clue 4), and must be Matthew, being served by Wendy (clue 6). Annie is serving the beans (clue 1), so Kay, who is not serving either the pies or the potatoes (clue 1), must be serving Lee with his fish sticks. By elimination, Lee must be in 11th grade and Mavis must be serving Rosie. The potatoes are not being served to Nicky or Shelley (clue 2), so they must be the item being served by Mavis to Rosie. Nicky is not being served with a pie (clue 3), so he must be receiving beans from Annie, and, by elimination, Hazel must be serving the pies to Shelley of 8th grade.

Annie, beans, Nicky, 9th grade.
Hazel, pie, Shelley, 8th grade.
Kay, fish sticks, Lee, 11th grade.
Mavis, potatoes, Rosie, 7th grade.
Wendy, peas, Matthew, 10th grade.

Fruitless Following, p. 94

Spike Spanner is behind tree 4 (clue 8), so the man behind tree 3, who isn't Nicky Nail, Dick Drill, or Ricky Wrench (clue 3) must be Mike Mallet, who has followed his prey from the Kwikee Mart (clue 2). So Ricky Wrench and Dick Drill must each be behind tree 1 or 2. The detective behind tree 1 is trying to advance his diamond theft case (clue 4), so Dick Drill, currently involved in a missing persons inquiry (clue 3) must be behind tree 2, with Ricky Wrench behind tree 1 looking for some diamonds, leaving Nicky Nail behind tree 5, having followed his suspect from the bus station (clue 4). Now, from clue 6, the detective who has followed a suspect from the railway station can't be behind tree 1 or 2 and we know it's not 3 or 5, so he must be Spike Spanner behind tree 4. The man with the dog was followed as a potential lead in the dog-napping case (clue 1), so the man who Ricky Wrench followed in connection with the diamond theft, who wasn't the man with the basket (clue 4), must be the man in the straw hat and he must have followed him to the park from O'Malley's bar (clue 5). By elimination, Dick Drill behind tree 2 must have followed his

suspect from the tram stop. So, from clue 7, the woman carrying the package must be being followed by Mike Mallet behind tree 3. She's not involved in the infidelity case (clue 7), so Mike Mallet must be looking into corruption in local government. So, from clue 7, the woman with the parasol must have been followed from the tram stop by Dick Drill behind tree 2. Finally, from clue 1, the potentially dog-napping man with the dog must be the prey of Spike Spanner behind tree 4 and must have been followed by him from the railway station, leaving Nick Nail behind tree 5 having followed a man with a basket from the bus station in connection with the infidelity case.

1, Ricky Wrench, man in straw hat, O'Malley's bar, diamond theft.
2, Dick Drill, woman with parasol, tram stop, missing person.
3, Mike Mallet, woman with package, Kwikee Mart, corruption.
4, Spike Spanner, man with dog, railway station, dog-napping.
5, Nicky Nail, man with basket, bus station, infidelity.

Court in the Act, p. 96

The two officers referred to in clue 4, who are both male, must be James and Barry. Since James was assigned to the drunk in public case (clue 5), Barry must have dealt with the offender guilty of vandalism, and the drunk must be Christian (clue 4). We know Martin, who dealt with the shoplifter (clue 3), is not Barry or James and clue 3 rules out Nathan. Since Rachel's surname is Atkins (clue 2), Martin's first name must be Pamela. We know Farouk was not the drunk, and, since his officer's surname is Lowther (clue 6), he cannot be the shoplifter, nor had he committed the disorderly conduct offense (clue 6). Since Jonathan was convicted of taking without consent (clue 1), Farouk must have been found guilty of vandalism, so Lowther is Barry's surname. So James, who is not Holloway (clue 5), must be Berryman. We have now fully identified four officers, so the fifth must be Nathan Holloway. Rachel, who did not deal with the disorderly conduct offender (clue 2), must have taken on the taking without consent offender, Jonathan. Now, by elimination, Nathan Holloway must have dealt with the disorderly conduct offender. Since Marlon was not the shoplifter (clue 3), Pamela's client must have been Craig, leaving Marlon as the disorderly conduct offender allocated to Nathan Holloway.

Christian, drunk in public, James Berryman.
Craig, shoplifting, Pamela Martin.
Farouk, vandalism, Barry Lowther.
Jonathan, taking without consent, Rachel Atkins.
Marlon, disorderly conduct, Nathan Holloway.

Lippie Service, p. 98

The film for which Rachel Morris has been nominated was released in November and has a two-word title (clue 1), and Miranda Kemp has been nominated as Best Actress (clue 1), so the female director of *The Marked Man* (clue 2) must be Imogen Penn. The May release has been nominated for its special effects (clue 3), but not by Hugh Talbot (clue 3). Rachel Morris' film was released in November, so the nominee for the May film must be Duncan McKee. *Queen of Manhattan* was released in July (clue 6), so, from clue 4, the nominee is not Imogen Penn, and the costume design nomination cannot be for the November film. Therefore the costume designer is not Rachel Morris and must be Hugh Talbot. We now know that the costume design award is not for the films released in May or July (clue 4), and as Duncan McKee is the nominee for the May film, it is also not for the September film (clue 4). Rachel Morris has been nominated for the November film, so the costume

design nomination must be for the January 2020 film. Therefore *The Marked Man*, with its nominated director Imogen Penn, must have been released in September (clue 4), leaving Miranda Kemp as the nominated leading actress in the July release. Therefore her performance must have been in *Queen of Manhattan*. By elimination, Rachel Morris must have written the nominated score. Therefore it was for a film with a two-word title, but not *Desert Ice* (clue 5), so it must have been *Funny Business*. *One Rainy Day* is not up for the special effects award (clue 3), so that must be for May's *Desert Ice*, leaving *One Rainy Day* as the film for which Hugh Talbot has been nominated for his costume designs.

May, *Desert Ice*, special effects, Duncan McKee.
July, *Queen of Manhattan*, leading actress, Miranda Kemp.
September, *The Marked Man*, director, Imogen Penn.
November, *Funny Business*, score, Rachel Morris.
January, *One Rainy Day*, costume design, Hugh Talbot.

Domino Search, p. 100

1	6	6	1	4	5	5	4
2	0	4	3	1	1	6	2
3	3	3	5	0	3	2	0
6	2	5	2	6	0	6	6
3	4	5	0	0	1	4	3
0	4	1	3	5	2	2	4
2	0	5	5	1	6	1	4

Art Dekko, p. 101

The artist behind canvas 5 isn't Bonny Kneah (clue 1), Della Kwah (clue 3), or Donna Tellow (clue 4). Artist 3 is hoping to attain cubism (clue 4), so, from clue 1, artist 5 can't be

Matt Ease and must be Dave Inchy, the would-be expressionist (clue 2). The art on canvas 4 can't be in the Dadaist style (clue 3) and isn't pointillist (clue 2), so it must be impressionist. So, from clue 1, Bonnie Kneah must be the cubist at canvas 3 and Matt Ease must be behind canvas 2. Now, from clue 3, Della Kwah can't be artist 1 and must be artist 4 and Matt Ease at canvas 2 must be the Dadaist, leaving Donna Tellow behind canvas 1 painting in style of the pointillists.

1, Donna Tellow, pointillism.
2, Matt Ease, Dadaism.
3, Bonnie Kneah, cubism.
4, Della Kwah, impressionism.
5, Dave Inchy, expressionism.

Odometer, p. 102

Since no car's first digit on the display is a zero (clue 6), and none has reached 50,000 miles (clue 2), and no digit appears in the same position on more than one display (clue 1), the four first digits must be 1, 2, 3 and 4. So that of automobile 3 must be 1 or 2, and that of automobile 1 must be 3 or 4 (clue 3). But the fourth number on its odometer is 4 (clue 7), so its first cannot be (clue 1). Therefore it must begin with a 3, and that of automobile 3 must start with 1 (clue 3). So, from clue 2, automobile 2's display must start with a 2, leaving the first digit on automobile 4's odometer as 4. So this vehicle is blue, and automobile 3 must be the Fiat (clue 4). We know automobile 1's fourth digit is 4, so this automobile cannot be the black Volvo, whose last three digits are 735 (clue 8). We know this vehicle is not number 3 or number 4, so it must be number 2. So, from clue 5, automobile 4's display ends in a 7. So this automobile cannot be the Audi (clue 9), which must, by elimination, be automobile 1, leaving automobile 4 as the Ford. The Audi's final digit is a 1 (clue 9), so this cannot be the automobile with a zero in that position (clue 6). We know the last digits on the odometers

of automobile 2 and automobile 4, so it must be automobile 3's display which ends in 0. So, from clue 6, 0 must be the third digit on automobile 1's odometer. We have now identified four of the digits on its odometer, so, from clue 3, its second must be an 8. So this automobile is not red (clue 4), and must be green, leaving automobile 3, the Fiat, as the red vehicle, whose second digit is a 9 (clue 4). We can now see, from clue 10, that 6 and 5 must be in third and fourth position on either automobile 3 or automobile 4, as must 9 and 8. But the display on automobile 3 already has a 9, so, from clue 1, its full display must be 19650, and that of automobile 4 must end with 987 (clue 10). One 2 and one 6 still remain to be assigned (clue 1). The 2 cannot be on automobile 2, since its display starts with that digit (clue 1), so it must be the second digit on automobile 4's odometer, leaving the 6 in that position on the odometer of automobile 2.

1, green Audi, 38041; 2, black Volvo, 26735; 3, red Fiat, 19650; 4, blue Ford, 42987.

Hot Wheels, p. 104

The automobile from Herring Street was burned out (clue 3) and Mr. Mason's automobile was repainted (clue 7). His automobile wasn't the Ford stolen from Spice Street (clue 1), nor did he keep it in York Street (clue 7), so it must have been lifted from Myrtle Street and, from clue 7 again, the Ford from Spice Street must have been found abandoned. Mr. Mason's automobile wasn't the BMW, which was dismantled (clue 6), the Renault (clue 4), or Mr. Kennedy's Toyota (clue 2), so it must have been the Volvo. Mr. Green's automobile from Barracks Street wasn't crashed (clue 5), so, by elimination, it must have been dismantled and was therefore the BMW, leaving the automobile from York Street as the one that crashed. It wasn't the Renault (clue 4), so must have been Mr. Kennedy's

Toyota, leaving the Renault as the burned-out automobile from Herring Street. This didn't belong to Mrs. Robins (clue 4), so must have been Ms. Wells', while Mrs. Robins owned the abandoned Ford.

Barracks Street, BMW, Mr. Green, dismantled.
Herring Street, Renault, Ms. Wells, burned out.
Myrtle Street, Volvo, Mr. Mason, repainted.
Spice Street, Ford, Mrs. Robins, abandoned.
York Street, Toyota, Mr. Kennedy, crashed.

Celebrity Sprouts, p. 106

Fleet Rosendal's garnish is sprout powder (clue 6) and Ollie James is responsible for the Sprout Ice Cream (clue 1), so the male chef who has developed the back-to-front Christmas dinner with Pulled Sprouts and turkey slices, who is not Anton Petitchou must be Don Corrode and, from clue 3, it is washed down with the sprout smoothie (clue 3). The chef who is matching his sprouts with snails isn't Celia (clue 5) or Ollie (clue 1), so it must be Anton Petitchou. The sprout texture isn't used by Celia Jones (clue 5), so it must be Ollie James' garnish to his Sprout Ice Cream, leaving sprout foam with Celia's dish. Anton's snails-and-lager additions don't go with the Sprout Brownie (clue 5), and the Sprout Kiev goes with a shot of vodka and a dash of tonic (clue 4), so Anton's dish must be the Sprout Porridge. Celia doesn't make the Sprout Brownie (clue 5), so she must make the Sprout Kiev with sprout foam and a vodka & tonic, leaving Fleet Rosendal as the creator of Sprout Brownie, sprinkled with sprout powder. He doesn't serve it with cranberry juice (clue 2), so it must arrive with a cup of appropriately green tea, leaving Ollie's ice cream and textures washed down with the cranberry juice.

Pulled Sprouts, Don Corrode, sliced turkey, sprout smoothie.
Sprout Brownie, Fleet Rosendal, sprout powder, green tea.
Sprout Ice Cream, Ollie James, textures of sprout, cranberry juice.
Sprout Kiev, Celia Jones, sprout foam, vodka & tonic.
Sprout Porridge, Anton Petitchou, snails, pint of lager.

The Balloon Goes Up, p. 108

David was terrified (clue 3), and Ronald landed on the road (clue 5), so, from clue 1, the man who landed among the grazing cows after feeling airsick must be John. The birthday tripper landed in a pond (clue 7), which rules out John and Ronald, nor was this passenger Pauline (clue 7). Mary had passed her exams (clue 4), so, by elimination, it must have been David's birthday. Therefore, the person who landed in the garden must be Mary or Pauline, so, from clue 2, one of these two must have remained calm and serene. We know Ronald was not airsick or terrified, nor did he enjoy his trip excitedly (clue 5), so he must be the one who couldn't look down and was therefore celebrating his job promotion (clue 6). So John, who was not marking his retirement (clue 4), must have been celebrating his ruby wedding, and, by elimination, it must have been Pauline who had retired. So she did not land in the garden (clue 2) and must have come down on the beach, leaving Mary's landing place as the garden. So, from clue 2, Pauline must have remained calm and serene, and Mary must therefore have enjoyed her trip excitedly.

David, birthday, terrified, pond.
John, ruby wedding, airsick, herd of cows.
Mary, passing exams, enjoyed excitedly, garden.
Pauline, retirement, calm and serene, beach.
Ronald, job promotion, couldn't look down, road.

Cruise Missing, p. 110

The cruiser spending the afternoon in the cooking class said, "Cakes, I hope," (clue 5), Mrs. Thomas planned to spend the afternoon sleeping (clue 3), and a woman was eating the green salad (clue 2), so Mr. Grey, who noted how much he wife would have enjoyed the food but who wasn't going to the pottery class (clue 1), must have been planning to spend the afternoon on the quoits court. The woman eating the avocado noted the similarity of its color to the one recently adopted by her husband (clue 3), so the woman with the green salad for lunch and the afternoon art class (clue 2), who wasn't the cruiser who promised to pop back later in the afternoon (clue 3), must have asked, "What time is tea?" Mrs. Thomas didn't liken her husband to an avocado (clue 3), so she must have said she'd pop back to the cabin to check on Mr. Thomas a little later, probably. We now know either the cruiser or the lunch to go with four quotes, so Mr. Simkin, who was having pea soup (clue 5), must have been the cruiser going to the cooking class and hoping to make unhealthy cakes. The cruiser who finished a green salad and then asked "What time is tea?" before going to the art class wasn't Mrs. Shepherd (clue 5), so it must have been Mrs. Lewes, leaving Mrs. Shepherd as the woman who spotted the likeness between her husband's current pallor and the color of her lunch. By elimination, she must have signed up for the pottery class. Finally Mr. Grey didn't say that his wife would have loved the asparagus (clue 1), so he must have been talking about the prawns, leaving Mrs. Thomas with the asparagus.

Mr. Grey, prawns, quoits, Wife would love this.

Mrs. Lewes, green salad, art class, What time is tea?

Mrs. Shepherd, avocado, pottery class, Color of husband.

Mr. Simkin, pea soup, cooking class, Cakes, I hope.

Mrs. Thomas, asparagus, sleeping, I'll pop back . . .

A Charmed Life, p. 112

The green juju engenders wealth (clue 2), so it is not adorned with shells (clue 1), cloth (clue 2), or beads (clue 3), and must be feathered. The blue beady mojo does not convey love (clue 3), wealth (clue 2), or power (clue 1), so it must deliver fame. The power amulet is ornamented with shells, so the love charm must be made of cloth. It is not purple (clue 3) so must be red. It cannot be D (clue 2), and since power and wealth are adjacent (clue 1) and fame is not next to love (clue 3), the red cloth love charm must be A, the green feathery wealth talisman B, the purple shell power amulet C, and the blue beads of fame D.

A, red cloth, love.

B, green feathers, wealth.

C, purple shells, power.

D, blue beads, fame.

Battleships, p. 113

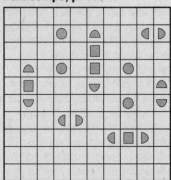

Top Deck, p. 114

The two women sitting in seats 7 and 8 can't include Naomi (clue 1), Helen (clue 5), or Janice (clue 6), so must be Laura and Pamela. Pamela is not in seat 8, so she must be in seat 7, with Laura in seat 8. From clue 2, Laura must be browsing the sports website. So the man in seat 5 reading the movie website (clue 2) can't be Kevin (clue 4). Nor is he Ian (clue 2), and Martin is referencing Wigglypedia (clue 3), so he must be Oliver. So the lady is seat 6 isn't Helen (clue 5) or Naomi (clue 1) and must be Janice. So, from clue 6, the person using the music website on the row of seats in front of Janice, but not next to the aisle (clue 6), must be Pamela in seat 7. So, from clue 6, the person playing World of Peace in an aisle seat must be the man in position 9. We know it's not Martin or Oliver and nor is it Kevin (clue 4), so it must be Ian. From clues 1 and 3, the occupants of seats 4 and 6 must each be using either Mugbook or Yourscraft. So Martin, looking up Wigglypedia, must be in seat 2, leaving the man in seat 4 as Kevin. Now, from clue 3, the person chirping on Chirrup can't be in seat 1 and must be in seat 3, leaving the woman in seat 1 playing Scribble. So, from clue 5, Helen must be chirping in seat 3, leaving the Scribble player in seat 1 as Naomi. So, from clue 1, Kevin in seat 4 must be updating his Mugbook profile and Janice in seat 6 must be playing Yourscraft.

1, Naomi, Scribble; 2, Martin, Wigglypedia; 3, Helen, Chirrup; 4, Kevin, Mugbook; 5, Oliver, movie website; 6, Janice, Yourscraft; 7, Pamela, music website; 8, Laura, sports website; 9, Ian; World of Peace

Hospital Exit, p. 116

Peter Redman played Dr. Scotty Gordon (clue 3), and Dougie Eliot's character is emigrating (clue 6), so Dr. Patrick Mulligan, who becomes a psychic, must be played by Larry Munro. Bonnie Corder didn't play Dr. CJ Forrest (clue 5), nor, since she's lost her job due to viewers' complaints (clue 5), was her role Dr. Jean Doumis, played by the unreliable actor (clue 4), so she must have

played Dr. Ginger McKay. Therefore, she isn't lost in the Bermuda Triangle (clue 1) or abducted by aliens, the fate of the character whose actor was convicted of theft (clue 3), so Dr. McKay must defect to Korea. Peter Redman's character, Dr. Scotty Gordon, isn't abducted by aliens (clue 3), so must be lost in the Bermuda Triangle and, by elimination, the theft-convicted actor whose character is abducted by aliens must be Helen Gauss. From the reason she's been fired, her character wasn't Dr. Jean Doumis, so must have been Dr. CJ Forrest, and Dougie Eliot's emigrating character must have been Dr. Jean Doumis (a French-Canadian) and Dougie is therefore unreliable. Finally, Larry Munro didn't demand a pay raise (clue 6), so he must have retired and the demand for a raise must have come from Peter Redman, who, as Dr. Gordon, is lost in the Bermuda Triangle.

Bonnie Calder, Dr. Ginger McKay, viewers' complaints, defected to Korea.
Dougie Eliot, Dr. Jean Doumis, unreliable, emigrated to Australia.
Helen Gauss, Dr. CJ Forrest, theft conviction, abducted by aliens.
Larry Munro, Dr. Pat Mulligan, retired, became psychic.
Peter Redman, Dr. Scotty Gordon, demanded raise, Bermuda Triangle.

Lunch in the Park, p. 118

The woman with 5 minutes left can't be figure E or figure F (clue 5), so figure D can't have 5 or 10 minutes left (clue 6), or, from the same clue, 15, 25, or 30 minutes, so she must have 20 minutes left. Therefore figure F has 15 minutes left and figure E has 25 minutes (clue 6). The woman with 30 minutes left can't be figure B (clue 2) or figure A (clue 5), so must be figure C, and the woman with 5 minutes left is figure B (clue 5). By elimination, figure A must have 10 minutes left. So Carol Bell must be figure B (clue 3) and Diane Eliot must be figure

D (clue 1), with the woman who is dozing, as figure E (clue 1). The woman reading a book, who is east of figure C but isn't figure F (clue 5), must be Diane Eliot, figure D. We now know figure E has 25 minutes of lunch left, so Vicky Unwin must have half an hour to go and is therefore figure C. Sue Ross can't be figure E or F (clue 4), so must be figure A and, from the same clue, the woman on the cell phone must have 15 minutes of her break left. Figure B, Carol Bell, with 5 minutes left, can't be eating ice cream (clue 2), or eating a banana (clue 5), so she must be listening to music. Molly Lane has more than 5 minutes left (clue 2), so the ice cream eater can't have 10 minutes and must have 30 minutes left, and is therefore Vicky Unwin, and the banana eater must be figure A, Sue Ross, with 10 minutes left. So, from clue 2, Molly Lane must have 25 minutes of her lunch hour left and must be figure E, leaving Jill Irving as figure F, with 15 minutes before she's expected back at the office.

A, Sue Ross, eating banana, 10 minutes.
B, Carol Bell, listening to MP3, 5 minutes.
C, Vicky Unwin, eating ice cream, 30 minutes.
D, Diane Eliot, reading book, 20 minutes.
E, Molly Lane, dozing, 25 minutes.
F, Jill Irving, talking on cell phone, 15 minutes.

Area 52, p. 120

From clue 1, the cylinder-shaped UFO came down in1960 and the Taurus Green one in 1988, so, from clue 4, the dumbbell-shaped UFO's collision with a pylon can't have been in 1974, nor was that the year of the sphere-shaped UFO's crash (clue 6). It was in 1967 that the UFO crashed while evading a fighter (clue 2), so clue 3 rules out 1974 for the flying saucer's crash, which was 7 years after a UFO suffered an onboard explosion, so the 1974 UFO must have been triangular and, also from clue 4, the collision with the pylon must have been

at Taurus Green in 1988. Now, the flying saucer must have crashed in 1967 or 1981, so it wasn't at Trantor Fell (clue 2). From clue 3, it wasn't at Pern Bridge and clue 5 rules out the Marsford incident, when a UFO flew into a hill, so the flying saucer must have crashed at Moonbury. It didn't have an onboard explosion (clue 3) and wasn't struck by lightning (clue 7) so must have been evading a fighter in 1967. Now, from clue 3, the onboard explosion must have been in 1960. From clue 5, the UFO which flew into a hill can't have been triangular, so must have been spherical and, by elimination, the triangular UFO must have been struck by lightning. From clue 3, the 1960 crash wasn't in Pern Bridge, so it must have been in Trantor Fell, and the Pern Bridge crash must have been in 1974.

1960, Trantor Fell, cylinder, onboard explosion.
1967, Moonbury, flying saucer, crashed avoiding fighter.
1974, Pern Bridge, triangular, struck by lightning.
1981, Marsford, sphere, flew into hill.
1988, Taurus Green, dumbbell, collision with pylon.

Rs and Js, p. 122

The Last Goodbye appeared in 2011 (clue 3). Rupert featured in the 2013 romance (clue 5), and Josephine in the one published in 2015 (clue 7), so clue 1 now rules out 2011, 2012, 2013, and 2015 as the year when the book featuring Raymond and Jeanette was published, so it must have appeared in 2014, and, from clue 1, *Amour No More* must have been the 2013 title featuring Rupert. Clue 4 now tells us neither Roland nor Roger can have been Josephine's lover in the 2015 work, so Rory must have been, and, from clue 4, Roger must have been the hero of *The Last Goodbye*, the 2011 book, and Roland must have appeared in the 2012 novel. Clue 6 now tells us Raymond and Jeanette must be the hero and heroine of *The Loneliest Nights*, which must have been published in 2014. This fact rules out 2015 for *A Heavy Heart* (clue 2), which must have appeared in 2012, leaving 2015 as the publication date of *A Fond Farewell.* From clue 2, Julia must have been Roger's star-crossed lover in the 2011 novel *The Last Goodbye,* so Rupert, whose female friend was not Jayne (clue 5), must have appeared with Jacqueline in *Amour No More,* leaving Jayne as the heroine of *A Heavy Heart.*

2011, *The Last Goodbye*, Roger, Julia.
2012, *A Heavy Heart*, Roland, Jayne.
2013, *Amour No More*, Rupert, Jacqueline.
2014, *The Loneliest Nights*, Raymond, Jeanette.
2015, *A Fond Farewell*, Rory, Josephine.

Take a Part, p. 124

The thriller is based on a bestseller (clue 2), one of the films had a great script but is a remake (clue 3), and *Deep Water*, which has a hot director, doesn't involve any of Donna's ex-boyfriends (clue 1); so the war film whose producer is an ex-boyfriend and is being made entirely in the studio (clue 4) and so can hardly have great locations and doesn't have a superb script must, therefore, have a hot co-star. It is not *Road Hog* (clue 2), *Blue Devil*, which is science fiction (clue 3), or *Night Watch*, which has nude scenes as its con factor (clue 5), so it must be *Wild Wings*. We now know that *Deep Water*, which has a hot director, isn't a remake and doesn't have an ex-boyfriend as producer, while its title rules out the nude scenes; from clue 1, it doesn't have an ex-boyfriend as director, so it must have a low budget. We know that it isn't the thriller, based on a bestseller, or the war film, and the title tells us it's not science fiction; nor is it the horror film (clue 1), so it must be the comedy. As the movie with the great script isn't *Blue Devil*, the sci-fi film (clue 3), it must be horror, and, by elimination, *Blue Devil* must have great

locations. *Night Watch*, with its nude scenes, can't be the film with a great script, whose con factor is being a remake, so it must be based on a bestseller, and is therefore the thriller. By elimination, the movie with the great script must be *Road Hog*, and *Blue Devil* must have a director who's one of Donna's ex-boyfriends.

Blue Devil, science fiction, great locations, ex-boyfriend director.
Deep Water, comedy, hot director, low budget.
Night Watch, thriller, based on bestseller, nude scenes.
Road Hog, horror, great script, remake.
Wild Wings, war, hot co-star, ex-boyfriend producer.

Cruising Home, p. 126

Mr. Simkin was sent to buy a djellaba (clue 1) and Mr. Thomas brought back a lantern (clue 2), so the man who went to buy a small rug and came back with a large carpet, who wasn't Mr. Lewes or Mr. Shepherd (clue 3), must have been Mr. Grey. Mr. Lewes tried the "I thought you said . . ." excuse, the man sent to buy a tagine asked, "What is a tagine?" (clue 2), and the man who bought the box of spices had by then run out of money (clue 4), so Mr. Grey, who didn't say that the salesman was very insistent, must have excused himself by saying that his large carpet was a bargain. Mr. Lewes didn't buy the basket (clue 3) and his excuse rules out the spices, so he must have bought the coasters. Mr. Thomas hadn't been send to buy the tagine or the jewelry box (clue 2), so he must have been sent to buy a leather bag, so the man sent to buy a tagine without the knowledge of what one is (clue 2) must have been Mr. Shepherd, and Mr. Lewes must have been sent to buy the jewelry box and returned with the line "I thought you said coasters." Also by elimination Mr. Thomas' excuse for buying a lantern rather than a leather bag must have been a very insistent salesman, leaving Mr. Simkin running out of money after buying a box of spices before he could get to the djellaba shop.

Mr. Grey, small rug, large carpet, was a bargain.

Mr. Lewes, jewelry box, coasters, "I thought you said . . .".

Mr. Shepherd, tagine, basket, "What is a . . .?".

Mr. Simkin, djellaba, box of spices, no money left.

Mr. Thomas, leather bag, lantern, insistent salesman.

I'm All Right Jack, p. 128

The Plummers live on Brick Road (clue 1), so the Joyners, who live on neither Millers Way nor Cobblers Drive (clue 2), or Locksmith Lane, where Jack Gardner is working (clue 4), must live on Tyler Street. The carpet-layer is working on Cobblers Drive (clue 3), so his employers are not the Plummers, the Joyners, the Bakers, for whom the sweep is working (clue 5), or the Butchers (clue 3), so he must be Jack Painter, working for the Pipers (clue 6). Jack Glaser is an electrician (clue 6), so Jack Naylor, who is neither a builder nor a decorator (clue 1), must be the chimney sweep working for Mr. and Mrs. Baker and by elimination, they must live on Millers Way. Also by elimination, Jack Gardner must be working for the Butchers. The builder is not working for the Joyners on Tyler Street or the Plummers (clue 1), so he must be Jack Gardner, doing work for the Butchers. The Joyners are not employing the decorator (clue 2), so it must be electrician Jack Glaser, and, by elimination, the decorator must be Jack Carpenter, who must be working for the Plummers on Brick Road.

Jack Carpenter, decorator, Plummer, Brick Road.

Jack Gardner, builder, Butcher, Locksmith Lane.

Jack Glaser, electrician, Joyner, Tyler Street.

Jack Naylor, chimney sweep, Baker, Millers Way.

Jack Painter, carpet layer, Piper, Cobblers Drive.

Troubled Waters, p. 130

There are at least two floors below Peter's apartment (clue 4) and Wilf Wynger lives above him, so Peter must live on the 2nd floor. One of the complaining residents lives in apartment 6 (clue 5), so Peter's apartment must be number 5 and Wilf, who does not live in apartment 7 (clue 2), must be in apartment 8. So the three complainers who share the same side of the block, one of whom must be on the 1st floor (clue 1), must live in apartments 4, 6, and 8, with the owner of apartment 2 absent. Apartment 7 doesn't have a complaining resident (clue 1) so must be absent, with apartments 3 and 1 being homes to malcontents. Tony Trubble is separated from the owner of the red Audi by one floor (clue 3), so they must each be in apartments 1 or 6. Apartment 6's owner has a black VW (clue 5), so this must be Tony, with the parking-obsessed Audi driver (clue 3) in apartment 1. So, from clue 6, Davina Dotty must be in apartment 4. Paul Petty drives the Ford (clue 4), so the Audi driver in apartment 1 must be Nora Newsance, leaving Paul Petty in apartment 3. The Mazda driver lives lower than Peter (clue 4), so that must be Davina Dotty in apartment 4, leaving Wilf Wynger in apartment 8 as the Toyota owner. Neither Davina with her Mazda nor Paul in his Ford is demanding automatic doors (clue 4), so that must be Tony Trubble's whine from apartment 6. Finally, Davina isn't complaining about planters, so this must be Paul Petty's complaint from apartment 3, leaving lighting in the garages as Davina Dotty's complaint from apartment 4.

Apartment 1, Nora Newsance, red Audi, parking in driveway.

Apartment 3, Paul Petty, white Ford, planters at entrance.

Apartment 4, Davina Dotty, gray Mazda, lighting in garage area.
Apartment 5, Peter Payshant (director).
Apartment 6, Tony Trubble, black VW, self-opening front door.
Apartment 8, Wilf Wynger, blue Toyota, puddle on roof.
Apartments 2 and 7 do not have complaints . . . at the moment.

After School, p. 132

Sam attended Miss Evans' class for 4 weeks (clue 5), so Miss Price's sessions, which Sam attended for an even number of weeks (clue 4), must have been the dance class he tried for 2 weeks (clue 1). Mrs. Barnes is the history teacher (clue 3), the French teacher runs the judo club (clue 3), and the English teacher was blessed with Sam's presence for three weeks (clue 2), so Miss Price, who doesn't teach science (clue 4), must be the math teacher. Mr. Abbot doesn't teach a language subject (clue 2), and we know it's not math or history, so it must be science. Mr. Gale doesn't teach French (clue 3), so he must teach English, leaving Miss Evans as the French teacher who also coaches judo (clue 3) and whose sessions Sam attended for four weeks. So, from clue 3, Sam must have attended history teacher Mrs. Barnes' after school sessions for 5 weeks. By elimination, Mr. Abbot's guitar classes (clue 2) must have held Sam's attention for 7 weeks. Finally Sam didn't stick at the chess club for 5 weeks (clue 7), so must have managed only 3 weeks, and so chess was the activity offered by English teacher Mr. Gale, leaving history teacher Mrs. Barnes holding the drumming sessions which Sam went to for 5 weeks.

Chess, 3 weeks, Mr. Gale, English.
Dance, 2 weeks, Miss Price, math.
Drums, 5 weeks, Mrs. Barnes, history.
Guitar, 7 weeks, Mr. Abbot, science.
Judo, 4 weeks, Miss Evans, French.

Logi-5, p. 134

A	E	D	B	C
B	A	C	D	E
C	D	B	E	A
E	B	A	C	D
D	C	E	A	B

Killer Sudoku, p. 134

8	6	7	4	9	2	5	3	1
5	3	1	7	6	8	2	4	9
4	2	9	3	1	5	6	7	8
3	1	4	5	2	6	8	9	7
7	8	6	1	4	9	3	2	5
2	9	5	8	3	7	1	6	4
9	5	8	2	7	3	4	1	6
6	4	2	9	5	1	7	8	3
1	7	3	6	8	4	9	5	2

Apostrophe's, p. 135

The total cost of the vegetable's is $3.40, so, from clue 3, the prices per pound of the veg on the back row must be $1.45 and that of the veg on the front row must be $1.95. The artichoke's, and the combinations of cabbage's and lettuce's, onion's and turnip's, and carrot's and tomato's each amount to the same price (clue 2). From the options available, the price of three pairings must each be 70 cents and so that must be the price of the artichokes. So, by elimination, the pepper's, at B (clue 4) are the only veg that can cost 60 cents. The cabbage's are in the top row (clue 5) and on the left-hand side (clue 1) so they must be in position A with, from clue 5, the artichoke's at E and, from clue 1, the lettuce's at F. The turnip's and tomato's are on the bottom row (clue 6) and the tomato's are right of the turnip's (clue 6), so the turnip's must be at G and the tomato's at H. Also from clue 6, the carrot's must be in position C, leaving the onion's at D. The pepper's cost 60 cents and there is no 10 cents or 35 cents offer, so the cabbage's, carrot's, and onion's on the back row, which must total 85 cents, must cost any of 20 cents, 25 cents, and 40 cents, and the lettuce's, tomato's, and turnip's must cost any of 30 cents, 45 cents, and 50 cents. The tomato's cost 5 cents more than the turnip's (clue 6), so they must be 50 cents and the turnip's 45 cents, leaving the lettuce's at 30 cents. From clue 2, the cabbage's are 40 cents, the carrot's 20 cents, and Know Your Onion's' onion's 25 cents.

A, cabbage's, 40 cents; B, pepper's, 60 cents; C, carrot's, 20 cents; D, onion's, 25 cents; E, artichoke's, 70 cents; F, lettuce's, 30 cents; G, turnip's, 45 cents; H, tomato's, 50 cents

Matter of Course, p. 136

Edward, whose total was 108, cannot have had his mishap at the seventeenth hole (clue 2), nor can he have been the man stuck in the bunker at the thirteenth, whose total was an odd number of strokes (clue 1). The Drone whose bad experience was at the eighth finished in 101 (clue 5), and it was Gerald who had a problem at the tenth (clue 7), so Edward must have suffered his mishap at the third. We know he did not linger in the bunker, nor did he lose his monocle in the rough (clue 2), while the Drone whose ball was lost down the hollow tree finished with 96 (clue 3) and it was Montague who tore his plus fours on the brambles (clue 6), so Edward's ball must have been taken by a squirrel. So, from clue 4, it must be Archie who scored 101 after a mishap at the eighth. His score rules him out for the hollow tree incident and the hole rules him out for the bunker, so he must have lost his monocle in the deep rough. We have now matched four holes with a name or a mishap, so it must have been at the seventeenth that Montague tore his plus fours. This leaves Gerald as the

Drone who lost his ball down a hollow tree but scored 96, and Rupert as the one who spent twenty minutes in the bunker. From clue 6, he must have taken 115 strokes to complete his round, and Montague must have gone round in 99.

Archie Fotheringhay, lost monocle in rough, 8th, 101.
Edward Tanqueray, ball taken by squirrel, 3rd, 108.
Gerald Huntington, lost ball in hollow tree, 10th, 96.
Montague Ffolliott, tore plus fours, 17th, 99.
Rupert de Grey, spent 20 minutes in bunker, 13th, 115.

Subtitles, p. 138

Saturday's movie will not be *Paws* or *Fifty Grades of Shale* (clue 1), *Kitties Insane* (clue 2) or *Slow and Serene* (clue 4), so must be *Six on the Settee*. So Friday's film must have Hungarian subtitles to its Bengali soundtrack (clue 3). This is not *Paws* or *Fifty Grades of Shale* (clue 1), so it must be *Slow and Serene* and Wednesday's movie must be screened in Dutch (clue 4). We have placed three films, so, from clue 1, *Paws*, a day after *Fifty Grades of Shale,* must be shown on Thursday and *Fifty Grades of Shale* on Wednesday. The Catalan film subtitled in Japanese (clue 1) won't be on Tuesday or Wednesday (clue 1), Thursday's *Paws* is subtitled in Icelandic (clue 1), and Friday's *Slow and Serene* is filmed in Bengali (clue 3), so the Catalan/Japanese film must be Saturday's *Six on the Settee*. We have matched three movies with subtitle languages, and we know *Kitties Insane* is not filmed in Afrikaans or subtitled in Filipino (clue 2), so it must be filmed in Estonian and subtitled in Georgian, leaving *Paws* filmed in Afrikaans and *Fifty Grades of Shale* subtitled in Filipino.

Tuesday, *Kitties Insane*, Estonian, Georgian.
Wednesday, *Fifty Grades of Shale*, Dutch, Filipino.
Thursday, *Paws*, Afrikaans, Icelandic.
Friday, *Slow and Serene*, Bengali, Hungarian.
Saturday, *Six on the Settee*, Catalan, Japanese.

Diving Expedition, p. 140

Jon dived to a depth of 32m (clue 1), Ben didn't exceed 20m (clue 4), and Gary was Marc's dive buddy, so Pippa, who dived to 30m but wasn't Heather's dive buddy (clue 5), must have been Emily's dive buddy, and that pair found the brooch (clue 2). Marc and Gary didn't dive to a depth of 20m or 23m (clue 3), so they must have dived to 15m. So, from clue 4, Ben must have dived to 20m, where he and his dive buddy found the old leather boot (clue 5), leaving Heather diving to 23m. Jon didn't dive with Kerry or Russ (clue 1), so must have dived to 32m with Tina. Russ found the silver goblet (clue 1), so Jon and Tina, who didn't find the coin (clue 6), must have seen the seal pup. We now know either the dive buddy or the item to go with four novices, so Russ must have found the goblet when diving to 23m with Heather. By elimination, Kerry must have dived to 20m with Ben and found the boot, and Marc and Gary must have found the coin at 15m.

Ben, Kerry, boot, 20
Emily, Pippa, broach, 30
Gary, Marc, coin, 15
Heather, Russ, goblet, 23
Jon, Tina, Seal pups, 32

Watch the Skies, p. 142

The object in Orion was spotted on Wednesday (clue 1), so Monday's sighting, which wasn't in Pegasus (clue 2), Ursa Minor (clue 4), or Taurus (clue 5), must have been in Ursa Major. Nor could Tuesday night's vision have been in Pegasus or Ursa Minor

(clues 2 and 4), and so it must have been in Taurus. So, from clue 5, the weather balloon must have been flying through Ursa Major on Monday, and the motorcycle headlamp must have confused Seamus on Wednesday in Orion. Now, we know it wasn't mistaken for a UFO (clue 1), the meteor was actually a spider (clue 3), and the supernova was observed in Pegasus, so he must have taken the Orion headlamp reflection for a moon of Jupiter. Clue 2 now reveals that the Pegasus supernova sighting occurred on Friday, leaving, by elimination, the British Airways plane in the second half of the week (clue 4) to have flown across Ursa Minor on Thursday. The only day now left available for the meteor/spider combination is Tuesday. Finally, the UFO which appeared before the firework must have been on Thursday, with the end-of-week firework display taking place on Friday.

Monday, Ursa Major, comet, weather balloon.
Tuesday, Taurus, meteor, spider.
Wednesday, Orion, moon of Jupiter, motorcycle lamp.
Thursday, Ursa Minor, UFO, airplane.
Friday, Pegasus, supernova, firework.

Spinning Off, p. 144

Kenny Young studied archaeology (clue 6) and in his new series George Todd dies and becomes a ghost (clue 2), so the theology student, who gets a job in TV and who is also male (clue 3), must be Ian Vickers. We know that in her new series Brenda Owen doesn't die and become a ghost or get a job in TV. It's called *Pinkies* (clue 5), so she can't move to London, which is the premise of *City Lights* (clue 1) or inherit a title, the premise of a series with a number in its title (clue 7), so she must marry a politician. She wasn't the drama student (clue 8) or the engineering student, whose new series is *Room 102* (clue 4), so, as we've identified the archaeology student and the theology student, Brenda Owen must have studied medicine. The series in which Ian Vickers gets a job in TV isn't *Number 7* (clue 3) and, as he studied theology, it can't be *Room 102*. We already know the ideas for *City Lights* and *Pinkies*, so Ian Vickers' new job must feature in *Hard Times*. We now know the subjects studied by three students. George Todd's subject wasn't drama (clue 8), so must have been engineering, and his new series, in which he becomes a ghost, is therefore *Room 102*. By elimination, Esther Reid must have studied drama. So her new series isn't *Number 7* (clue 8) and must be *City Lights*, in which she moves to London. Finally, it must be former archaeology student Kenny Young who will appear in *Number 7*, in which he must inherit a title.

Brenda Owen, medicine, *Pinkies*, marries politician.

Esther Reid, drama, *City Lights*, moves to London.

George Todd, engineering, *Room 102*, dies and becomes ghost.

Ian Vickers, theology, *Hard Times*, gets job in TV.

Kenny Young, archaeology, *Number 7*, inherits title.

Curry Favor, p. 146

Mille had the bean meal (clue 5), Alicia chose to drink beer (clue 4), and Liam risked the 5-chili meal, so the prawn meal and water, which wasn't the hottest and wasn't ordered by Danny (clue 2), must have been chosen by Fran. Alicia's meal was rated two chilies lower than the vegetable meal (clue 4), so hers wasn't rated 4 or 5. The fish meal has a 3-chili rating (clue 3), so Alicia's couldn't have been rated 1 chili, and the cola drinker had the 2-chili dish (clue 6), so beer-drinking Alicia must have had the 3-chili fish meal, with Liam's 5-chili choice being vegetable meal. By elimination Danny must have had the eggplant meal. The fruit juice didn't accompany the 4-chili meal or Liam's 5-chili

veg meal, so it must have gone with the 1-chili dish. By elimination Fran's prawn meal, accompanied by water, must have been the 4-chili dish and the lager must have gone with Liam's 5-chili vegetable meal. Finally Danny's eggplant meal wasn't the mildest (clue 5), so it must have been the 2-chili meal and he must have ordered cola, leaving Millie's bean meal as the 1-chili choice ordered with fruit juice.

Alicia, fish, 3, beer.
Danny, eggplant, 2, cola.
Fran, prawn, 4, water.
Liam, vegetable, 5, lager.
Millie, bean, 1, fruit juice.

Vacation Booking, p. 148

Audrey recommended the book by Kate Lovel (clue 1), so the one recommended by Zoe, which can't be by Lucy Mowiss (clue 3) or Coral Carey or Saul Snape (clue 5), must be by Greta Hallaby. Its one-word title (clue 4) can't be *Constantinople* (clue 3), so must be *Empress*. So, from clue 4, Patsy recommended *Constantinople*, which, from clue 3, must be the Lucy Mowiss book, and which Ivy thought was pornographic (clue 2). The book recommended by Dawn wasn't by Coral Carey (clue 6), so must have been by Saul Snape, and Jane must have recommended the Coral Carey. *Passion Fruit* can't have been the Coral Carey book recommended by Jane or the Kate Lovel book (clue 4), so must be the Saul Snape book recommended by Dawn. Audrey didn't recommend *Rupert's Woman* (clue 1), so must have recommended *Lord of Eagles*, and, by elimination, it must have been Jane who recommended *Rupert's Woman*, which Ivy thought boring (clue 1). Zoe's recommended book, *Empress*, can't have been described by Ivy as infantile (clue 3) or mildly amusing (clue 5), so she must have said it was badly researched. The book Ivy called infantile can only have been Dawn's recommendation, *Passion Fruit* (clue 3), and, by elimination, Audrey's recommendation, *Lord of Eagles* by Kate Lovel, must have struck Ivy as mildly amusing.

Audrey, *Lord of Eagles*, Kate Lovel, mildly amusing.
Dawn, *Passion Fruit*, Saul Snape, infantile.
Jane, *Rupert's Woman*, Coral Carey, boring.
Patsy, *Constantinople*, Lucy Mowiss, pornographic.
Zoe, *Empress*, Greta Hallaby, badly researched.

Battleships, p. 150

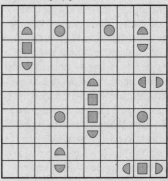

Sunny Specs, p. 151

From clue 3, the sum of the pairs on the top shelf must total $230 and that of the pairs on the bottom shelf $205. So the $60 pair must be on the bottom shelf and the $85 pair must be on the top shelf. The $65 pair is on the lower shelf (clue 3), so the third pair on the lower shelf must be $80, leaving the prices on the top shelf being $70, $75, and $85. Pair 3 is priced at $5 lower than pair 5, so they can't be $85 or, since $75 is a top-shelf price, $70, so they must be priced at $75 and pair 5 must be the $80 pair. So, from clue 3, pair 1 must be $70 and pair 4 must be $65, leaving pair 2 at $85 and pair 6 at $60. Now, from clue 1, the Shades model can only be number 2 at $85. So the Seafarer and Poolwear, which are adjacent

(clue 1) must be on the lower shelf and the Beachcool pair and Glider, which share a shelf (clue 2), must be on the top shelf with, from clue 2, Beachcool being pair 1 at $70 and Glider being pair 3 at $75. The EyeSpy specs aren't the cheapest pair 6 (clue 2) or, since Seafarer and Poolwear are adjacent, pair 5, so they must be pair 4 at $65, leaving Seafarer as pair 5 at $80 and Poolwear as pair 6 at $60.

1, Beachcool, $70; 2, Shades, $85; 3, Glider, $75; 4, EyeSpy, $65; 5, Seafarer, $80; 6, Poolwear, $60

Maiden Cruisers, p. 152

The new cook is joining the ship at Santorini (clue 3), so the job of the maiden from Harwich joining the ship at Monte Carlo, which isn't cabin steward, IT Facilitator, or receptionist (clue 5), must be working as the cabaret dancer and she is therefore Pippa. Sandy doesn't come from Portsmouth or Southampton (clue 3) and the Liverpool lady is Jane, so Sandy must be from Felixstowe. She is not joining at Gibraltar (clue 6) or Santorini (clue 3), and Marie is joining the ship's company at Barcelona, so Sandy must be joining at Naples. Jane isn't joining at Gibraltar either (clue 6), so she must be getting on board at Santorini and is therefore the cook. By elimination, Laura must be joining at Gibraltar. Sandy isn't the cabin steward (clue 6), or, since she is joining at Naples, the IT Facilitator (clue 1), so she must be joining as a receptionist. Laura, joining at Gibraltar, won't be the cabin steward (clue 6), so she must be the new IT Facilitator and Marie must be the new cabin steward. So she's not from Southampton (clue 6) and must be from Portsmouth, leaving Laura as the Southampton lady joining the *Moonshadow* in Gibraltar as IT Facilitator.

Jane, Liverpool, cook, Santorini.
Laura, Southampton, IT Facilitator, Gibraltar.

Marie, Portsmouth, cabin steward,
Barcelona.
Pippa, Harwich, dancer, Monte Carlo.
Sandy, Felixstowe, receptionist, Naples.

Pool Party, p. 154

Ms. Prentice is number 5 (clue 5). From clue
1, Ms. Myers cannot be 1, 4, 7, 8, or 9, nor
can she be Harriet, in position 6 (clue 7),
and this clue, combined with clue 1, also
rules her out as number 3, so she must be in
position 2. Therefore Alicia is Alicia Prentice,
in position 5 and number 4 is Ms. Jordan
(clue 1). From clue 4, Cassandra Orton
cannot be 3, 7, 8, or 9, and we know she is
not 2, 4, 5, or 6, so she must be in position
1. So, from clue 4, Ms. Lawson must be
number 3. We have now placed Ms. Jordan,
Ms. Lawson, and Ms. Prentice, so, from
clue 7, Harriet, number 6, must be Harriet
Ryan. So Diane is either 7 or 8 (clue 3). From
names already placed, Beverley and Ines
cannot be at either end of the front or middle
rows, so they must be in the back row, and
Ms. Quigley must be number 8 (clue 2).
From clue 3, since we now know number 7
must be either Ines or Beverley, Diane must
be Diane Quigley in position 8. Clue 8 now
tells us Frances must be Frances Jordan
in position 4 and Gill must be Gill Myers
in position 2. So, by elimination, number 3
must be Eve. Therefore, from clue 2, Ines
cannot be number 9 and must be number 7,
leaving number 9 as Beverley. Finally, from
clue 6, the latter must be Beverley Kettley
and Ines must be Ines Nolan.

1 Cassandra Orton; 2 Gill Myers; 3 Eve
Lawson
4 Frances Jordan; 5 Alicia Prentice; 6
Harriet Ryan
7 Ines Nolan; 8 Diane Quigley; 9 Beverley
Kettley

Steaks Are High, p. 156

Charlie Chomp doesn't touch wine, nor is he
sampling yak-in-cola (clue 3). Nicky Nibble is
sticking to the soda water (clue 7), so Charlie
must be drinking orange juice. So, since this
doesn't go with bison or wildebeest (clue 5)
and Chester Chewett has been treated to
squirrel (clue 2), Charlie must be enjoying
a whale burger, combined with the wombat
steak (clue 1). Chester isn't drinking cola
with his squirrel and Terry Trencher-Manne is
on something stronger (clue 6), so the guinea
pig for the yak/cola combination along with
his camel steak must be Gordon Guzzler.
We have assigned the cola and the orange
juice, and the red wine is washing down an
alligator steak (clue 4), so the emu cutlet,
which isn't matched with white wine (clue
6), must be being tempered with soda water
and is therefore Nicky Nibble's first course.
By elimination, the white wine must now be
accompanying the zebra steak, which isn't
Terry Trencher-Manne's choice, so he must
be the guest trying to forget his alligator
steak with the help of a bottle of red wine
(clue 4), leaving Chester Chewett tucking
into zebra. By elimination, the bison eater
must be Terry T-M, leaving Nicky Nibble
contemplating a sleepless night trying to
digest his wildebeest-burger.

Charlie Chomp, wombat, whale, orange
juice.
Chester Chewett, zebra, squirrel, white
wine.
Gordon Guzzler, camel, yak, cola.
Nicky Nibble, emu, wildebeest, soda
water.
Terry Trencher-Manne, alligator, bison,
red wine.

Late Cut, p. 158

Douglas will be 20 mins. late (clue 5). The
person delayed on the bus will be 5 mins.
late (clue 3), so Annabel, who will be 5 mins.
more late than the customer on the school
run and 5 mins. less later than Kathryn's

customer (clue 3) must be running 15 mins. late. So, from clue 3, Kathryn's customer must be the 20-mins. late Douglas and the school run problem must be delaying one customer for 10 mins. before they occupy seat 2 (clue 4). Gordon's customer is stuck in a traffic jam (clue 6), so they're not delayed for 5 or 10 mins. Nor are they delayed for 25 mins. (clue 6) so this must be the 15-mins. delayed Annabel. So, from clue 1, Justin's customer can't be delayed by any of 10, 15, 20 or 25 mins. and must be the customer who will be 5 mins. late because of a tardy bus and, also from clue 1, Hannah's customer must be the seat 2 customer delayed for 10 mins. on the school run. Eleanor will have seat 3, so Douglas, who will be seen to by Kathryn but who isn't in seat 1 (clue 5) or seat 4 (clue 3), will be in seat 5. So he can't be delayed waiting for a delivery (clue 1) and must be having a problem because his automobile won't start. So, from clue 1, Barnaby can't be the customer booked at seat 4 and must be due to sit in seat 2 to be dealt with by Hannah when he arrives 10 mins. late after the school run, the customer in seat 1 must be waiting at home for a delivery, and Justin will deal with Eleanor in seat 3 when she arrives 5 mins. late off the bus. By elimination, Claudia must be Imogen's customer due for seat 1 but running 25 mins. late because of late delivery. This leaves empty chair 4 waiting for Gordon's customer Annabel who will be 15 mins. late after being stuck in a traffic jam.

1, Claudia, Imogen, delivery late, 25 mins.
2, Barnaby, Hannah, school run, 10 mins.
3, Eleanor, Justin, bus, 5 mins.
4, Annabel, Gordon, traffic jam, 15 mins.
5, Douglas, Kathryn, automobile won't start, 20 mins.

Traveling Player, p. 160

The man for whom Laurinda substituted on Monday (clue 4) wasn't Christopher Peddle (clue 1) or Charles Stopps (clue 3), so it must have been Frank Flatts. On Tuesday she stood in for Joanne Keyes (clue 4), so the day that she took the place of Susan Pypes, which wasn't Thursday or Friday, must have been Wednesday. So, from clue 2, Thursday's recital must have started at 7 p.m. and St. Jethro's must have been the location for the Friday appointment. Monday's engagement wasn't at Christchurch (clue 1) or St. Mildred's (clue 2) nor, since Tuesday's regular player wasn't Charles Stopps, was it at All Saints (clue 3), so it must have been at St. Seymour's. Since she substituted for Frank Flatts, it wasn't at 7:15 p.m. or 7:30 p.m. (clue 1) and wasn't at 6:45 p.m. (clue 5), so must have been at 6:30 p.m. We know the regular players for Monday, Tuesday, and Wednesday, so Charles Stopps must have had the evening off on Thursday or Friday and the appointment at All Saints must have been on Wednesday or Thursday (clue 3). It wasn't Wednesday (clue 3), so All Saints must have been the Thursday engagement and Charles Stopps must be the regular organist at St. Jethro's where Laurinda played on Friday. By elimination, Christopher Peddle must be the organist at All Saints, where Laurinda played at 7 p.m. on Thursday. So, from clue 3, the recital standing in for Charles Stopps couldn't have begun at 6:45 p.m. or 7:30 p.m. and must have been at 7:15 p.m., with the playing at St. Mildred's beginning at 7:30 p.m. So this wasn't on Wednesday (clue 3) and must have been on Tuesday when Laurinda replaced Joanne Keyes, leaving Wednesday's engagement as the one at Christchurch where Laurinda covered for Susan Pypes and began at 6:45 p.m.

Monday, St. Seymour's, Frank Flatts, 6:30 p.m.
Tuesday, St. Mildred's, Joanne Keyes, 7:30 p.m.
Wednesday, Christchurch, Susan Pypes, 6:45 p.m.

Thursday, All Saints, Christopher Peddle, 7:00 p.m.
Friday, St. Jethro's, Charles Stopps, 7:15 p.m.

In the House, p. 162

The former politician was voted out first (clue 2). The eventual winner was not the TV personality (clue 1), or the retired athlete (clue 4), and clue 5 rules out the gossip columnist, so the winner must have been the male radio presenter (clue 3). He cannot be Clyde Crowe (clue 1), or Max, who was voted out second (clue 6), so he must be Steve. The third to go was not the gossip columnist (clue 5), and clue 1 rules out the TV personality, who departed next after Clyde Crowe, and we know neither the former politician nor the radio presenter was expelled third, so the retired athlete must have been. So Pushey, who was not the winner, must have been voted out fourth (clue 4). This person is not Linda (clue 4), and we know Clyde is Crowe and the positions in which Max and Steve finished, so Pushey must be Adrienne Pushey. Steve, the winner, cannot be Headstrong (clue 7), nor is he Boast (clue 3), and we know he is not Crowe or Pushey, so he must be Steve Loudleigh. Adrienne is not the gossip columnist (clue 7), so she must be the TV personality. Therefore, from clue 1, Clyde Crowe must be the retired athlete expelled third, leaving Linda as the politician voted out first. She is not Headstrong (clue 2), so she must be Linda Boast, leaving Headstrong as Max Headstong, who must be the gossip columnist.

Adrienne Pushey, TV personality, fourth.
Clyde Crowe, retired athlete, third.
Linda Boast, former politician, first.
Max Headstrong, gossip columnist, second.
Steve Loudleigh, radio presenter, winner.

Orbis in Urbis, p. 164

The 113 orbs were not found by Terry Pathic (clue1), Claire Voyant (clue 3), Sy Kick (clue 3), or Sue Pernatural (clue 4), so must have been counted by Misty Cal. The 5 orbs were not seen by Terry Pathic (clue 1), Claire Voyant (clue 3), or Sy Kick (clue 3), so Sue Pernatural photographed them and the 15 orbs were attributed to time travelers (clue 4). The orbs around Ashcliffe Library were not blamed on dust (clue 5), time travelers, or aliens (clue 4), and the ghosts haunted the Radleian Museum (clue 3), so the Ashcliffe must have been buzzing with ideas, of which there were 20 (clue 2). The River Pits Institute did not have 5, 10, or 113 orbs (clue 1) so must have had 15 time travelers. So, from clue 1, Terry Pathic must have photographed 10 orbs and Sue Pernatural's 5 orbs must have been aliens. We have already matched 3 phenomena with landmarks and the aliens were not at Circus (clue 5), so they must have infested the Bodmolean Camera. Sy Kick spotted more orbs than Claire Voyant (clue 3), so he must have logged 20 ideas and she must have counted 15 time travelers. Finally, Misty Cal's 113 orbs weren't at the Radleian Museum (clue 3), so they must have been dusty orbs at Circus, leaving Terry Pathic finding 10 ghosts at the Radleian Museum.

Claire Voyant, River Pits Institute, 15 time travelers.
Misty Cal, Circus, 133 dust particles.
Sue Pernatural, Bodmolean Camera, 5 aliens.
Sy Kick, Ashcliffe Library, 20 ideas.
Terry Pathic, Radleian Museum, 10 ghosts.

In the Jug, p. 166

The two jugs containing mango add up to 7 (clue 3), so they must be 2 and 5 or 4 and 3. No two adjacent jugs have the same flavor (clue 3), so the mangos can't be 4 and 3 and must be 5 and 2. Jug 1 doesn't have any banana juice (clue 3) or lemon juice (clue 4), so it must have pineapple and orange and, from clue 4, jug 2 must have mango and lemon. The two banana flavors aren't in adjacent jugs (clue 2), so they must now be in jug 3 and in jug 5 with the mango. The second lemon can't be in jug 3 (clue 2) so must be in jug 4. So, from clue 4, the second pineapple must be in jug 3, with the banana, leaving jug 4 having a blend of lemon and orange.

1, orange and pineapple.
2, mango and lemon.
3, pineapple and banana.
4, lemon and orange.
5, banana and mango.

Sign-In, p. 167

4	6	2	3	5	1
3	1	4	5	2	6
1	2	6	4	3	5
5	3	1	6	4	2
6	4	5	2	1	3
2	5	3	1	6	4

Sudoku, p. 167

4	7	5	3	8	6	2	9	1
8	6	2	4	1	9	5	3	7
3	9	1	2	7	5	8	4	6
2	8	3	9	4	7	6	1	5
6	1	4	5	3	2	9	7	8
9	5	7	1	6	8	3	2	4
5	2	8	7	9	1	4	6	3
7	3	9	6	5	4	1	8	2
1	4	6	8	2	3	7	5	9

Domino Search, p. 168

2	1	1	3	6	2	3	0
6	6	6	4	0	5	1	3
4	5	1	5	6	3	5	3
2	4	2	0	0	1	4	4
2	6	3	4	5	5	0	2
5	0	0	1	2	4	4	1
1	6	2	3	0	6	3	5

Candy Crush, p. 169

The boy served last wasn't in position 4 (clue 1), 3 (clue 4), or 1 (clue 3), so he must have been in position 2 and, from clue 3, the boy in position 1 must have wanted pear drops. Wesley wasn't in positions 3 or 4 (clue 4). He was served immediately after the boy in position 3 (clue 3) who, from clue 1, couldn't have been served third, so Wesley couldn't have been the fourth-served boy in position 2. So Wesley must have been in position 1. The boy served second wasn't Sidney or standing next to Sidney (clue 2), so he can't have been in position 3. So the boy in position 3, who we know wasn't served third or fourth, must have been served first, and from clue 4, Wesley, in position 1 must have received his pear drops second, leaving the boy served third in position 4. So, from clue 2, the boy in position 3 must have wanted aniseed balls and, from clue 4, he must have been Rodney. Now, from clue 2, Sidney wasn't in position 2, so he must have been in place 4. He didn't order gobstoppers so must have wanted a sherbet fountain, leaving boy number 2 as Barney ordering gobstoppers and being served last.

1, Wesley, pear drops, second.
2, Barney, gobstoppers, fourth.
3, Rodney, aniseed balls, first.
4, Sidney, sherbet fountain, third.

On Your Bikes, p. 170

From clues 1 and 4, the riders on bikes 1 and 2 have each either won 1 or 2 races. So the rider of bike 3, who has won a least once (clue 3), must have won 3 times so far this season and the rider of bike 4 must have yet to win. The bike ridden by the rider with one win isn't the Dash 50 or the Rapide MKlll (clue 1). Since the rider with no wins is in position 4, from clue 2, Graham Gere on the Scuttle Buzz, who has won more times than rider 2, can't have won just 1 time, so the single win rider must be riding the Flite XXR. This isn't the bike in position 1 (clue 4), so it must be bike 2, leaving the rider of bike 1 as the rider with 2 wins. The Flite XXR isn't being ridden by Colin Crouch (clue 4) or, from its 1 win, Theresa Twist (clue 1), so it must be ridden by Lorinda Leane. Also from clues 1 and 4, bike 1 isn't being ridden by Theresa Twist or Colin Crouch and so must be Graham Gere on his Scuttle Buzz with 2 wins so far. Theresa Twist isn't on bike 4 (clue 1), so she must be riding bike 3, leaving Colin Crouch on bike 4. From clue 1, he must be on the Rapide MkIII and not won yet this season, with Theresa Twist having won 3 times on her Dash 50.

1, Graham Gere, Scuttle Buzz, 2 wins.
2, Lorinda Leane, Flite XXR, 1 win.
3, Theresa Twist, Dash 50, 3 wins.
4, Colin Crouch, Rapide MkIII, no wins.

Battleships, p. 171

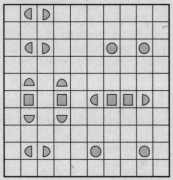

Summer Shows, p. 172

Andrew was in *Hooray for Vacations!* in 2014 (clue 5), so, from clue 1, he can't have been in *Fun in the Sun!* in Brightbourne in 2010, 2013, or 2015, so he must have been there in 2012. From the same clue, it must have been 2013 when he was at the Galleon in *Summer Stars!* The Neptune is in Swanmouth (clue 2), so Andrew can't have been there in 2012. Nor did he appear at the Marine Pier or Pierhead in that year (clue 2), so the theater in Brightbourne must be the Anchorage. We now know the locations of the Anchorage and the Neptune. Neither the Marine Pier nor the Pierhead is in Havensands (clue 3), so that must be where Andrew was at the Galleon in *Summer Stars!* Now, from clue 2, Andrew can't have been at the Neptune in 2010 or 2015 and we know the theaters at which he performed in 2012 and 2013, so he must have been at the Neptune in Swanmouth in 2014, when he was in *Hooray for Vacations!* and, from the same clue, he was at the Marine Pier in 2015, leaving the theater in 2010 as the Pierhead. He wasn't in Dingle-on-Sea in 2010 (clue 4), so the Pierhead must be in Marlcliff, leaving Dingle-on-Sea as the location of the Marine Pier, the 2015 theater. Therefore the 2015 show wasn't *Seaside Sensation!* (clue 4) and must be *Song of*

Summer!, leaving *Seaside Sensation!* as the show in which Andrew appeared in 2010 at Marlcliff's Pierhead Theater.

2010, Marlcliff, Pierhead, *Seaside Sensation!*
2012, Brightbourne, Anchorage, *Fun in the Sun!*
2013, Havensands, Galleon, *Summer Stars!*
2014, Swanmouth, Neptune, *Hooray for Vacations!*
2015, Dingle-on-Sea, Marine Pier, *Song of Summer!*

Cool Cats, p. 174

Giles Davis plays the castanets (clue 4*), Bop and Hop* features the washboard player (clue 1), and the guitar player is also a virtuoso on the pan pipes (clue 5), so Tammy Dorsey, who blows her first instrument on her album *Far Out* but doesn't also blow on the kazoo (clue 2), must play the spoons. So she isn't the alto sax player (clue 3) and the tenor saxophonist has released *Bluer than Green* (clue 3), so Tammy Dorsey must play the trumpet and spoons on her album *Far Out*. We now know the guitar and pan pipe player isn't Tammy Dorsey or Giles Davis, nor is it Jet Baker (clue 5), and Fizzy Gillespie plays the piano (clue 1), so the guitar and pan pipe player must be Charlie Barker. His album isn't *Kinda Cool* (clue 2) and we know at least one instrument for three others, so Charlie Barker must play guitar and pan pipes on *Mellow Mood*. Fizzy Gillespie's album isn't *Bop and Hop* and her piano rules out *Bluer than Green*, so she must have released *Kinda Cool*. She doesn't play the washboard (clue 1), so she must play piano and kazoo. By elimination, Jet Baker must be the washboard player on *Bop and Hop*. So he doesn't play tenor sax and must play alto sax and washboard, leaving Giles Davis playing tenor sax and castanets on *Bluer than Green*.

Charlie Barker, *Mellow Mood*, guitar and pan pipes.
Fizzy Gillespie, *Kinda Cool*, piano and kazoo.
Giles Davis, *Bluer than Green*, tenor sax and castanets.
Jet Baker, *Bop and Hop*, alto sax and washboard.
Tammy Dorsey, *Far Out*, trumpet and spoons.

Party Animals, p. 176

The boy who won at musical chairs and broke Miranda's new toy (clue 3) was not Dylan, who poured juice into the chips (clue 2), or Frankie (clue 3), so he must have been Jackson. The boy who refused to hand over his present was not Dylan (clue 2) so must have been Frankie. We have identified the ways in which the boys disgraced themselves, so the child who punched Miranda must have been a girl. She did not give the fruit (clue 1), the jigsaw puzzle or the automobile (clue 4), and Frankie gave the dinosaur (clue 3), so she must have given the crayons. So she was not Daisy (clue 3) and must have been Betty, and Daisy, who won hide the thimble (clue 3) must have given the fruit and eaten Miranda's cake (clue 1). From her gift, Betty did not win blind man's buff (clue 4) or pin the tail on the donkey (clue 5), so she must have won pass the package. By elimination, it was Dylan who gave the jigsaw puzzle and won blind man's buff (clue 4), Jackson who gave the toy automobile, and Frankie who won pin the tail on the donkey after refusing to hand over the dinosaur.

Betty, crayons, pass the package, punched Miranda.
Daisy, fruit, hide the thimble, ate cake.
Dylan, jigsaw puzzle, blind man's buff, poured orange juice on chips.
Frankie, dinosaur, pin the tail on the donkey, refused to give present.
Jackson, car, musical chairs, broke toy.

What a Scorcher, p. 178

Mr. Chard lives at no. 2 (clue 4), so the man who is burning sausages immediately between the houses belonging to Mr. Sinder and Mr. Krisp (clue 1) must live at no. 6 or no. 8. The man at no. 6 is burning pork chops (clue 2), so the man burning sausages must live at 8 Charcoal Avenue. He's not Mr. Sinder or Mr. Krisp (clue 1), and Mr. Sere is cremating an ear of corn (clue 3), so it must be Mr. Synge who's burning sausages at no. 8. The man at 10 Charcoal Avenue must now be either Mr. Krisp or Mr. Sinder, so Mr. Sere must be charring his sweet corn at no. 4. Mr. Chard isn't cooking chicken (clue 4), so he must be burning the steak, leaving the chicken drumsticks on the barbecue at no. 10. They aren't being cooked by Mr. Krisp (clue 4), so they must be being burnt by Mr. Sinder, leaving Mr. Krisp crisping his pork chops at no. 6.

No. 2, Mr. Chard, steak.
No. 4, Mr. Sere, sweet corn.
No. 6, Mr. Krisp, pork chops.
No. 8, Mr. Synge, sausages.
No. 10, Mr. Sinder, chicken drumsticks.

Battleships, p. 179

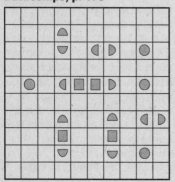

Domino Search, p. 180

0	1	5	6	6	6	5	4
6	1	5	4	4	0	2	4
6	5	4	3	1	0	2	3
3	2	2	0	5	0	5	6
2	0	3	6	2	1	4	2
5	3	0	2	5	0	1	6
4	1	3	3	1	4	3	1

Cyber Caves, p. 181

Egg's search engine is not cave 5, home of the web log, or cave 3 (clue 4), or, since it is not adjacent to cave 5, caves 1 or 4 (also clue 4). So the search engine must be cave 2, and the social network is cave 3 (clue 1). Now, from clue 2, Tweeter can't be in cave 1 and must be run from cave 4 and Agg must be the social networking host in cave 3. We have placed 4 web sites, so cave 1 must host Flicker. It is adjacent to Igg's site and is not the property of Ogg (clue 3), so Flicker must be Ugg's domain, Igg must be the web logger, and Ogg and his flock of birds must run Tweeter.

1, Ugg, Flicker.
2, Egg, search engine.
3, Agg, social network.
4, Ogg, Tweeter.
5, Igg, web log.

Martial Arts, p. 182

The Thai boxing demo lasted 25 mins. (clue 1), so, from clue 3, the 20-min. demonstration by Bridget and her club (clue 2) couldn't have been a demonstration of kendo or ju jitsu, nor was it aikido (clue 2), so Bridget's 20-min. demonstration must have been for the Tae kwon do club. Callum is the chief instructor of the ju jitsu club (club 3) and aikido signed up 11 members, so Matthew, whose club signed up 8 members but isn't the instructor of the Thai boxing (clue 1), must be the instructor of the kendo club. The club that performed for 35 mins. signed up 5 new members (clue 4), so the 25-min. Thai boxing demonstration, which didn't sign up only 2 members (clue 1), must have signed up 9 new members. We now know the martial art, the length of demonstration, or the instructor for four numbers of new members, so the 20-mins. of Tae kwon do by Bridget must have attracted 2 new members. The 9 new members at the Thai boxing club weren't attracted by Lizzie (clue 5), so the Thai boxing instructor must be Andy, leaving Lizzie as the aikido instructor. By elimination, the club which attracted 5 members after a 35-min. performance must be the ju jitsu club coached by Callum. So, from clue 3, Matthew's kendo demonstration must have lasted 40 mins. and Lizzie's aikido demonstration must have been for 30 mins.

Aikido, 30 mins., Lizzie, 11 members.
Ju jitsu, 35 mins., Callum, 5 members.
Kendo, 40 mins., Matthew, 8 members.
Tae kwon do, 20 mins., Bridget, 2 members.
Thai boxing, 25 mins., Andy, 9 members.

Fancy That!, p. 184

Andy Anagram, Chris Conundrum, and Terry Teaser were all in the same row of cells and none was dressed as Miss Raffles (clue 2), so, from the same clue, the man dressed as Miss Raffles must have been in the same row of cells as Percy with a cell number half of his. So the Miss Raffles impersonator must have been in cell 1 and Percy Puzzle must have been in cell 2. So Andy, Chris, and Terry must have occupied cells 4, 5, and 6. From clue 3, Chris Conundrum, in a cell numbered one higher than Quentin Quiz, must be in cell 4, with Quentin in cell 3, leaving Eddie Enigma in the guise of Miss Raffles in cell 1. Also from clue 3, we know that either Quentin in cell 3 or Percy in cell 2 must be dressed as Beau Tighe, so

neither can be the man disguised as Hamish Hazel, who isn't in the adjoining cell (clue 4). So the man in the Sir Coward de Custarde costume must have had cell 4 or 5 (clue 3). He wasn't Chris Conundrum in cell 4 (clue 3) so must have been in cell 5, and Beam Tighe must have been in cell 2. We have already seen that the Hamish Hazel costume isn't in cells 2 or 3, so it must have been Chris Conundrum's costume with, from clue 1, Quentin Quiz in cell 3 in the Ugg costume. By elimination, Percy Puzzle must have gone to the party as Beau Tighe, Terry Teaser must be dressed as Montague Ffollliot in cell 6, and the man dressed as Sir Coward de Custarde in cell 5 must be Andy Anagram.

1, Eddie Enigma, Miss Raffles.
2, Percy Puzzle, Beau Tighe.
3, Quentin Quiz, Ugg.
4, Chris Conundrum, Hamish Hazel.
5, Andy Anagram, Sir Coward de Custarde.
6, Terry Teaser, Montague Ffolliott.

Rocket Full of PIE, p. 186

Bruce Bean is in pod 5 (clue 1) and the ship's commander is in pod 3 (clue 5), so engineer Amanda Armstrong must be in pod 2 (clue 4). The crew member in pod 1 isn't the communications officer (clue 3), the doctor (clue 4), the geologist (clue 7), or the physicist (clue 8), so it must be the biologist. From clue 3 and the arrangement of pods, the crew member who will be woken 7th must be in either pod 1 or 3. So it's not Amanda Armstrong or Bruce Bean. Nor is it Sheila Shepard (clue 3), Andrea Aldrin (clue 4), or Sidney Scott (clue 6), and Caroline Conrad will be 6th to be woken (clue 7), so the 7th person to be woken must be Marcus Mitchell. So he isn't in pod 7. Nor is that person Sheila Shepard (clue 3), Andrea Aldrin (clue 4), or Sidney Scott (clue 6) and so must be Caroline Conrad. She isn't the communications officer (clue 3), the doctor, who will be woken first (clue 4), or the geologist, who is in an even-numbered pod (clue 7), so she must be the physicist. Now, the only level left that can accommodate both Andrea Aldrin and the doctor (clue 4) is pods 4 and 5, with Andrea in pod 4, being woken 4th (clue 8) and Bruce Bean in pod 5 being the doctor who will be woken 1st. So, from clue 3, Sheila Shepard must be the commander in pod 3, the biologist in pod 1 must be the 7th crew member to be woken, Marcus Mitchell, and Andrea Aldrin in pod 4 must be the communications officer. By elimination, Sidney Scott must be in pod 6 and must be the geologist and, from clue 6, he will be woken 5th. Finally Commander Sheila Shepard in pod 3 won't be woken 2nd (clue 3) so must be due to be woken 3rd, leaving Engineering Officer Amanda Armstrong in pod 2 being woken 2nd.

1, Marcus Mitchell, biologist, 7th.
2, Amanda Armstrong, engineer, 2nd.
3, Sheila Shepard, commander, 3rd.
4, Andrea Aldrin, communications, 4th.
5, Bruce Bean, doctor, 1st.
6, Sidney Scott, geologist, 5th.
7, Caroline Conrad, physicist, 6th.

Cut It Out!, p. 188

The news reporter was shown struggling to pronounce the word statistics (clue 6). The outtake from the drama serial didn't involve the collapse of the scenery or a broken prop (clue 3), nor did the star trip and fall, as in the third clip (clue 1), so they must have forgotten their lines. Doris Tuckfast broke the prop (clue 4) but not during a news broadcast, a drama, a quiz, which clip featured Laura Murphy (clue 6), or a soap (clue 4), so it must have been the sitcom, which was the fifth outtake (clue 2). The second outtake showed Charlie Wright (clue 1), and since the fourth extract didn't involve Betty Stumbles or Gladys Over (clue 2), it must have been Laura Murphy in the quiz show. She didn't have trouble with the word "statistics," forget her lines, break a prop, or

trip and fall, which was the third clip, so the scenery must have collapsed. By elimination, the third clip must have been from the soap. Since Betty Stumbles didn't forget her lines in a drama and isn't a news reporter (clue 5), she must have been the soap star in the third extract. The star in the drama outtake wasn't Gladys Over (clue 3), so it must have been Charlie Wright in the second clip, and, by elimination, Gladys Over must have featured in the first extract, and she must have been the news reporter unable to pronounce the word "statistics."

1, Gladys Over, news, statistics stumble.
2, Charlie Wright, drama, forgot lines.
3, Betty Stumbles, soap, tripped and fell.
4, Laura Murphy, quiz, scenery collapsed.
5, Doris Tuckfast, sitcom, broke prop.

Kings of the Castle, p. 190

Donna Tellow and her child placed first (clue 6), so the parent of third-placed Paula (clue 2), who isn't Michael Angelo (clue 2) or Bernie Knee (clue 3) or Rho Danne, whose child is a boy (clue 6), must be Polly Clytus, and they won 3rd prize with the Willis Tower sculpture. Now, from clue 3, Bernie and Shelley Knee didn't finish 1st, 3rd, or 5th (clue 3), so the T Rex model must have been 3rd or 5th. We now know it wasn't 3rd, so it must have been 5th with the Knees in 4th place. The T Rex wasn't built by Polly, or Donna or Rho (clue 6), so must be the work of Michael Angelo. By elimination, Rho Danne must have come 2nd with the Smart Car. Bernie and Shelley didn't build the Tower, the T Rex, the roller coaster (clue 5), or the automobile, so must have carved the Mermaid, leaving Donna Tellow winning the competition with Claire and their spectacular roller coaster. Finally, Robbie didn't build the automobile (clue 4), so he isn't Rho Danne's son and so must have helped his dad, Michael, with the T Rex, leaving James keeping his mom, Rho, up to the mark with their automobile.

Bernie Knee, Shelley, 4th, mermaid.
Donna Tellow, Claire, 1st, roller coaster.
Michael Angelo, Robbie, 5th, T Rex.
Polly Clytus, Paula, 3rd, Willis Tower.
Rho Danne, James, 2nd, automobile.

Ones Who Got Away, p. 192

Ellie served table 4 (clue 1) and the Dale family was served at table 2 (clue 3), so the Artois family's even-numbered table where they were served by Daniel (clue 2) must have been table 8. The Harris family was served on Saturday (clue 5), Amy served on Wednesday (clue 3), and Tuesday's tip-skippers were at table 7 (clue 4), so the Artois family, served by Daniel at table 8, must have had their breakfast on Thursday. We now know the table or day for three families, so the family served at table 7 on Tuesday (clue 4), who weren't the Curtises (clue 4), must have been the Talbots. We know they weren't served by Amy, Daniel, or Ellie, nor was it Clare (clue 6), so it must have been Blake. Amy didn't wait at table 2 (clue 3), so she must have served table 5 on Wednesday, leaving Clare dealing with the Dales at table 2. From the family, we know this wasn't on Saturday so must have been on Sunday, leaving Ellie waiting on the Harrises on Saturday at table 4 and Amy dealing with the Curtis family at table 5 on Wednesday.

Amy, 5, Wednesday, Curtis.
Blake, 7, Tuesday, Talbot.
Clare, 2, Sunday, Dale.
Daniel, 8, Thursday, Artois.
Ellie, 4, Saturday, Harris.

Vacation Park, p. 194

Flora Forrest is a ranger at Ferndale Woods Country Park (clue 6), the date of the Minibeast Day at Manorfield Hills must be after the 11th (clue 3), and the Hawthorn Chase activity is taking place on the 20th or 22nd (clue 4), so Becky Brook, who is organizing the event on the 11th (clue 1), but does not work at Littletoft Country Park (clue 1), must work at Grangelands. Dale Moore's Kingfisher Watch is taking place more than seven days earlier than the Minibeast Day at Manorfield Hills (clue 3), so it cannot be the Hawthorn Chase event on either the 20th or 22nd (clue 4) and must be taking place at Littletoft Country Park on the 5th or 13th (clue 1). It is not the 5th (clue 1), so the Kingfisher Watch must be the Littletoft event on the 13th. So the Manorfield Hills Minibeast Day must be on the 22nd, and therefore the Hawthorn Chase activity must be on the 20th and, by elimination, Ferndale Woods must be planning their event on the 5th. The Pond Dipping is taking place before the 13th (clue 1), but not at Grangelands Country Park (clue 2), so it must be at Ferndale Woods. The Hawthorn Chase event is not the Adventure Trail (clue 4), so that must be taking place at Grangelands, leaving Hawthorn Chase as the venue for the Teddy Bears' Picnic. This is not being organized by Hazel Coppis (clue 5), so it must be Will Denness, leaving Hazel as the ranger in charge of Manorfield Hills' Minibeast Day.

5th, Ferndale Woods, Pond Dipping, Flora Forrest.
11th, Grangelands, Adventure Trail, Becky Brook.
13th, Littletoft, Kingfisher Watch, Dale Moore.
20th, Hawthorn Chase, Teddy Bears' Picnic, Will Denness.
22nd, Manorfield Hills, Minibeast Day, Hazel Coppis.

Seaside On Air, p. 196

On Monday, Dee visited Saxham Market (clue 3), on Tuesday she was with the police officer (clue 5), and on Thursday she was with Louise Moor (clue 4), so her day with Denise Ellis, the tourist guide, which was in a town with a one-word name and can't have been on Friday (clue 1), must have been on Wednesday. Therefore, from clue

1, Louise Moor, Dee's Thursday contact, must work in North Allingham. We know that Dee wasn't with Jill Keely on Wednesday or Thursday. Clue 6 rules out both Friday and Tuesday, when she was with the police officer, so Jill Keely must have been her Monday contact, at Saxham Market. Since the parking enforcement officer was in Mundham (clue 6), Dee didn't see her on Monday or Thursday and we know she didn't see her on Tuesday or Wednesday, so she must have done so on Friday. From clue 2, the police officer visited on Tuesday must have been Sandra Trent, leaving the parking enforcement officer as Patsy Quinn. Clue 2 also tells us that Wednesday's contact, tourist guide Denise Ellis, works in Kingswell, so, by elimination, the Tuesday contact Sandra Trent must work in Wanstoft. Finally, from clue 4, Thursday contact Louise Moor isn't the hotel housekeeper, who must therefore be Monday's contact Jill Keely, leaving Louise Moor as the diner waitress.

Monday, Jill Keely, hotel housekeeper, Saxham Market.

Tuesday, Sandra Trent, police officer, Wanstoft.

Wednesday, Denise Ellis, tourist guide, Kingswell.

Thursday, Louise Moor, diner waitress, North Allingham.

Friday, Patsy Quinn, Parking Enforcement Officer, Mundham.

Hat'll Do, p. 198

The owner of hat 7 is drinking water (clue 5) and the owner of hat 9 has come to see Spike Spanner (clue 4), so Mike Mallet, who has an alcoholic drink and who is talking to the lady who owns the hat immediately to the left of his (clue 1), must have hat 3 and the owner of hat 2 must have come to see him. Since, the lady who owns hat 10 has come to see Spike Spanner, from clue 1, Spike can't own either hat 8 or hat 9. Hat 1 belongs to Nicky Nail (clue 6), so

Spike Spanner must be the water-drinking owner of hat 7. Cassie Harrison's hat is number 6 (clue 2) and the lady who owns hat 5 is drinking cognac (clue 2), so the non-alcoholic drink-drinking Ellie Johnson, talking to the private eye who owns hat 8 (clue 5), must own hat 4. From clue 3, cherryade-drinking Dolly Ingles can't own either hat 2 or hat 5 and so must own hat 9. Becky Garcia doesn't own hat 5 (clue 2), so she must own hat 2 and have come to see Mike Mallet, leaving Addie Foster as the cognac-drinking owner of hat 5. Cassie Harrison's private eye's hat is on the lower shelf (clue 2). It can't be Spike Spanner's hat 7 (clue 1) and we know it isn't hat 8, so it must be hat 10. So this doesn't belong to Ricky Wrench (clue 2) and must belong to Dick Drill, leaving hat 8 belonging to Ricky Wrench, who is meeting with Ellie Johnson. Dolly's cherryade rules her out as Nicky Nail's client (clue 6), so Nicky Nail must be talking to Addie Foster, leaving Dolly Ingles talking to Spike Spanner. Now, from clue 7, Nicky Nail must be drinking a whisky sour and Ellie Johnson must be drinking a lime soda. The cola drinker's hat is on the top shelf (clue 8). It's doesn't belong to Mike Mallet (clue 1), so cola must be Becky Garcia's drink, leaving the woman drinking a gin and tonic (clue 8) as Cassie Harrison. Mike Mallet's alcoholic drink can't be the martini (clue 8), so it must be the bourbon. Finally, the owner of hat 10, Dick Drill, isn't drinking lemonade (clue 4), so he must have the martini, leaving Ricky Wrench drinking the lemonade.

1, Nicky Nail talking to Addie Foster, whisky sour; 2, Becky Garcia talking to Mike Mallet, cola; 3, Mike Mallet talking to Becky Garcia, bourbon; 4, Ellie Johnson talking to Ricky Wrench, lime soda; 5, Addie Foster talking to Nicky Nail, cognac; 6, Cassie Harrison talking to Dick Drill, gin and tonic; 7, Spike Spanner talking to Dolly Ingles, water; 8 Ricky Wrench talking to Ellie Johnson,

lemonade; 9, Dolly Ingles talking to Spike Spanner, cherryade; 10, Dick Drill talking to Cassie Harrison, martini.

Logi-5, p. 200

A	E	C	D	B
B	C	D	A	E
D	B	E	C	A
C	A	B	E	D
E	D	A	B	C

Killer Sudoku, p. 200

5	4	6	1	2	9	7	8	3
7	2	3	6	4	8	9	5	1
8	1	9	5	3	7	6	4	2
2	5	8	9	7	3	4	1	6
4	6	1	2	8	5	3	7	9
9	3	7	4	6	1	5	2	8
1	7	5	8	9	6	2	3	4
6	8	2	3	5	4	1	9	7
3	9	4	7	1	2	8	6	5

Battleships, p. 201

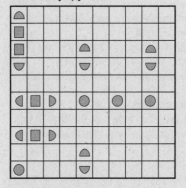

Not in Service, p. 202

NRC-1293 is *Vasa* (clue 5). *Mary Rose* isn't the NRC-1124 or the NRC-1293 (clue 1), and *Hesperus*, whose certificate has been revoked, has an odd number (clue 2), while *Titanic*, whose loss was reported by POLARIS2C, has a number under 1000 (clue 4), so the NRC-1124 must be *Waratah*. We know that *Titanic* isn't NRC-1124 or NRC-1293, nor can it be NRC-846 (clue 4), while the NRC-973 has been reported lost by a SOL space station (clue 3), so *Titanic* must be NRC-571. It has neither had its certificate revoked (clue 2) nor suffered a meteor strike (clue 1) and it can't have been lost to an antimatter explosion, which was the fate of NRC-846 (clue 3), while the alien attack was reported from SOL4C (clue 6), so *Titanic* must have been withdrawn for scrapping. From either the registration number or the reason for loss, we can rule out *Vasa*, *Hesperus*, *Titanic*, and *Waratah* as the NRC-846, lost to an antimatter explosion, which must therefore be *Mary Rose*. By elimination, *Hesperus*, whose certificate was revoked, must be NRC-973. So its loss was reported from a SOL space station (clue 3). We know that SOL4C reported the loss owing to alien attack, so *Hesperus*' certificate revocation must have been reported from SOL3C. Therefore the ship lost to alien attack must be the one with a registration number over 1000 reported from a SOL space station (clue 1). It can't be NRC-1124 (clue 6) so must be NRC-1293, *Vasa*. By elimination, NRC-1124 *Waratah* must have suffered a meteor strike. This wasn't reported from ISD40 (clue 5), so must have been reported by DELOS1C, and ISD40 must have reported the loss of NRC-846 *Mary Rose*.

NRC-571, *Titanic*, withdrawn for scrapping, POLARIS2C.

NRC-846, *Mary Rose*, antimatter explosion, ISD40.

NRC-973, *Hesperus*, certificate revoked, SOL3C.

NRC-1124, *Waratah,* meteor strike, DELOS1C.

NRC-1293, *Vasa*, alien attack, SOL4C.

Drawn Together, p. 204

Robin Trotter and his illustrator are cousins (clue 2). Gerald Irving and his illustrator aren't father/daughter or uncle/niece (clue 2), nor the son/mother responsible for *Magic Words* (clue 3), so they must be brother/sister. Judy Liddle and her writer are father/daughter (clue 4). He is not Clive Escott, whose book was illustrated by Maxine Ovett (clue 5), or Ian Keiller (clue 4), so must be Daniel Frame and the book on which Judy worked with him was therefore *Warren Hill* (clue 6). *Sunhunters* was illustrated by Amanda Clark, so *Oak And Ash*, which wasn't illustrated by Linda Naylor or Theresa Vealy (clue 1), must have pictures by Maxine Ovett and it was therefore written by Clive Escott. They are not, we know, the son/mother pair who produced *Magic Words*, so must be uncle/niece. By elimination, Ian Keiller must have written *Magic Words*. Theresa Vealy didn't illustrate Gerald Irving's book, which had pictures by his sister, nor Robin Trotter's (clue 1), so she must have illustrated Ian Keiller's *Magic Words* and is therefore his mother. Gerald Irving's sister-illustrator isn't Linda Naylor (clue 2), so she must be Amanda Clark, and Gerald Irving therefore wrote *Sunhunters*. By elimination, Linda Naylor must have illustrated *Black Roses*, which must have been written by Robin Trotter, her cousin.

Black Roses, Robin Trotter, Linda Naylor, cousins.
Warren Hill, Daniel Frame, Judy Liddle, father/daughter.
Magic Words, Ian Keiller, Theresa Vealy, son/mother.
Oak and Ash, Clive Escott, Maxine Ovett, uncle/niece.
Sunhunters, Gerald Irving, Amanda Clark, brother/sister.

I Won't Keep You . . ., p. 206

Monday's call, delaying the visit to the bank, did not come from Maggie's cousin (clue 4) or her boss (clue 3). Her tennis partner phoned when she was on her way to visit her aunt (clue 2) and the dentist phoned on Friday (clue 5), so the first caller of the week must have been her boyfriend, preventing her from getting to her meeting before the power outage. So, from clue 1, she must have been heading to the Passport Office on Tuesday and been sent back indoors by the thunderstorm on Wednesday. Tuesday's caller couldn't have been her tennis partner (clue 2) or her boss (clue 3) so must have been her cousin. Also from clue 3, the train cancellations must have been Tuesday. Her tennis partner didn't cause the missed bus (clue 2) so must have kept her chatting until the storm prevented her visit to her aunt. Also from clue 2, the disappointing journey to the garden center must have been on Thursday caused, by elimination, by her frantic boss, leaving the dentist's call on Friday causing her to miss her bus to the Post Office.

Monday, boyfriend, bank, power outage.
Tuesday, cousin, passport office, trains canceled.
Wednesday, tennis partner, visit aunt, thunderstorm.
Thursday, boss, garden center, item sold out.
Friday, dentist, post office, missed bus.

Roommates, p. 208

The first name of the lady in picture 3 isn't Carol (clue 1) or Tracy (clue 2). Hannah Tracy (clue 3) can't be in picture 1 (clue 2), so picture 3 must be Lesley who works in finance (clue 3). So, from clue 2, Lesley in picture 3 must be Lesley Hannah and the lady in picture 4 must be the scientist. She isn't Tracy or Hannah Tracy (clue 2), so she must be Carol. From clue 1, picture 1 must be Ms. Carol, leaving picture 2 as Hannah

Tracy and therefore picture 1 as Tracy Carol, leaving picture 4 as Carol Lesley. Finally, Hannah Tracey isn't in marketing (clue 3), so she must be the advertising executive, leaving Tracy Carol as the marketer.

1, Tracy Carol, marketing; 2, Hannah Tracy, advertising; 3, Lesley Hannah, finance; 4, Carol Lesley, scientist.

Men of Straw, p. 209

Scarecrow 4, looking after a field of strawberries, isn't Strawbry (clue 2), Stalky (clue 1), or Bailer (clue 3), so must be Hayman. Since the barley field scarecrow isn't number 3, the birds troubling scarecrow 1 aren't starlings (clue 1), nor are they blackbirds or crows (clue 3), so they must be gulls. Since the crow-scaring scarecrow is either 2 or 4, the one scaring off the blackbirds can't be number 3 (clue 3), so scarecrow 3 must be having trouble with starlings. So, from clue 1, scarecrow 2 must be Stalky and scarecrow 1 must be guarding a field of barley from gulls. From clue 4, the wheat field scarecrow can't be number 2 and must be number 3, leaving scarecrow 2 in the field of rapeseed. So, from clue 3, the blackbirds aren't scarecrow 2's problem and must be attacking Hayman's strawberries, leaving the crows attacking Stalky's rapeseed. Finally, also from clue 3, Bailer must be scarecrow 3 in the wheat field with the starlings, leaving scarecrow 1 as Strawbry, scaring the gulls off the barley.

1, Strawbry, barley, gulls.
2, Stalky, rapeseed, crows,
3, Bailer, wheat, starlings.
4, Hayman, strawberries, blackbirds.

The Small Five, p. 210

The mosquitoes in the valley did not accompany the lions (clue 1), elephants (clue 2), buffaloes (clue 3), or leopards (clue 4) so they must have bitten us while we admired the rhinoceroses on Thursday (clue 5). On Monday we were tormented

by ants, so we did not view the lions (clue 1), elephants (clue 2), or buffaloes (clue 3) and must have watched the leopards in the forest (clue 4). We have matched pests with three animals, so the elephants, which were not accompanied by tsetse flies, must have exposed us to swarms of stinging bees, leaving the tsetse flies with the buffaloes. Neither the lions nor the elephants were in the swamp (clue 1), so the buffaloes must have been, and since we saw the rhinoceroses in the valley on Thursday, we must have seen the elephants in the mountains on Friday. Now, from clue 1, we must have visited the swamp on Tuesday and been bitten by fleas in the grassland on Wednesday.

Monday, forest, leopards, ants.
Tuesday, swamp, buffaloes, tsetse flies.
Wednesday, grassland, lions, fleas.
Thursday, valley, rhinoceroses, mosquitoes.
Friday, mountains, elephants, bees.

Chase the Lady, p. 212

Card 7 can't have been chosen by Ann, Cyd, Eve or Dan (clue 1), Bob (clue 2) or Fay (clue 3), so it must be Guy's card. So, from clue 3, Fay must have picked card 5. Dan's card can't be any of 1, 2, or 3 (clue 1) or, since it was numbered lower than Fay's, card 6, so it must be card 4. Ann's card isn't 1 or 2 (clue 1), so it must be card 3 with, also from clue 1, cards 1 and 2 chosen by Cyd and Eve. Eve didn't choose card 1 (clue 1), so must have selected card 2 with Cyd picking card 1 and, by elimination, Bob choosing card 6. The Queen of Spades wasn't next to Ann's card (clue 1), so wasn't card 2 or 4. Nor was it immediately right of Eve's card (clue 1), so it wasn't card 1. It's not card 7 (clue 3) or, from the same clue, card 3 or card 6, so it must be Fay's card 5.

1 Cyd; 2 Eve; 3 Ann; 4 Dan; 5 Fay (Queen of spades); 6 Bob; 7 Guy

Battleships, p. 213

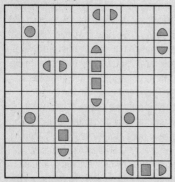

Stake Out, p. 214

The grocery boy was recorded delivering to the apartment during the 0600-0900 shift (clue 3), so the man and woman leaving recorded by Moynihan, which was two hours before the two men were recorded arriving (clue 1), must have been at 1200, and the two men must have arrived during Stockley's 1400 shift (clue 6). From clue 5, Moynihan must also have seen the automobile cruising past suspiciously. Detective Palmer recorded loud music being played (clue 2), so this was not when one man left the apartment, as that coincided with something being thrown from the rear window (clue 2). Those two events were also not recorded by Lewis (clue 2), so it must have been Tucker who saw the one man leave. Detective Stockley did not record the bag of garbage being brought out (clue 6), so he must have seen the two men arrive and heard the argument, leaving Lewis as the detective who recorded the garbage being brought out. Detective Tucker didn't see one man leave during the 0900 shift (clue 4), so it must have been after 0400, leaving the arrival of the woman as having been recorded during the 0900 shift. Now, from clue 2, Detective Palmer must have recorded the grocery boy and the loud music during his 0600 shift, and Lewis

must have seen the woman arrive and the garbage being brought out after 0900.
0400, Tucker, one man left and something thrown from window.
0600, Palmer, grocery boy delivered and loud music played.
0900, Lewis, woman arrived and garbage brought out.
1200, Moynihan, man and woman left and suspicious car.
1400, Stockley, two men arrived and argument heard.

Math Phobia, p. 216

Kevin offered help with art (clue 1) and help with food technology was offered just as one TA went to lunch (clue 4), so Brad, who claimed to have mislaid his glasses (clue 2) and isn't knowledgeable in music or history (clue 2), must have offered help with French. The fourth TA to be approached confessed to having difficulties with math (clue 3), so the TA who is knowledgeable on history, but wasn't the one who claimed someone else was a math expert or Brad with his mislaid specs (clue 2), must have said they were helping another pupil. The food tech help wasn't offered by Abbi or Jill (clue 4) so must have been offered by Sonia. Jill was the 2nd TA asked (clue 4), so the 3rd TA asked who offered help with history, who wasn't, from either their excuse or offer, Sonia, Brad, or Kevin, must have been Abbi. By elimination, the 4th TA to be asked and who confessed their lack of math skills must be Kevin, who offered help with art. Also by elimination, Jill must have suggested another TA but offered help with music. Finally, Brad wasn't the first TA Sam approached (clue 2), so he must have been asked fifth, leaving Sonia as the first TA Sam tried.
First, Sonia, lunch, food tech.
Second, Jill, suggests another, music.
Third, Abbi, helping other pupil, history.
Fourth, Kevin, not good at math, art.
Fifth, Brad, mislaid glasses, French.

Marked Men, p. 218

Slim had the birthmark (clue 1) and Doc Cassidy was wanted for stagecoach robbery (clue 4), so the bank robber with the broken nose, which didn't belong to Jed Junior (clue 2) or Bronco (clue 5), must have been Wild Willis. $5,000 was offered for the cattle rustler (clue 3) and Doc Cassidy was the stagecoach robber, so Jed Junior, who had a price of $1,000 on his head (clue 2) but wasn't the gunslinger (clue 2), must have been the arsonist. From his bounty he didn't have the scar, which was the mark on the man with $2,000 on his head (clue 4), so Jed Junior the arsonist, who didn't have the wart (clue 6), must have the bitten ear. Doc Cassidy didn't have the scar (clue 4), so he must have had the warty chin, leaving Bronco with the scar and the $2,000 bounty. So he's not the cattle rustler (clue 3) and must be the gunslinger, leaving Slim with the birthmark as the cattle rustler with the $5,000 reward. Finally, the bank robber's head didn't carry the largest bounty (clue 5), so he must have had the $750 reward, leaving Doc Cassidy the stagecoach robber with the warty chin attracting a reward of $6,000.

Bronco, gun slinging, $2000, scar.
Doc Cassidy, stage robbery, $6000, wart.
Slim, cattle rustling, $5000, birthmark.
Jed Junior, arson, $1000, bitten ear.
Wild Willis, bank robbery, $750, broken nose.

Sign-In, p. 220

6	4	1	5	3	2
5	3	4	2	1	6
2	6	3	4	5	1
1	5	2	6	4	3
3	2	5	1	6	4
4	1	6	3	2	5

Sudoku, p. 220

1	4	3	8	2	9	7	6	5
2	6	7	1	4	5	3	8	9
9	5	8	7	6	3	4	2	1
6	3	5	2	9	4	1	7	8
7	1	2	3	5	8	9	4	6
4	8	9	6	7	1	2	5	3
5	7	4	9	1	6	8	3	2
3	9	6	4	8	2	5	1	7
8	2	1	5	3	7	6	9	4

Canal Turn, p. 221

Gary Gates' team was at the Old Wharf (clue 1), so Wendy Waterman's group, which wasn't working at the locks (clue 3), must have been at the Bridge, leaving Betty Barge's team pulling bicycles (clue 1) from the canal by the lock. Wendy's team at the bridge wasn't pulling out automobile tires (clue 2), so they must have been dragging out shopping carts, and so must have numbered 7 (clue 2). So, from clue 3, Betty must have led a team of 5 at the locks and, by elimination, Gary must have had a team of 3 at the Old Wharf where they spent some time pulling automobile tires from the water.

Betty Barge, 5, lock, bicycles.
Gary Gates, 3, wharf, automobile tires.
Wendy Waterman, 7, bridge, shopping carts.

Fussy Cats, p. 222

Ambrose refuses to eat chicken or duck (clue 5), fresh fish (clues 3 and 5) or fresh lamb (clue 4), so he must like fresh beef for breakfast. So, from clue 4, Jarvis must like dried beef and Ninja must prefer fresh lamb. Ambrose is not ginger (clue 1), gray (clue 2), or tabby or black (clue 5) so he must be white. Lucy is not tabby or black (clue 5), so she must be gray and is therefore the fan of the fresh duck breakfast (clue 2). So she doesn't like dried lamb (clue 2) or dried fish (clue 3 and intro), so must like dried chicken for her dinner. Now, the cat who eats fresh fish and dried duck, who isn't Ninja (clue 3), must be Kittycat. She isn't tabby (clue 5), so she is black and Ninja is tabby. By elimination, Jarvis must start the day with a bowl of fresh chicken, Ninja must have dried fish for dinner, and Ambrose must be the fan of dried lamb in the evening.

Ambrose, white, fresh beef, dried lamb.
Jarvis, ginger, fresh chicken, dried beef.
Kittycat, black, fresh fish, dried duck.
Lucy, gray, fresh duck, dried chicken.
Ninja, tabby, fresh lamb, dried fish.

Missed the Boat, p. 224

Tom missed a 5-hour island tour (clue 2) and 9 hours was spent in Ibiza (clue 6), so Majorca, where they stayed for 2 hours longer than Corsica (clue 1), must have been the island with the 7-hour stay, missed by Ken (clue 1) and, from clue 5, Ken must have suffered the food poisoning. Also from clue 1, the stay on Corsica must have been for 5 hours and so was missed by Tom (clue 2). Sheila was sunburnt (clue 3), and the person who had a hangover missed the stopover at Sardinia (clue 4), so Tom, who missed the trip to Corsica, which wasn't missed by the person who overslept (clue 2), must have overeaten. Sheila was sunburnt (clue 3), so Vikki, who didn't have a hangover (clue 4), must have overslept, leaving Grace with the hangover missing the stopover at Sardinia (clue 4). By elimination, this must have been the 8-hour stay. Sheila didn't miss the stopover at Sicily (clue 3), so she must have missed the 9-hour stop in Ibiza nursing her sunburn, leaving Vikki missing the 3-hour trip to Sicily, after oversleeping.

Grace, Sardinia, hangover, 8 hours.
Ken, Majorca, food poisoning, 7 hours.
Sheila, Ibiza, sunburnt, 9 hours.
Tom, Corsica, over-ate, 5 hours.
Vikki, Sicily, overslept, 3 hours.

No Need to Worry . . ., p. 226

Emma's text arrived at 7:30 (clue 1), so the last text to arrive, which wasn't to Kathryn (clue 5), Laura (clue 4), or Melanie (clue 3), must have been to Jane. So, since Emma received her call half an hour before Jane, Jane's call can't have been about the TV warranty (clue 3) or the HVAC tech (clue 5). Nor was it about the plumber (clue 4) and Melanie received the text about the fire extinguisher (clue 3), so Jane must have received the text about the dog and her husband must be Quentin. The 7:45 text was not to Melanie (clue 3) or Kathryn (clue 5) and so must have been to Laura, and so her husband must be Richard (clue 1). So Oliver didn't text Emma at 7:30 (clue 4) and Kathryn is married to Norman (clue 5), so Oliver must have texted Melanie about the fire extinguisher. He didn't text at 7:00 (clue 4), so must have texted at 7:15, leaving Norman texting Kathryn at 7:00 and Patrick texting Emma at 7:30. From clue 4, Norman must have been inquiring about the plumber and, from clues 3 and 5, Patrick must have texted Emma at 7:15 about the HVAC tech and Richard must have texted Laura at 7:45 about the TV warranty.

7 p.m., Kathryn, Norman, plumber.
7:15 p.m., Melanie, Oliver, fire extinguisher.
7:30 p.m., Emma, Patrick, HVAC tech.
7:45 p.m., Laura, Richard, television.
8:00 p.m., Jane, Quentin, dog.

Background Check, p. 228

Russell Quinn is a restaurateur (clue 7). The naval surgeon is male (clue 6) so can't be Liz Kirk or Olive Norbert, nor is he the accountant's creation, Charles Barbet (clue 6), so he must be Isaac Hunter, the creation of Donald Elgin (clue 4). We know that Donald's not an accountant, nor is he a solicitor (clue 4). Anita Bixby is the funeral director (clue 5) and the consular officer's detective is a vet (clue 3), so Donald Elgin must be the dentist. We know that the consular officer who created the vet detective isn't Donald Elgin or Anita Bixby and clue 3 rules out Gail Hilbert. James Knight's detective is a mystery writer (clue 1), so Martin Norman must be the consular officer. His vet detective isn't Liz Kirk (clue 2), so must be Olive Norbert. Charles Barbet isn't the Professor of math (clue 6), so must be the mystery writer created by James Knight. Since Gail Hilbert's detective is male (clue 3), he must be Russell Quinn the restaurateur. By elimination, Gail must be the solicitor and funeral director Anita Bixby's detective must be Liz Kirk, who must be a Professor of math.

Anita Bixby, funeral director, Liz Kirk, Professor of math.
Donald Elgin, dentist, Isaac Hunter, naval surgeon.
Gail Hilbert, solicitor, Russell Quinn, restaurateur.
James Knight, accountant, Charles Barbet, mystery writer.
Martin Norman, consular officer, Olive Norbert, vet.

Back to School, p. 230

Melinda, from Miami, isn't Van Der Byl, the martial arts expert (clue 1). The army officer comes from Fort Bragg (clue 2), it's Billy who's a CIA agent (clue 7), and the bank robber is male (clue 6), so Melinda must be an explosives expert. We know her surname isn't Van Der Byl, nor can she be Kruger (clue 6), while Patrick is Reilly (clue 5) and Piretta comes from Chicago (clue 4) not Miami, so Melinda's surname must be La France. We know the first names of the explosives expert and the CIA agent. Faith can't be the male bank robber (clue 6) nor is she the army officer (clue 7), so she must be Faith Van Der Byl, the martial arts expert. We know that she's not from Miami or Fort Bragg and that Piretta comes from Chicago. Faith isn't from Denver (clue 7), so must have flown in from San Diego. We now know the surnames to

go with three first names. From clue 3, Tony can't be Kruger, so he must be Tony Piretta from Chicago and, by elimination, he must be the bank robber. Also by elimination, Patrick Reilly must have flown in from Fort Bragg and is therefore the army officer, while Billy the CIA agent must be Billy Kruger and have flown in from Denver.

Billy Kruger, Denver, CIA agent.
Faith Van Der Byl, San Diego, martial arts expert.
Melinda La France, Miami, explosives expert.
Patrick Reilly, Fort Bragg, army officer.
Tony Piretta, Chicago, bank robber.

Piece of Cake, p. 232

The old people's home received the Dundee cake (clue 4) and the Playgroup was holding the tea party (clue 6), so the Madeira cake for the yard sale, which was not being held by either the church or the Sunday School (clue 5), must have been for the British Legion. The cake baked on Wednesday was for the Sunday School (clue 3), so the tea loaf wasn't Monday's cake for the bring and buy sale (clue 2). Nor was this the plate of rock cakes (clue 1) or the Madeira cake, so it must have been the Victoria sponge that was baked on Monday. By elimination, this must have been for the church. The Dundee cake was not to be eaten on the coach trip (clue 4) nor could it have been for the tea party, so it must have been for sale at the Summer Fair, leaving the cake for the coach trip as the one baked on Wednesday for the Sunday School. The cake for the Summer Fair must have been baked on Thursday (clue 2), so the tea loaf must have been made on Wednesday and the cake for the yard sale on Friday (clue 2). Therefore the tea loaf was intended for the coach trip, and, by elimination, the cakes for the Playgroup tea party must have been the rock cakes, which Madeleine must have baked on Tuesday.

Monday, Victoria sponge, church bring and buy sale.
Tuesday, rock cakes, Playgroup tea party.
Wednesday, tea loaf, Sunday School coach trip.
Thursday, Dundee cake, old people's home Summer Fair.
Friday, Madeira cake, British Legion yard sale.

Just Browsing, p. 234

Loretta Linger browsed the DVDs first (clue 1) and a man first stopped at the greeting cards (clue 4), so Imelda Idol, who didn't look first at the reference books or the pens and paper (clue 1), must have spent her first few rain-dodging minutes with the cookbooks. The person who browsed the DVDs second wasn't Loretta Linger (clue 1 and intro), Imelda Idol (clue 1) or, since he spent his second browsing period in the spot that Wendy Waite had spent her first which, as we know, wasn't the DVDs, Larry Loyter (clue 3), so it must have been Wendy Waite who looked at the DVDs second. Wendy Waite couldn't have looked at the greeting cards first (clue 4), so it wasn't Larry Loyter who went there second (clue 3). Nor, since Imelda looked at the cookbooks first, could she have moved on to the greeting cards (clue 5), so it must have been Loretta Linger who browsed the greeting cards second. A man looked at the reference book section second (clue 4), so Imelda must have browsed the pens and papers second, leaving Larry Loyter as the person who browsed the reference books second, and, from 3 Wendy Waite must have started her rain dodging at the reference books. Now, from clue 4, Larry Loyter did not start his rain dodging with the greeting cards, so he must have started by browsing the pens and paper, leaving Brian Brows browsing the greeting cards and then the cookbooks and staying for 14 minutes (clue 4). The person who stayed for only 6 minutes wasn't Loretta

Linger or Imelda Idol (clue 1) or Larry Loyter (clue 3), and so must have been Wendy Waite, whose reference book and DVD browsing must have taken 6 minutes. So, from clue 1, Imelda Idol must have spent 8 minutes browsing the cookbooks and pens and paper and Larry Loyter must have spent 10 minutes looking at the pens and paper and reference books, leaving Loretta Linger lingering over the DVDs and the greeting cards for 12 minutes before venturing back out into the rain.

Brian Brows, greeting cards, cookbooks, 14 minutes.
Imelda Idol, cookery books, pens and paper, 8 minutes.
Larry Loyter, pens and paper, reference books, 10 minutes.
Loretta Linger, DVDs, greeting cards, 12 minutes.
Wendy Waite, reference books, DVDs, 6 minutes.

Bad Form, p. 236

Wednesday's lesson is Technology, but isn't taught to a 2nd year class (clue 2), so 2E's lesson that is the day before a Physics class but isn't on Monday (clue 3) must be on Thursday, with the Physics on Friday. So 2M's Biology lesson, which isn't on Tuesday (clue 5), must be on Monday. The Wednesday Technology lesson will not be taught by Mr. Markham or Mrs. Boord (clue 2), Senora Escuela, the Spanish teacher (clue 1), or Miss Graydes (clue 4), so that must be Mr. Kane's worst day of the week. Mr. Markham teaches 1J (clue 2) and 3M are taken by a woman Mr. Kane's dreaded lesson, which isn't with 2E or 2M (clue 2), and 3C are being "taught" by a woman (clue 4), so it must be 4B. By elimination, 1J's lesson with Mr. Markham must be on Tuesday. So it's not Biology, Technology, or Physics, and Senora Escuela teaches Spanish (clue 1), so it must be History. We know the Physics lesson isn't being taught to 1J, 4B, 2E (clue 3), or

2M (clue 5), so it must be to 3C, and 2E's Thursday class must be Spanish, leaving the day for Miss Graydes' lesson early in the week as Monday, when she tries to instill some Biology into 2M. Finally, by elimination, 3C's Physics lesson must be taught by Mrs. Boord.

Mrs. Boord, Physics, 3C, Friday.
Senora Escuela, Spanish, 2E, Thursday.
Mr. Kane, Technology, 4B, Wednesday.
Miss Graydes, Biology, 2M, Monday.
Mr. Markham, History, 1J, Tuesday.

Enforced Stoppages, p. 238

The chemical spill caused one team to retire to the bar at 12:45 (clue 3), so Betty's team, who stopped after discovering a number of dead rats (clue 2) but not at 12:30, must have gone to the bar at 1:00. Therefore, from clue 2, it must have been Wendy's team who spotted the chemical spillage and went for a drink at 12:45. This leaves Gary's team spotting the mannequin and settling their nerves with a stiff drink at 12:30 in The Towpath (clue 1). Wendy's team didn't go to The Old Barge (clue 2), so must have gone to The Lighterman at 12:45 after the chemical spillage, leaving Betty's team going to The Old Barge at 1:00 after encountering the dead rats.

Betty Barge, 1:00, dead rats, The Old Barge.
Gary Gates, 12:30, body, The Towpath.
Wendy Waterman, 12:45, chemical spillage, The Lighterman.

Domino Search, p. 239

1	6	0	4	5	1	2	4
3	6	0	6	3	5	6	5
0	3	2	2	0	1	4	3
5	3	5	1	4	4	2	0
6	6	5	1	2	3	2	3
1	1	3	0	4	2	4	1
4	5	2	6	0	5	0	6

Selling Point, p. 240

Mrs. Wells sold her teapot (clue 5), and the plate was sold for $55 (clue 6). Mrs. Inman's item, sold for $85 (clue 2), can't have been the book or the vase, which were both sold by men (clue 1), so must have been the music box. The vase, found in a garden shed, sold for more than the book (clue 1); since the plate sold for $55, this rules out $55 or $70 for the vase and we know that the music box sold for $85, while clue 4 tells us that the $100 item came from a garage, not a garden shed, so the vase must have sold for $115. Its male vendor was therefore not Mr. Shaw (clue 7), nor Mr. Owen, as his item was in the basement (clue 3), not the garden shed, so must have been Mr. Clark. Mr. Shaw didn't sell the plate for $55 (clue 7), so Mr. Owen must have done so, and, by elimination, Mr. Shaw must have sold the book. Mrs. Wells' teapot didn't sell for $70 (clue 5), so it must have been the $100 item that had been in a garage and Mr. Shaw's book must have sold for $70. From clue 2, Mrs. Inman's music box, sold for $85, hadn't been kept under her stairs, so it must have been in her attic, and the item kept under the stairs must have been Mr. Shaw's book.

Mr. Clark, vase, garden shed, $115.
Mrs. Inman, music box, attic, $85.
Mr. Owen, plate, basement, $55.
Mr. Shaw, book, under stairs, $70.
Mrs. Wells, teapot, garage, $100.

Emergency Roster, p. 242

The roofer was needed in August (clue 2) and Millie took a day off in July (clue 4), so Danny, who waited for the glazier but not in June or October (clue 1), must have taken a day off in September and so must have read the whole of a novel (clue 3). Fran used her day to practice her guitar playing (clue 2), so Millie, who didn't play video games or watch the TV (clue 4), must have listened to the radio. Nor was Liam the video games player (clue 4), so he must have watched TV all day, leaving Alicia as the video game player who waited for the electrician (clue 4). Fran didn't wait for the roofer or the locksmith (clue 2), so she must have waited for the plumber. This couldn't have been the June event (clue 5), so must have happened in October, leaving Alicia's day off playing video games while waiting for the electrician in June. By elimination, Liam's day off watching the TV must have been for the August visit of the roofer, leaving Millie's July day listening to the radio as the day the locksmith came.

Alicia, electrician, June, played video games.
Danny, glazier, September, read book.
Fran, plumber, October, played guitar,
Liam, roofer, August, watched TV.
Millie, locksmith, July, listened to radio.

Lone Star Rangers, p. 244

Ben Cooper had been a soldier (clue 4) and Jed Kinsman wore red shirts (clue 6), so the man not known by a nickname who had been a horse breaker and had a mustache (clue 1) must have been Mike Nealey, who had been born in New York (clue 5). Ben Cooper didn't wear a buckskin jacket (clue 4), and we know he didn't wear red shirts or have a mustache; the man from Brownsville who wore a sombrero was known by a nickname (clue 2), so Ben Cooper must have had a scar on his cheek. We know that he wasn't born in New York or Brownsville; nor was he born in San Antonio (clue 4), or El

Paso, where the trail boss was born (clue 3), so Ben Cooper must have been born in Phoenix. We now know the former jobs to go to with three birthplaces; the ex-cowhand wasn't born in Brownsville (clue 2), so that must have been where the former laborer was born, and the ex-cowhand must have been born in San Antonio. We know that Jed Kinsman wore red shirts, so he wasn't the former horse breaker, soldier, or laborer; nor had he been a trail boss (clue 6), so he must have been the ex-cowhand from San Antonio. By elimination, the El Paso-born ex-trail boss must have worn a buckskin jacket. Red Samson hadn't been a laborer (clue 5), so he must have been the ex-trail boss from El Paso, and Dutchy Ernst must have been the Brownsville-born former laborer who wore a sombrero.

Ben Cooper, Phoenix, soldier, scar on cheek.
Dutchy Ernst, Brownsville, laborer, sombrero.
Jed Kinsman, San Antonio, cowhand, red shirt.
Mike Nealey, New York, horse breaker, mustache.
Red Samson, El Paso, trail boss, buckskin jacket.

A Haunting We Will Go, p. 246

Ben was dressed as a vampire (clue 1) and the skeleton encountered the spider (clue 5), so Hannah, who was covered in leaves but who wasn't the devil or ghost (clue 2), must have been dressed as a zombie. The ghost found the licorice (clue 2), so Courtney, who found the toffee (clue 3) but wasn't dressed as the skeleton (clue 5), must have been dressed as a devil. The skeleton attacked by a spider wasn't Joseph (clue 5), so must have been Daniel, leaving Joseph as the ghost who found the licorice. The scout who was the victim of the flour bomb found the chocolate cookies (clue 4), so toffee-finding Courtney, who didn't get a maple-syrup covered hand (clue 3), must have been sprayed with water, leaving Joseph dressed as a ghost, finding both the licorice and the maple syrup. We now know the surprise for four scouts, so Ben the vampire must have suffered the flour bomb while finding the chocolate cookies. Finally, Daniel didn't find the fudge (clue 6), so he must have dressed as a skeleton, and found the assorted candy bars and the realistic spider, leaving Hannah the zombie finding the fudge and being covered in leaves.

Ben, vampire, chocolate cookies, flour.
Courtney, devil, toffee, water.
Daniel, skeleton, candy bars, spider.
Hannah, zombie, fudge, leaves.
Joseph, ghost, licorice, maple syrup.

Bring to Book, p. 248

Naomi Franklin is the author of the romantic novel (clue 4). D. R. Goodman is not the author of either the historical or the biographical work (clue 2), nor is he the author of the detective novel being borrowed by Mr. Tomes (clue 4), so he must have written the travel book. *Looking Back* is from the biography section (clue 3), but its author is not Arthur Brewer, author of *After the Storm*, or Gareth Morgan (clue 3), so it must be the book by Alexander Shaw being borrowed by Miss Plott (clue 5). Mr. Paige is borrowing *Touch the Hills* (clue 5), and since Mrs. Wordley is not borrowing either *Midnight Hags* or *The Temple Gates*, it must be *After the Storm*. This is not romantic fiction, travel, biography, or detective fiction, which is being borrowed by Mr. Tomes, so it must be history. By elimination, Mr. Tomes' chosen detective fiction writer must be Gareth Morgan. *Midnight Hags* is not the travel book by D. R. Goodman, nor the work by Naomi Franklin (clue 2), so it must be Mr. Tomes' Gareth Morgan thriller. D. R. Goodman is not the author of *The Temple Gates* (clue 2), so he must have written *Touch the Hills*, Mr. Paige's choice, and, by

elimination, *The Temple Gates* must be Mrs. Reade's choice, and must be the romantic novel by Naomi Franklin.

Mr. Paige, *Touch the Hills*, D. R. Goodman, travel.
Miss Plott, *Looking Back*, Alexander Shaw, biography.
Mrs. Reade, *The Temple Gates*, Naomi Franklin, romantic fiction.
Mr. Tomes, *Midnight Hags*, Gareth Morgan, detective fiction.
Mrs. Wordley, *After the Storm*, Arthur Brewer, history.

Borrowed Heroes, p. 250

The killer in *Fratricide*, detected by Sir Percy Blakeney, doesn't use snake venom (clue 5), nor a knife (clue 2). Captain Ahab investigates the murder with a club (clue 1) and the cyanide is used in *Deathwatch* (clue 6), so the victim in *Fratricide* must be killed with arsenic and is therefore a smuggler (clue 3). The victim in *Manslayer* is a wine merchant (clue 4). The victim in *Swansong* isn't a physician (clue 3) and the length of the title rules out the Army officer whose killer is caught by Lord Fauntleroy (clue 2), so he must be a musician. We know the detectives who figure in the cases involving a club and arsenic. The knife-user isn't detected by Lord Fauntleroy (clue 2), nor Lemuel Gulliver (clue 7), so must be Bilbo Baggins. He doesn't feature in any of the stories with ten-letter names (clue 2), nor in *Manslayer* (clue 4), so he must solve the musician's murder in *Swansong*. In *Deathwatch*, the cyanide victim isn't a physician (clue 6), so he must be the Army officer whose murder is solved by Lord Fauntleroy. By elimination, Lemuel Gulliver must solve the case involving snake venom. Therefore he doesn't feature in *Breathless* (clue 7) and must therefore solve the wine merchant's murder in *Manslayer*. By elimination, Captain Ahab must investigate the clubbing of a physician in *Breathless*.

Breathless, physician, club, Captain Ahab.
Deathwatch, Army officer, cyanide, Lord Fauntleroy.
Fratricide, smuggler, arsenic, Sir Percy Blakeney.
Manslayer, wine merchant, snake venom, Lemuel Gulliver.
Swansong, musician, knife, Bilbo Baggins.

Hits for Six, p. 252

The number 1 hit was released in August (clue 5) and the January release was before 2013 (clue 3), so the 2014 single, which reached number 3 in the charts and which was released earlier in the year than *Whisper Goodbye* in September (clue 2), must have been released in May. The song concerned was not the number 9 hit *Don't You Understand* (clue 6), nor was it 2010's *See My Heart* (clue 1), and *Always Sometimes* was a hit before 2013 (clue 3), so the 2014 hit must have been *Lost and Gone*. The number 9 hit, *Don't You Understand*, was not released in January (clue 3), May, August, or September, so it must have been November. From clue 1, the 2011 hit must have reached number 1 and was therefore released in August (clue 5). By elimination, it must have been *Always Sometimes* and the 2010 hit *See My Heart* must have been released in January. Now, from clue 4, the 2016 hit must have been released in September (clue 3) and the 2012 hit in November. Since 2010's *See My Heart* got higher in the charts than the 2014 release (clue 3), it must have been number 4, and 2016's *Whisper Goodbye* must have reached number 7.

January 2010, *See My Heart*, 4.
May 2014, *Lost and Gone*, 3.
August 2011, *Always Sometimes*, 1.
September 2016, *Whisper Goodbye*, 7.
November 2012, *Don't You Understand*, 9.

Skiffit, p. 254

Red Moon can't run for 126, 130, or 133 minutes (clue 1), so must run for 127 or 128 minutes. But the film directed by Leigh Kinnison must run for 126 or 127 minutes (clue 5) and the one directed by Hank Graeme must also run for 126 or 127 minutes (clue 1). Neither of these two directed *Red Moon* (clue 1), so it can't run for 127 minutes and must therefore run for 128 minutes, and it was therefore directed by Benny Atreides (clue 2). *Cold Dragon*, which, from clue 5, can only run for 127 or 128 minutes, must therefore run for 127 minutes so, from the same clue, Leigh Kinnison must have directed the 126-minute film. Hank Graeme must therefore have directed the 127-minute *Cold Dragon*. *Night Wind* can't run for 126 or 133 minutes (clue 4) so must run for 130 minutes and, from the same clue, Walt Van Rijn must have directed the 133-minute film. By elimination, the 130-minute *Night Wind* must have been directed by Damien Carter. *Zero Zone* doesn't run for 126 minutes (clue 3), so it must run for 133 minutes and the 126-minute film must be *Iron Range*. The film scripted by Moses Lytton runs for more than 128 minutes but not 133 minutes (clue 1), so it must be the 130-minute *Night Wind*. The male writer of *Zero Zone* (clue 3) can't have been Earl Dickens (clue 6), so it must have been Darren Chaucer. Cheryl Bronte didn't script *Iron Range* or *Red Moon* (clue 2) so must have written *Cold Dragon*. So Earl Dickens must have scripted the 126-minute *Iron Range* and Becky Austen must have scripted *Red Moon*.

Cold Dragon, 127 minutes, Hank Graeme, Cheryl Bronte.
Iron Range, 126 minutes, Leigh Kinnison, Earl Dickens.
Night Wind, 130 minutes, Damien Carter, Moses Lytton.
Red Moon, 128 minutes, Benny Atreides, Becky Austen.

Zero Zone, 133 minutes, Walt Van Rijn, Darren Chaucer.

Select Committee, p. 256

The first person to speak called the novel "disgraceful" (clue 1) and the fourth foresaw it being a chart topper (clue 5), so Bertram Bach, who expected the book to make fortune and who spoke immediately after the board member who said the book was appalling and that it would be a publishing sensation (clue 2), must have spoken third with the appalled person speaking second. Peregrine Payper spoke fifth and then summed up (clue 6), so Percival Pulp, who thought the book shameful (clue 3) and so couldn't have spoken first, second, or third must have spoken fourth and imagined the book would be a shameful chart topper. The first speaker wasn't Pandora Pulp (clue 1), so it must have been Petula Payper, leaving Pandora Pulp piping up second and so describing the book as appalling and a probable publishing sensation. Petula Payper, who we know kicked off the discussion with her description of "disgraceful," didn't say it would be a big hit (clue 4), so she must have said "It is disgraceful. It'll sell millions." By elimination, Peregrine Payper speaking last must have said that the novel would be a big hit. So he didn't describe it as "outrageous" and must have used the word shocking (among other non-printable ones), leaving Bertram Bach butting in third saying, "The book is outrageous, it'll make a fortune."

First, Petula Payper, "It's disgraceful. It'll sell millions."
Second, Pandora Pulp, "It's appalling. It'll be a publishing sensation."
Third, Bertram Bach, "It's outrageous. It'll make a fortune."
Fourth, Percival Pulp, "It's shameful. It'll be a chart topper."
Fifth, Peregrine Payper, "It's shocking. It'll be a big hit."

Logi-5, p. 258

A	B	C	D	E
E	C	D	A	B
B	D	E	C	A
D	E	A	B	C
C	A	B	E	D

Killer Sudoku, p. 258

3	4	5	8	1	9	6	7	2
8	9	7	6	3	2	5	4	1
2	6	1	7	4	5	9	8	3
4	1	9	2	5	8	3	6	7
5	3	6	4	9	7	1	2	8
7	8	2	3	6	1	4	5	9
6	7	4	1	2	3	8	9	5
1	5	8	9	7	4	2	3	6
9	2	3	5	8	6	7	1	4

Grounded, p. 259

One reindeer has nose rash (clue 1), so Comet, who has a hoof problem but not an ache (clue 2), must have hoof itch, leaving the third ailment as antler ache. It's not Prancer's problem (clue 3), so Donner must have antler ache and Prancer must have nose rash. The reindeer grounded for three days isn't Comet (clue 2) or Prancer (clue 3) and so it must be Donner. So, from clue 2, the hoof itch must be keeping Comet on the ground for 2 days, leaving Prancer grounded for just a day with nose rash.

Comet, hoof itch, 2 days.
Donner, antler ache, 3 days.
Prancer, nose rash, 1 day.

Lights in the Sky, p. 260

Joe saw three lights (clue 2) and Clare saw a silver craft (clue 1), so the spinning globe, which was not seen by Harry (clue 4) or Terry (clue 2), must have been seen by Ray over Little Green (clue 1). He didn't watch it for 2 minutes (clue 4), 5 minutes (clue 1), 3 minutes, which was the silver tube (clue 5), or 4 minutes, which was the sighting over Oddleigh (clue 3), so it must have lasted for just 1 minute. The red glow was not seen over Oddleigh or Marsham (clue 3), nor was it the silver disc over Weardon (clue 6), so it must have been observed in the sky over Fenomenham. We now know either the time or the description for four places so the 4-minute sighting over Oddleigh must have been the three lights watched by Joe. By elimination, the silver tube must have been seen above Marsham. This was not Clare's silver sighting (clue 1), so she must have seen the silver disc over Weardon. Harry didn't see his UFO above Marsham (clue 4), so it must have been the red glow over Fenomenham. It was not watched for 2 minutes (clue 4), so it must have been 5 minutes. By elimination, the UFO over Marsham must have been seen by Terry, and Clare must have watched the silver disc for 2 minutes.

Clare, Weardon, silver disc, 2 minutes.
Harry, Fenomenham, red glow, 5 minutes.
Joe, Oddleigh, three lights, 4 minutes.
Ray, Little Green, spinning globe, 1 minute.
Terry, Marsham, silver tube, 3 minutes.

Action Wedding, p. 262

Belinda was Gavin's bride (clue 1), and Glen traveled to Thailand (clue 4), so Bridget, who went to the Maldives (clue 2), but not to marry Gareth or George (clue 2), must now be married to Greg. The hot-air balloon wedding was in New Zealand and we have named the men who went to Thailand and the Maldives, so Gareth, who went waterskiing but not to the Bahamas (clue 2), must have gone to the Seychelles. So his new wife isn't Beth (clue 5) and Bonnie went scuba diving (clue 4), so Gareth must have married Beatrice on a water skiing trip to the Seychelles. Bonnie wasn't Glen's bride

(clue 4), so she must have married George while scuba diving, leaving Beth and Glen marrying in Thailand. Bonnie and George's scuba diving rules out New Zealand as their wedding location (clue 3), so they must have scuba dived in the Bahamas, leaving the New Zealand balloon trip as the wedding arrangement of Belinda and Gavin. Finally, Glen didn't go sky diving (clue 4), so he and Beth must have bungee jumped in Thailand, leaving Bridget and Greg saying I do while plummeting toward the ground on a sky diving trip to the Maldives.

Beatrice, Gareth, water skiing, Seychelles.
Belinda, Gavin, balloon, New Zealand.
Beth, Glen, bungee jump, Thailand.
Bonnie, George, scuba dive, Bahamas.
Bridget, Greg, sky dive, Maldives.

Music Makers, p. 264

The $45 event is on the 17th (clue 5) and the event on the 4th doesn't involve an orchestra (clue 2), so the Royal London Orchestra concert, for which tickets are $50 and which is earlier in the month than the 22nd, the date of the GBP-promoted event (clue 1), must be appearing on the 12th. The promoter is not GBP, Posh Frock Productions, who are selling tickets at $65 (clue 5), or Green House Productions, who is staging the Jeff Barclay concert (clue 6), and Wildwood is not promoting an orchestra (clue 2), so the Royal London Orchestra's promoter must be Hugo Lindsay. Therefore Barney and the Farmers must be the event on the 17th for which the tickets are $45 (clue 5). The $65 Posh Frock event is not on the 4th (clue 2), or the 17th (clue 5), so it must be on the 29th. The promoter is not Green House Productions, who is presenting Jeff Barclay, so it must be Wildwood. By elimination, the Jeff Barclay concert must be the Green House Productions one on the 4th. Now, from clue 3, the Norwich Symphony Orchestra must be appearing on the 22nd and Jennifer Earle on the 29th. The tickets for Jeff

Barclay cost less than those for the Norwich Symphony Orchestra (clue 2), so they must be $55 and for the NSO they must be $60.

4th, Jeff Barclay, Green House Productions, $55.

12th, Royal London Orchestra, Hugo Lindsay, $50.

17th, Barney and the Farmers, Wildwood, $45.

22nd, Norwich Symphony Orchestra, GBP, $60.

29th, Jennifer Earle, Posh Frock Promotions, $65.

On the Buses, p. 266

The No. 6 bus goes to Bank and the passengers have not been waiting either 11 or 12 minutes (clue 5). Nor is it 9 minutes, which is the time since the last No. 42 called (clue 2), or 4 minutes, which is the wait for the Chelsea bus (clue 4), so it must be 7 minutes. Six passengers have been waiting 12 minutes for their bus (clue 6), so the No. 98 is not the Tower Bridge bus that the group of four are waiting for (clues 1 and 3). The four are also not waiting for the No. 14 (clue 1) or the 42 (clue 2), so it must be the No. 207 and, by elimination, they must have been waiting for 11 minutes. The No. 42 does not go to Marylebone (clue 2) or Chelsea, so it must be Islington, leaving the Marylebone bus as the one for which six people have been waiting 12 minutes. Therefore, from clue 2, the group of seven are waiting for the No. 42 to Islington bus. Now, from clue 3, the six must be waiting for the No. 98 and the eight for the Bank bus. Finally, by elimination, the Chelsea bus must be the No. 14.

4 passengers, No. 207, 11 mins., Tower Bridge.

5 passengers, No.14, 4 mins., Chelsea.

6 passengers, No. 98, 12 mins., Marylebone.

7 passengers, No.42, 9 mins., Islington.

8 passengers, No. 6, 7 mins., Bank.

Rescue Dogs, p. 268

Ellen's dog was rescued on Wednesday (clue 3) and the German shepherd was rescued on Friday (clue 4), so Dom's poodle, which wasn't rescued on Saturday or Sunday (clue 1) must have been rescued on Tuesday. Bruce's dog fell from a speed boat (clue 2), so the Labrador, which found itself in trouble while playing with another dog but which doesn't belong to Corrine or Ellen (clue 6), must belong to Freddie. We now know either the day or the incident for four owners, so the owner of the dog that was rescued after chasing the stick which was saved from the surf on Sunday (clue 5) must have been Corrine. We have now linked either breed of dog or day with four owners, so the German shepherd rescued on Friday must belong to Bruce and it must have fallen from a speedboat. The Jack Russell isn't Ellen's dog (clue 3), so it must be Corrine's dog that chased the stick on Sunday, leaving Ellen's dog as the border collie and Freddie's Labrador's rescue as the Saturday event. Finally, Ellen's border collie didn't slip off the surfboard (clue 3), so it must have jumped off the jetty, leaving Dom's poodle slipping off the surfboard (Dom had fallen off quite some time before) on Tuesday.

Bruce, German shepherd, Friday, fell from boat.

Corrine, Jack Russell, Sunday, chased stick.

Dom, poodle, Tuesday, came off surfboard.

Ellen, border collie, Wednesday, slipped off jetty.

Freddie, Labrador, Saturday, played with dog.

Paintball, p. 270

Alicia was hit when she made a dash for the tower (clue 1), and the person hit on their helmet on the side of the head was hiding behind a wall at the time, so Liam, who was hit on the arm but who wasn't hiding behind the hedge or oak tree (clue 3), must have been hit as he opened the door of the hut after 20 mins. (clue 5). The player hit after 24 mins. was shot in the back (clue 4), so Alicia, who wasn't the last to be hit and who wasn't shot in the shoulder as she ran for the tower (clue 1), must have been hit in the thigh. Nor was Danny hit in the back after 24 mins. or on the side of the head (clue 4), so he must have been hit on the shoulder. So he wasn't hit first (clue 1). Fran was hit after 12 mins. (clue 2) and we know the body parts for 20 and 24 mins, so Danny must have been hit after 17 mins. So Alicia, who was eliminated earlier, must have been hit on the thigh after 10 mins. We now know the hiding place or body part hit for four times, so the person hit on the side of the head as they crouched behind a wall must have been hit after 12 mins. and was therefore Fran. By elimination, it must have been Millie who was shot in the back after 24 mins. She wasn't behind the oak tree (clue 3), so she must have been hiding under the hedge, leaving Danny hiding behind the oak tree when he was hit on the shoulder after 17 mins.

Alicia, tower, thigh, 10 mins.
Danny, oak tree, shoulder, 17 mins.
Fran, wall, head, 12 mins.
Liam, hut, arm, 20 mins.
Millie, hedge, back, 24 mins.

Tunnel Trouble, p. 272

Someone caught the wrong train on Wednesday (clue 7). The Monday mishap was not Alain's beret falling on the track (clue 1), or failing to beat the barrier (clue 4), while clue 5 rules out tripping on the stairs at the Champ de Mars, so it must have been on Monday that someone trapped their foot in the door. We know Alain did not lose his beret at the Champ de Mars and clue 1 rules out the Invalides, while Sylvie's mishap occurred at the Concorde station (clue 2). We also know that Alain's mishap did not occur on Monday or Wednesday, while Marcel was the Gnome's Thursday victim (clue 3), so

Alain must have suffered on either Tuesday or Friday. So he was not at the Etoile station (clue 6) and, by elimination, must have lost his beret at the Gare du Nord. Clue 8 now tells us this was not on Tuesday, so, by elimination, it must have been on Friday and, from clue 1, the station where Marcel suffered on Thursday must have been the Invalides. So he cannot have tripped on the stairs and we have matched days with three other mishaps, so it must have been Marcel who failed to beat the barrier. Now, by elimination, the tripping incident at the Champ de Mars must have occurred on Tuesday. So, from clue 5, Jacqueline must have trapped her foot in the door on Monday. We have now matched a name or a station with four days, so it must have been on Wednesday at Concorde station that Sylvie caught the wrong train. This leaves Henri as the passenger who tripped on the stairs on Tuesday and Etoile as the station where Jacqueline trapped her foot on Monday.

Monday, Jacqueline, trapped foot in door, Etoile.
Tuesday, Henri, tripped down stairs, Champ de Mars.
Wednesday, Sylvie, caught wrong train, Concorde.
Thursday, Marcel, failed to beat barrier, Invalides.
Friday, Alain, beret on track, Gare du Nord.

Bagging a Bargain, p. 274

The tie was part of the purchase that totaled just $7 (clue 6) and the books part of a purchase amounting to $12 (clue 6), so the shirt and vinyl LP, which were not bought from Age UK and did not come to either $25 or $36 (clue 2), must have cost $13. Therefore the Oxfam purchases must have come to $36 (clue 2). The purchase from the Salvation Army shop included the sweater but did not amount to $7 or $13 (clue 3), so it must have been $12 and the other item must have been some books. The $36 purchase from Oxfam didn't include the suit (clue 5), so it must have been the dress, and by elimination, the suit must have been part of the $25 purchase. The shirt wasn't bought from Age UK and since it was bought with the vinyl LP (clue 2), it wasn't from Scope, where we got the wineglasses (clue 1), so it must have been the Mind shop. Our purchases at Scope did not come to $25 (clue 1), so they must have been the tie and another item for $7. By elimination, our Age UK purchases must have included the suit, for a total of $25. The other item was not the lamp (clue 4), so it must have been the jigsaw puzzle and the $36 Oxfam purchase must have been the dress and lamp.

Age UK, suit and jigsaw puzzle, $25.
Mind, shirt and LP, $13.
Oxfam, dress and lamp, $36.
Salvation Army, sweater and books, $12.
Scope, tie and wineglasses, $7.

Curious Couriers, p. 276

The arrival in Dorchester was in the second week (clue 2) and the package was in Manchester on the Monday of the second week (clue 6), so the package's first location, where it was "being processed" must have been in Croydon. So, from clue 4, the package must have been "at the hub" at 5:00 a.m. on the Thursday of week 1. This wasn't in Dorchester (clue 2) and the package was in Exeter at 6:00 p.m. one day (clue 3), so the hub must be in Norwich. So, from clue 5, the package must have been "being processed" in Croydon at 3:00 p.m. and it must have been marked as "Courier in transit" in Manchester on Monday of the second week. The arrival in Exeter wasn't on a Tuesday (clue 3), so it must have been there on Thursday of week 2 at 6:00 p.m., leaving Tuesday of the second week as the day the package was delivered to the wrong Dorchester, leaving the Exeter status as "at depot." Finally, the timing in Manchester

wasn't 8:00 a.m. (clue 6), so the package must have been "in transit" at 1:00 p.m., leaving 8:00 a.m. on the second Tuesday as the time the package was delivered to the wrong Dorchester.

Tues. week 1, Croydon, 3:00 p.m., order being processed.
Thurs. week 1, Norwich, 5:00 a.m., at the hub.
Mon. week 2, Manchester, 1:00 p.m., courier in transit.
Tues. week 2, Dorchester, 8:00 a.m., package delivered.
Thurs. week 2, Exeter, 6:00 p.m., at depot.

Find the Lady, p. 278

The operation in March was to destroy some memoirs (clue 2) and the May crime was in St. Petersburg (clue 5), so the month in which Mata traveled to Cairo to steal the sacred scarab, which wasn't in July (clue 1) or September (clue 5), must have been in November. The July keepsake was the silk scarf (clue 1), the locket of hair was left behind in Florence (clue 3), and the ruby ring was left behind after the dagger was stolen (clue 4), so the keepsake left after the theft of the scarab in Cairo in November, which wasn't the white orchid (clue 2), must have been the handkerchief. The scheme to annoy Rick by substituting the stolen dagger with an even more valuable ring wasn't in September (clue 5), so it must have taken place at St. Petersburg in May. Mata's visit to Singapore wasn't to murder the ambassador (clue 6), and couldn't have been the trip to destroy her former lover's memoirs (also clue 6), so it must have been to intercept some secret plans. So, from clue 6, the murder of the ambassador must have been in July and the Singapore crime must have been in September. By elimination, it must have been the occasion Rick found a white orchid. Also by elimination, the July murder must have taken place in New York and Rick must have been left a silk scarf, leaving the March incident as the destruction of memoirs in Florence after which Rick discovered the locket of hair.

March, Florence, destroy memoirs, locket of hair.
May, St. Petersburg, steal dagger, ruby ring.
July, New York, murder ambassador, silk scarf.
September, Singapore, intercept plans, white orchid.
November, Cairo, steal scarab, handkerchief.

Battleships, p. 280

Training Days, p. 281

Zachary's problem was during loading practice (clue 2) and Blitzen slipped over (clue 4), so the reindeer who managed to get their hocks tangled up during emergency harnessing practice (clue 1) must have been Cupid, leaving Blitzen slipping over during reversing practice on Tuesday (clue 3) and Zachary tipping the sleigh during loading practice. Finally, from clue 4, Cupid's harness and hocks problem must have been on Monday, leaving Zach tipping over the sleigh with poor loading on Wednesday.

Monday, harnessing, Cupid, hocks caught.
Tuesday, reversing, Blitzen, slipped over.
Wednesday, loading, Zachary, tipped sleigh.

Band on the Run, p. 282

Isabella plays the cornet (clue 3) and Joanna was distracted by the sight of the new yFone in the phone shop (clue 1), so the woman who plays the piccolo and was distracted by the smells from the food stall (clue 4) must have been Heather. The musician who spotted their aunt didn't stop marching when they should have (clue 5), so Gareth, who played the wrong song but not after being distracted by Santa on his sleigh (clue 2), must have had his eye caught by the toy in the toy shop window. So he doesn't play the clarinet (clue 3), and the drummer split the drum (clue 1), so Gareth must be the flute player. We now know either the instrument or the distraction for three accidents, so Heather, distracted from her piccolo playing by the food stall smells, who didn't trip (clue 4), must have resumed playing in the wrong key. It wasn't Kenny who spotted his aunt (clue 5) and we know it wasn't Joanna, so it must have been Isabella, the cornet player, who spotted her aunt and kept marching when she should have stopped. Finally, Joanna isn't the drummer (clue 1), so she must be the clarinet player and, by elimination, must have tripped after spotting the new yFone, leaving Kenny splitting the skin on his bass drum after being surprised by the arrival of Santa Claus.

Gareth, flute, toy shop, wrong song.
Heather, piccolo, food stall, wrong key.
Isabella, cornet, spotted aunt, didn't stop.
Joanna, clarinet, phone shop, tripped.
Kenny, drum, Santa Claus, split drum

Band of Sisters, p. 284

Number 5 is known as Aurora (clue 3). So Angela, who is number 2, but who isn't Medusa (clue 7), Juno (clue 2), or Nemesis (clue 5), must be referred to as Lucrezia and is therefore the toxicologist (clue 1). The judge cannot be number 4 or number 5 (clue 2) and we now know she is not number 2. Number 3 is the psychologist (clue 6), so the judge must be number 1. We now know Harriet, the university professor (clue 4), is none of numbers 1, 2, or 3, and clue 4 rules her out as number 5, so she must be number 4. So, from clue 4, the attorney must be number 5, Aurora. She cannot be Susan (clue 2), nor is she Katherine (clue 3), and we know she is not Angela or Harriet, so she must be Lorna. Susan is not the judge, number 1 (clue 2), so she must be number 3, the psychologist, leaving the judge as Katherine. Clue 2 now tells us Juno must be number 4, Harriet. Katherine, the judge, is not known within the Band of Sisters as Nemesis (clue 5), so she must be Medusa, leaving Nemesis as the code name chosen by Susan.

Angela, toxicologist, 2, Lucrezia.
Harriet, university professor, 4, Juno.
Katherine, judge, 1, Medusa.
Lorna, attorney, 5, Aurora.
Susan, psychologist, 3, Nemesis.

Needles and Tinsel, p. 286

The silver tinsel tree has 4 presents (clue 1); the alternative tree has a robin on top (clue 3), and the traditional real tree has at least 3 presents (clue 5), so the tree topped with a star and 2 presents underneath it, which doesn't have a fiber-optic light display (clue 2), must be the green plastic one. The star is attached to the tree that sits over 2 presents (clue 2), so the traditional tree, which has more than 2 presents but isn't topped with a fairy or a snowflake (clue 5), must have the angel. The Furghs' tree with the snowflake can't be the green plastic one with the two presents (clue 5) and the Scots' tree is the fiber-optic option (clue 2), so the Furghs must have the silver tinsel tree, topped with a snowflake and sitting above four presents. So, from clue 5, the Forrest family must have 3 presents under their tree. The Douglas family has 6 presents under their tree, so the Scot family must have 5 presents beneath their fiber-optic tree. So the traditional real

tree with the angel, which has more presents than the Furgh's four (clue 5), must have the six presents placed by the Douglas family, leaving the Pignes as the couple with the very restrained 2 presents under the green plastic tree, the Forrest family as the owners of the alternative tree with its robin and with 3 presents beneath its MDF branches, and the fairy atop the Scots' fiber-optic tree with 5 presents beneath.

Douglas, traditional real, angel, 6 packages.
Forrest, alternative, robin, 3 packages.
Furgh, silver tinsel, snowflake, 4 packages.
Pigne, green plastic, star, 2 packages.
Scot, fiber-optic, fairy, 5 packages.

Christmas Mass, p. 288

The man who's playing solitaire is on duty because he has no family (clue 2), so the one who's watching TV, who isn't on duty for overtime or as punishment (clue 4) and isn't Anson Nader, who's on duty because of his religion (clue 3), must have been picked by rotation. The man at Police HQ who's on duty for the overtime isn't on the phone (clue 5) or listening to CDs, the pastime of the cop in the patrol car (clue 6); we know he isn't playing solitaire or watching TV, so he must be reading a book and is therefore Ben Overton (clue 6). Elmer Rogers is at the National Guard armory (clue 1), so Chuck Palowski, who isn't at the Forest Service HQ or the firehouse (clue 1), must be in the police patrol car listening to CDs. We know that he's not on duty because of the rotation, having no family, overtime, or because of religion, so Chuck Palowski must be serving punishment for "goofing off." By elimination, Anson Nader must be spending his time on the phone. The man at Forest Service HQ isn't the man watching TV who's on duty by the rotation, nor the solitaire player (clue 2), so he must be the religious phone caller Anson Nader. The TV watcher isn't at the firehouse (clue 1), so he must be at the National Guard armory and is therefore Elmer Rogers. By elimination, the man at the firehouse must be Dennis Quinn, who must be playing solitaire and on duty because it's his turn on the rotation.

Anson Nader, Forest Service HQ, on phone, religion.
Ben Overton, Police HQ, reading book, overtime.
Chuck Palowski, police patrol, listening to CDs, punishment.
Dennis Quinn, firehouse, playing solitaire, no family.
Elmer Rogers, National Guard armory, watching TV, rotation.

Hit the Right Note, p. 290

Ben Barton had the old harmonica (clue 2) and the boy with the panpipes was told he could have them back when he'd learned not to play them in the library, so Chris Cockroft who could have his items back "When the time is right" but wasn't the boy with the tin whistle (clue 4) must have had his paintbrush and pencil drumsticks confiscated by Mr. Grimm until the time is right. Mr. Stoney told one boy he could have his instrument back "When you can be trusted . . .," so Hamish Hazel, who lost his instrument to Mr. Gaunt but wasn't told he could have it back "When I say so" (clue 6) must have handed Mr. Gaunt his panpipes and been told he could have them back when he'd learned not to play them in the library. By elimination Martin Masters must have been struggling to get a note from the tin whistle. He didn't lose it to Mr. Stern (clue 1), so must have given it to Mr. Stoney, who said he could have it back when he could be trusted . . . (clue 4), leaving Ben Barton losing his two-note harmonica to Mr. Stern who said he could have it back when he said so.

Ben Barton, harmonica, Mr. Stern, "When I say so."
Chris Cockroft, drumsticks, Mr. Grimm, "When the time is right."
Hamish Hazel, pan pipes, Mr. Gaunt, "When you've learned . . ."
Martin Masters, tin whistle, Mr. Stoney, "When you can be . . ."

Battleships, p. 292

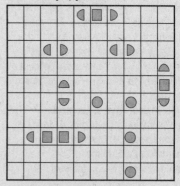

Domino Search, p. 293

1	0	6	1	3	1	5	6
5	1	4	0	2	3	6	1
5	2	4	6	5	0	0	6
5	1	4	2	0	4	2	6
3	1	0	4	6	5	1	4
4	2	3	2	2	3	3	0
5	6	0	3	4	3	5	2

Teacher, p. 294

Wednesday's session was at Netherlipp Arena (clue 1), so Monday's, which wasn't at Churchminster Sports Hall (clue 2), must have been at Stonekeigh Leisure Center and the session in Churchminster must have been on Friday. The 14-strong session wasn't on Wednesday (clue 1) or Monday (clue 2), so it must have been Friday's session. It's not the Pilates (clue 3), which also wasn't the session to which 18 people came (clue 3), so 16 people must have attended the Pilates and, from clue 3, 18 people must have gone to Stonekeigh on Monday, leaving the Wednesday's Netherlipp session as the 16-strong Pilates group. So, from clue 1, the 14-strong group at Churchminster on Friday must have been doing aerobics, leaving Monday's Stonekeigh session for 18 people as yoga.

Monday, yoga, Stonekeigh, 18.
Wednesday, Pilates, Netherlipp, 16.
Friday, aerobics, Churchminster, 14.

Student, p. 295

May Lern's course runs for 12 weeks (clue 3), so Alice Sonne's Egyptology course, which isn't 16 weeks long (clue 1), must be the 14-week course running on Saturday evenings (clue 3). So, from clue 1, the pottery lessons must last for 16 sessions and May Lern's 12 lessons must be about automobile mechanics on Tuesday nights (clue 2), leaving Will Preach teaching pottery on Thursdays for 16 weeks.

Tuesday, automobile mechanics, May Lern, 12 weeks.
Thursday, pottery, Will Preach, 16 weeks.
Saturday, Egyptology, Alice Sonne, 14 weeks.

A, B, Seeds, p. 296

Brian bought broccoli (clue 1) and Chris bought carrots (clue 2), so the person who bought cabbage seeds and broad bean seeds (clue 3) must have been Amanda, who also bought the aubergine seeds (clue 1), leaving Brian buying the celery. So he didn't also buy asparagus seeds (clue 3) and must have bought the seeds for artichokes, broccoli, and celery, leaving Chris' seeds as asparagus, beets, and carrots.

Amanda, aubergine, broad bean, cabbage.
Brian, artichoke, broccoli, celery.
Chris, asparagus, beets, carrot.

A, B, C, DIY, p. 297

Someone bought the Allen keys and the brush (clue 3), so the woman who bought the axe and the clamp but who didn't buy the bolt cutter (clue 1), must have bought the blowtorch. So the auger must have been bought along with the bolt cutter by a man (clue 1). So, from clue 1, Chris is male and the woman who bought the axe, the blowtorch, and the clamp must be Amanda. Chris didn't buy the auger, so that must have been bought by Brian along with the bolt cutter and the chisel (clue 1), leaving Chris buying the Allen keys, the brush, and the crowbar.

Amanda, axe, blowtorch, clamp.
Brian, auger, bolt cutter, chisel.
Chris, Allen keys, brush, crowbar.

Pier of the Realm, p. 298

Sheryl Schilling runs the rock shop (clue 2) and kiosk 3 is run by Tommy Tanner, so the owner of kiosk 1, the ice cream stall, who isn't Fenella Farthing (clue 4), must be Pete Penney. The pick'n'mix kiosk is offering a free scoop (clue 1), so kiosk 2, offering free postcards, which doesn't sell cotton candy (clue 3), must be Sheryl Schilling's Rock Emporium. So, from clue 2, Pete Penney's ice cream stall must have the "buy one get one free" promotion. By elimination Fenella Farthing must run kiosk 4. She isn't offering 50 cents off (clue 4), so must be offering a free scoop of her pick'n'mix, leaving kiosk 3 as Tommy Tanner's cotton candy store offering a 50 cent discount.

Kiosk 1, Pete Penney, ice cream, buy one get one free.
Kiosk 2, Sheryl Schilling, rock, free postcard.
Kiosk 3, Tommy Tanner, cotton candy, 50 cents off.
Kiosk 4, Fenella Farthing, pick'n'mix, free scoop.

Key Bay Selling, p. 300

Delilah is selling the digital radio (clue 1) and the lawn mower's sale will end on Sunday (clue 4), so Arnold, whose sale won't be last to finish and who isn't selling the games console (clue 3), must be selling his electric guitar, to be picked up by the buyer (clue 2). Colin isn't selling the lawn mower (clue 4), so that must be Belinda's item, which will be delivered by courier (clue 5) after the sale closes on Sunday, leaving Colin selling the games console. So, from clue 3, neither Arnold's nor Colin's sale will close on Saturday which must therefore be Delilah's digital radio auction. Now, still from clue 3, Colin's auction must end on Thursday, Arnold's guitar will be sold on Friday and Delilah's digital radio, to be sold on Saturday, will be personally delivered, leaving Colin sending his games console by package post.

Arnold, electric guitar, Friday, pick up.
Belinda, lawn mower, Sunday, courier.
Colin, games console, Thursday, package post.
Delilah, digital radio, Saturday, personal delivery.

Key Bay Buying, p. 302

Arnold's auction ends on Monday (clue 1), so the person who bid a maximum of $20 on the auction ending on Tuesday (clue 4), who, from the bid, can't be Belinda (clue 2) and who isn't Delilah (clue 4), must be Colin, who is bidding on a porcelain vase (clue 1). The maximum bid placed on the mirror was $40 (clue 3), so the wall clock, which didn't attract the $50 bid (clue 2), must have had the $30 bid. So, from clue 2, Belinda's maximum bid must have been $40 for the mirror. Since the vase auction ends on Tuesday, Belinda's mirror auction can't end on Monday (clue 2) and must end on Thursday, with the wall clock auction ending on Wednesday. So it's not Arnold and must be Delilah who has placed the maximum bid of

$30 on the wall clock, leaving Arnold placing a maximum bid of $50 on the painting.

Arnold, painting, Monday, $50.
Belinda, mirror, Thursday, $40.
Colin, porcelain vase, Tuesday, $20.
Delilah, wall clock, Wednesday, $30.

Keigh Bay Sellers, p. 304

Eric is selling his Wayfarer dinghy (clue 4) and Graham is selling the *Spicy Sal* (clue 1), so the Minto dinghy, the *Dainty Dot*, which doesn't belong to Felicity (clue 3) must be Hazel's vessel. Eric's *Wayfarer* isn't the yellow *Zesty Zoe* (clue 4), so must be the *Briny Bess*, leaving the *Zesty Zoe* as Felicity's boat. We now know the type or color of dinghy for three sailors, so the red Heron type dinghy must be Graham's *Spicy Sal*, leaving Felicity's yellow *Zesty Zoe* as the Mirror type dinghy. Finally, Eric's *Briny Bess* isn't green (clue 5) so must be navy blue, leading Hazel's Minto type *Dainty Dot* as the green boat.

Eric, Wayfarer, *Briny Bess*, navy blue.
Felicity, Mirror, *Zesty Zoe*, yellow.
Graham, Heron, *Spicy Sal*, red.
Hazel, Minto, *Dainty Dot*, green.

Keigh Bay Buyers, p. 306

Graham showed his Heron dinghy to Karen (previous puzzle and clue 1) so the seller hoping to sell to Jerry, who wasn't Eric with the *Briny Bess* or Hazel with her green boat (previous puzzle and clue 2), must have been Felicity. So the woman selling to Leonard (clue 3) must have been Hazel, leaving Eric trying to sell the *Briny Bess* to Isabel who therefore left with a dismissive, "I'll let you know" (clue 2). This wasn't at 11:00 a.m. or 2:00 p.m. (clue 2) or 12 noon (clue 4) and so must be at 1:00 p.m. So, from clue 2, Hazel must have tried to sell her green boat at 2:00 p.m. The 11:00 a.m. appointment wasn't Graham's (clue 1), so it must have been Felicity's meeting with Jerry, leaving Graham and Karen meeting at 12 noon. So, from clue 1, Felicity's 11:00 a.m. meeting with Jerry must have ended with, "I'll be in touch." Finally, Graham's noon meeting didn't finish with, "I'll get back to you" (clue 4), so must have ended with, "I'll think about it," leaving Leonard departing from the quay after meeting Hazel at 2:00 p.m. with, "I'll get back to you."

Eric, Isabel, 1:00 p.m., I'll let you know.
Felicity, Jerry, 11:00 a.m., I'll be in touch.
Graham, Karen, 12 p.m., I'll think about it.
Hazel, Leonard, 2:00 p.m., I'll get back to you.

Driving for Perfection, p. 308

The test that went wrong in Balmoral Close started at 9:30 (clue 5), Ron Gear made his mistake in Hawthorn Way (clue 1), and the driving error in Market Street took place later than Rex Chance's test (clue 3), so Roland Brake, whose test began at 9:00 and didn't come to grief in Mill Road (clue 2), must have made his failing maneuver in Church Hill and must therefore have fluffed the hill start (clue 6). Therefore Vera Swerve's test, which was half an hour after the one featuring the botched emergency stop (clue 3), did not begin at either 9:30 or 10:30. The parking error was during the 10:30 test (clue 4), so Vera's test also was not at 11:00 and must have been at 11:30. Therefore the test failed on the emergency stop must have been at 11:00 (clue 3). Helen Weales messed up her reversing (clue 1), so her test was not at 10:30 or 11:00 and must have been the 9:30 test, and the reversing was done in Balmoral Close. The driver who failed the maneuver in Market Street was not Rex Chance (clue 3), so it must have been Vera Swerve during her 11:30 test, and, by elimination, Rex Chance must have made his mistake in Mill Road. So his test must have been at 10:30 and therefore he failed on parking (clue 4) and the emergency stop during the 11:00 test must have been fluffed by Ron Gear in Hawthorn Way, leaving the

signaling mistake as made by Vera Swerve during her 11:30 test.

9:00, Roland Brake, hill start, Church Hill.
9:30, Helen Weales, reversing, Balmoral Close.
10:30, Rex Chance, parking, Mill Road.
11:00, Ron Gear, emergency stop, Hawthorn Way.
11:30, Vera Swerve, signaling, Market Street.

Minor Injuries, p. 310

Simon burnt his arm (clue 3) and Greg is studying geology (clue 4), so the male history student who limped in with a bruised knee (clue 3) must be Andrew. He wasn't dancing at the disco (clue 1), experimenting (clue 2), skateboarding (clue 3), or cooking (clue 4), so he must have been climbing the statue. Greg did not hurt himself dancing (clue 1), experimenting (clue 2), or cooking (clue 4), so he must have been the adventurous skateboarder. The student who was injured in a cooking accident was not studying chemistry (clue 2), geology, or English (clue 4) so must have been studying physics, leaving the overenthusiastic female dancer studying English. She isn't Delia (clue 4) so must be Pauline, leaving Delia as the chemistry student injured in an experiment. She didn't damage her nose (clue 2) so must have cut her hand, leaving Simon as the clumsy cook and Greg as the skateboarder with a nosebleed.

Andrew, history, climbing statue, bruised knee.
Delia, chemistry, experimenting, cut hand.
Greg, geology, skateboarding, nosebleed.
Pauline, English, dancing, sprained ankle.
Simon, physics, cooking, burnt arm.

Sales and Returns, p. 312

The sweater bought by Jane's brother wasn't too big and didn't have the wrong logo (clue 5). The scarf was the torn item (clue 3) and it was Jane's co-worker who bought the item that was frayed (clue 1), so the problem with the sweater must have been that it was too small. It didn't come from Sharks & Denser (clue 5) or G & J's (clue 4). The Supergirl purchase was the blouse (clue 2), and Tripark was visited by Jane's boyfriend (clue 3), so it must have been picked up at Bodenham's. The torn scarf wasn't found in Sharks & Denser, the item from which was too big (clue 5), or Tripark (clue 3), so it must have been picked up in G & J's. Its purchaser wasn't her cousin (clue 4), so must have been her aunt. We now know the buyer or the problem for four stores, so Jane's co-worker who bought the frayed item must have bought the blouse from Supergirl (clue 2). By elimination, Jane's cousin must have been bargain-hunting in Sharks & Denser, and Jane's boyfriend's Tripark purchase must have had the despised football logo. Finally, the hat wasn't bought by Jane's cousin (clue 4), so her find must have been the Sharks & Denser slippers that were too big, leaving the hat to have been snapped up by boyfriend Colin, emblazoned with a Netherlipp United logo.

Blouse, co-worker, Supergirl, frayed.
Hat, boyfriend, Tripark, wrong logo.
Sweater, brother, Bodenham's, too small.
Scarf, aunt, G & J's, has tear.
Slippers, cousin, Sharks & Denser, too big.

Jammy Winners, p. 314

Thirty-three jars of plum jam were produced (clue 5). So the 25 jars, which were not strawberry (clue 2), the gooseberry jam produced in Bottleham (clue 5), nor the blackberry and apple jam (clue 1), must have been Dorothy's raspberry jam, and 30 jars of blackberry and apple must have been produced (clue 1). Thirty-seven jars were made in Canefield (clue 4), so the Bottleham jam must have been the 42 jars of gooseberry. By elimination, the 37 jars must have been strawberry and Rosalind of Much Picking must have made the 33 jars (clue 2).

Barnaby didn't make the 30 jars, or the 37 jars of strawberry jam (clue 3), so his must have been the 42 jars of gooseberry jam and he must live in Bottleham. The Canefield resident is not Dorothy or Larry, as the Fullhedge jam-maker's name is shorter (clue 4), so it must be Elizabeth. Therefore Larry must have made the 30 jars of blackberry and apple. He does not live in Brambleigh (clue 6), so it must be Fullhedge, which leaves Dorothy as Brambleigh's jam-maker.

25 jars of raspberry jam, Dorothy from Brambleigh.
30 jars of blackberry and apple jam, Larry from Fullhedge.
33 jars of plum jam, Rosalind from Much Picking.
37 jars of strawberry jam, Elizabeth from Canefield.
42 jars of gooseberry jam, Barnaby from Bottleham.

Collision Course, p. 316

Demi Meare's character is in Wyoming (clue 6), so the female astronaut on the space station (clue 1) must be played by Kate Winett. Tom Hooks' character Mike McLaine isn't in Florida (clue 4), nor in California, the location of Sam Gomez (clue 2), so must be in New York. We now know that Kate Winett's character isn't Mike McLaine or Sam Gomez; nor is she Nic Leroy (clue 5) or Red Weber, who's a reporter, not an astronaut (clue 7), so she must be J P Burke. So, from clue 3, Demi Meare must play the ecologist. Brad Peat's character isn't Sam Gomez in California (clue 2), so that must be Al Pinici's role and Brad Peat's character must be in Florida. We have now matched four stars with a character, occupation, or location, so Red Weber the reporter must be Brad Peat's character in Florida. This leaves Demi Meare as Nic Leroy. Al Pinici's Sam Gomez isn't the police officer (clue 5), so he must be an astronomer, and the police officer must be Tom Hooks' Mike McLaine in New York.

Al Pinici, Sam Gomez, astronomer,
California.
Brad Peat, Red Weber, reporter, Florida.
Demi Meare, Nic Leroy, ecologist,
Wyoming.
Kate Winett, J P Burke, astronaut, space
station.
Tom Hooks, Mike McLaine, police officer,
New York.

Sign-In, p. 318

2	4	1	3	5	6
5	6	3	1	4	2
1	5	2	4	6	3
6	3	4	2	1	5
4	2	5	6	3	1
3	1	6	5	2	4

Sudoku, p. 318

4	1	5	3	6	8	2	7	9
3	7	9	4	2	1	8	6	5
6	8	2	7	9	5	4	3	1
2	6	4	9	1	3	5	8	7
7	5	3	2	8	4	1	9	6
1	9	8	6	5	7	3	4	2
5	2	6	8	4	9	7	1	3
8	3	1	5	7	6	9	2	4
9	4	7	1	3	2	6	5	8

Play these other fun puzzle books by USA TODAY

USA TODAY Sudoku

USA TODAY Everyday Sudoku

USA TODAY Crossword

USA TODAY Logic

USA TODAY Mini Sudoku / Sudoku X

USA TODAY Word Roundup / Word Search

USA TODAY Word Play

USA TODAY Jumbo Puzzle Book

USA TODAY Picture Puzzles

USA TODAY Everyday Logic

USA TODAY Jumbo Puzzle Book 2

USA TODAY Don't Quote Me®

USA TODAY Txtpert™

USA TODAY Picture Puzzles Across America

USA TODAY Word Finding Frenzy

USA TODAY Sudoku 2

USA TODAY Crossword 2

USA TODAY Logic 2

USA TODAY Sudoku 3

USA TODAY Up & Down Words Infinity

USA TODAY Crossword 3

USA TODAY Sudoku Super Challenge

USA TODAY Crossword Super Challenge

USA TODAY Jumbo Puzzle Book Super Challenge

USA TODAY Jumbo Puzzle Book Super Challenge 2

USA TODAY Logic Super Challenge

Andrews McMeel Publishing
a division of Andrews McMeel Universal
1130 Walnut Street, Kansas City, Missouri 64106

www.andrewsmcmeel.com

Logic puzzles copyright of Puzzler Media Ltd. All puzzles supplied
under license from Puzzler Media Ltd.—www.puzzler.com

20 21 22 23 24 PAH 10 9 8 7 6 5 4 3 2 1

ISBN: 978-1-5248-6038-7

Editor: Patty Rice
Art Director/Designer: Holly Swayne
Production Editor: David Shaw
Production Manager: Cliff Koehler

ATTENTION: SCHOOLS AND BUSINESSES

Andrews McMeel books are available at quantity discounts with bulk purchase for educational, business, or sales promotional use. For information, please e-mail the Andrews McMeel Publishing Special Sales Department: specialsales@amuniversal.com.